Getting Started in

ALTERNATIVE
INVESTMENTS

Getting Started in

ALTERNATIVE INVESTMENTS

Matthew Dearth
Swee Yong Ku

WILEY

Registered Office(s)
John Wiley & Sons, Inc., 111 River Street, Hoboken, NJ 07030, USA
John Wiley & Sons Singapore Pte. Ltd, 134 Jurong Gateway Road, #04-307H, Singapore 600134

Editorial Office
John Wiley & Sons Singapore Pte. Ltd, 134 Jurong Gateway Road, #04-307H, Singapore 600134

For details of our global editorial offices, customer services, and more information about Wiley products visit us at www.wiley.com.

Wiley also publishes its books in a variety of electronic formats and by print-on-demand. Some content that appears in standard print versions of this book may not be available in other formats.

Library of Congress Cataloging-in-Publication Data

Names: Dearth, Matthew, author. | Ku, Swee Yong, author.
Title: Getting started in alternative investments / Matthew Dearth, Swee Yong Ku.
Description: First edition. | Hoboken, NJ : Wiley, 2023. | Includes index.
Identifiers: LCCN 2023003045 (print) | LCCN 2023003046 (ebook) | ISBN 9781119860280 (paperback) | ISBN 9781119860297 (adobe pdf) | ISBN 9781119860303 (epub)
Subjects: LCSH: Asset allocation. | Investments. | Portfolio management. | Investment analysis.
Classification: LCC HG4529.5 .D43 2023 (print) | LCC HG4529.5 (ebook) | DDC 220.94/05—dc24
LC record available at https://lccn.loc.gov/2023003045
LC ebook record available at https://lccn.loc.gov/2023003046

Cover Design: Wiley
Cover Image: © Yuichiro Chino/Getty Images

Set in 12/14pt and Adobe Garamond Pro by Straive, Chennai, India

SKY10046167_042023

To Sebastian, Nicolas, and Mateo. Don't be scared by big ideas because they seem like a lot of work. Be stubborn, eat the elephant by pieces, and you will be surprised by what you can accomplish.

To the hardworking investors and learners seeking new opportunities and financial growth, I hope this book provides you with new insights to enhance your portfolio with Alternative Investments.

Contents

Chapter 4

Chapter 5

Appendix

Acknowledgments

Matthew Dearth: As a first-time author, writing this book was a magnificent, challenging experience. I naïvely assumed that because I had taught much of this material for five years, turning the course material into a book wouldn't be too difficult. Ha! I learned the hard way that the difference between 20 slide decks and 80,000 words is far greater than I expected. Still, reflecting on the journey and the finished product, I have more people to thank than the average Academy Awards winner, so cue the music. . .

I consider myself blessed to have had the opportunity to teach at SMU, and I owe a debt of gratitude to Guy Weyns, Lieven Demeester, and Ser Keng Ang in the MBA program, as well as Soon Huat Chan, Fangjian Fu, and John Sequeira in the GMF/MAF programs. Their support helped me grow as an instructor to the point where this book is even remotely possible. My students in FNCE695, FNCE6023, and FNCE6055 have been an immense help without knowing it, as every raised hand, confused look, and missed exam question forced me to sharpen my teaching and materials. Thank you for your interest and enthusiasm; it has been a pleasure and privilege to stand at the front of the room every week.

Tackling three smaller challenges—case writing—gave me the experience (and false confidence!) to tackle this book, and I must thank my colleagues for their assistance in bringing my ideas to reality, especially Philip Zerillo and Havovi Joshi. A special shout-out to Jaclyn Seow and Shane Chesson at Openspace Ventures, whose support was instrumental in the case writing that underpins the chapter on venture capital. Some of these chapters were based on scripts I prepared for a blended learning version of FNCE6055, and I would be remiss without thanking Ivy Seow for her tireless support despite many, many delays on my part.

In my career I have been incredibly fortunate to meet and break bread with so many thoughtful, knowledgeable, and wonderful people whose fingerprints are all over this text: my colleagues at Silvercrest, especially Robert Teeter and Mark Morris; Joanne Kwek and the team at Nordea Asset Management; a long list of subject matter experts, including Ryan Collins, James Cox, Anthony Huston, Ashish Jain, Scott Johnson, Robert Kraybill, Munib Madni, and Brian Toh; my intrepid guest "judges" for student projects, especially Eric Nietsch and Leon Toh; and in NY, Tom Adams, Matt Barnard, Jed Bonnem, Peter Boodell, Brian Gonick, Tom Kanter, and Claudio Macchetto.

At some point we probably wished we hadn't signed up for this special torture together, but it was my friend and co-author Swee Yong's idea in the first place, so I blame and thank him at the same time. The Wiley team of Syd, Purvi, Stacey, and Susan have been great to work with, and I'm grateful for their understanding with all my missed deadlines and naïve questions along the way.

Finally, a most special thanks to my family across the world who supported me on this path, even though it meant they saw less of me for weeks on end. I am so blessed to have your love and understanding, thank you.

Swee Yong Ku: The beginning of this journey seemed like an enjoyable stroll through a large beautiful garden. The overarching rain trees provided a canopy that corresponded to the key concepts in finance and investments, the footpaths and the shelters represented the various forms of real estate, and the vibrant colors of the roses highlighted the insights and intricacies of real estate investments.

I wanted to introduce our readers the ideas of real estate finance and real estate investments in simple terms. It would allow readers outside the real estate industry to gain a broad perspective of this field, with a bit more depth to lead inquisitive readers to more specialized publications.

But the stroll was not an easy one. The garden was indeed beautiful, but it had a challenging terrain with knolls and valleys that I had to navigate. The writing was more challenging than I had expected: Who is the reader? Which country is the reader from? What are the real estate laws and types of financial investment that the reader is familiar and unfamiliar with? I struggled with considering how to make the writing useful to readers from various countries who would view real estate from their specific local lenses.

However, the undulating landscape was made easier, more enjoyable, and more rewarding by the supportive people around me.

I would like to express my deepest gratitude to all of the people who helped me to write, edit, and fact check my work. First and foremost, I would like to thank my family: Annabelle, Trevor, and Simone, who provided constant support, sometimes nagging, and encouragement throughout the writing process. You know how much I dread writing, and your love and belief in me kept me motivated and inspired. I am grateful for your unwavering support, especially as I am making progress toward my thesis.

Additionally, I would like to thank Konstantina Barker, Steven Chan, Kok Keong Tan, Joel Kam, Guan Wei Tan, Heidi Tan, Benjamin Tay, and Tristan Yu for reading and improving my work and providing me with additional content. I am lucky to have your support. Your attention to detail and commitment to excellence were invaluable and allowed me more time to rest and reflect along the journey.

I would also like to thank my co-author Dr. Matthew Dearth and editors Stacey Rivera and Syd Ganaden for your patience and guidance. Your support made the whole process of putting this book together more enjoyable. Thank you.

These acknowledgments would not be complete if I do not express my appreciation for Emeritus Professor Francis Cher Chiew Koh from Singapore Management University. You have taught me how to deliver lessons more clearly, in class and through my writing, and to be more meticulous with research and methodologies. Thank you very much for your generous sharing.

About the Authors

Matthew Dearth is managing director at Silvercrest Asset Management, a leading independent advisory and financial services firm created to provide traditional and alternative asset management and focused family office services to wealthy families and select institutional investors. His 30 years of financial services experience also include roles with leading equity hedge fund manager Marshall Wace, global investment bank Goldman Sachs, and strategy consulting firm Booz Allen & Hamilton. Matt founded his own firm in 2013, advising clients in the United States, Asia, and Europe on new product development, performance attribution analysis, and portfolio manager decision-making.

In addition, since 2016 he has served as Adjunct Faculty (Finance) at the Lee Kong Chian School of Business at Singapore Management University, teaching graduate-level courses on alternative investments and sustainable investing. In recognition of his teaching, Matt has been awarded the Dean's Teaching Honor List for Top Adjunct Faculty (Postgraduate Programs) since 2019.

Matt holds a PhD (General Management) from Singapore Management University, an MBA from Massachusetts Institute of Technology (MIT), and a Bachelor of Science in Civil Engineering and Operations Research from Princeton University. He has written several teaching cases available through Harvard Business Publishing on topics ranging from investing in collectibles (Merlion Investments, ISB220-PDF-ENG) and sustainable venture capital (Openspace Ventures, SMU028-PDF-ENG).

A native of the American Midwest who spent 20 years living and working in the New York area, Matt has lived in Singapore since 2015.

Swee Yong Ku has been a director of a licensed property consulting firm International Property Advisor Pte Ltd since 2010. In the past two decades, he has also taken on the roles of chief marketing officer of Kasa Singapore, a real estate tokenization platform, and was the country CEO of Century 21 real estate agency in Singapore. Prior to running his own practice, he was a director in the Real Estate Centre of Expertise at Société Générale Private Banking, responsible for advising clients on real estate investments; the director of Marketing and Business Development at real estate consulting firm Savills Singapore and the general manager at property developer Far East Organization's Indonesia office.

He was an adjunct faculty at three institutions of higher learning: the Lee Kong Chian School of Business in the Singapore Management University, the Department of Real Estate in the National University of Singapore, and the School of Design and Environment in Ngee Ann Polytechnic.

He holds an MBA in marketing from University of Hull, UK, and completed his BSc in chemistry at the Imperial College, University of London, UK and the Institut Louis Pasteur, Université de Strasbourg, France.

Swee has written six books on the property market: *Real Estate Riches, Building Your Real Estate Riches, Real Estate Realities, Weathering a Property Downturn, Preparing for a Property Upturn*, and *The Future of Real Estate*.

Swee is now researching how new technologies impact the real estate market. In particular, he is focused on how autonomous vehicles will affect the built environment and bring about urban regeneration.

Introduction

For several years the authors co-taught a course called "Alternative Investments" for the Masters of Applied Finance (MAF) program at Singapore Management University. This course served several purposes. First and foremost, it provided a foundation for students studying for the Chartered Financial Analyst (CFA) exams. Because the MAF program at that time did not offer a separate elective in real estate, academic directors allocated two out of eight class sessions to cover this important part of the Level I and Level II exams. The university engaged two Adjunct Faculty—Dr. Dearth with a background in institutional equities and hedge funds, and Mr. Ku with deep experience in real estate investing—to teach these sessions, which is how the authors of this book met.

The course provided students with a high-level overview of the major alternative asset classes, including Venture Capital, Private Equity, Real Estate, and Hedge Funds. While other elective courses were available for these topics, not every student could fit all the electives into a single schedule, so by taking "Alternative Investments" students were assured of at least a base level of understanding of these asset classes.

Beyond catering to the CFA material, however, Dr. Dearth believed that a course on alternative investments would be more interesting and valuable if it covered a wider range of so-called "modern alternatives" such as catastrophe bonds, impact investments, and collectibles. These assets were not typically covered in a Master's program, but based on his 20+ year career in the financial markets, he understood that modern alternatives played an important role in many institutional and high net worth (HNW) investors' portfolios. Thus, the curriculum came to include a very broad range of alternative investments, from the traditional to the modern.

With such a wide range of assets to cover in their class, the authors were motivated to write this book because a suitable text on the topic did not yet exist. They believed alternatives to be increasingly important because of the relative scarcity of yield in more liquid public markets. Institutional investors such as US pension funds often require target returns of 8% to meet their funding obligations to their retirees. When interest rates were as low as they had been in much of the world after the Global Financial Crisis (GFC) of 2008–2009, that 8% would be a difficult hurdle to clear without more risk than pension funds might like to take. Many wealthy individuals and families faced similar pressures, though perhaps more self-imposed.

This book, therefore, provides the reader with an overview of the market for alternative investments, both traditional and modern. For traditional alternatives, Chapter 2 describes each asset class[1] in terms of a typical investment process, historical performance, and a review of more recent developments. As many readers may be familiar with real estate investing from personal experience, Chapter 3 contains a detailed description of the range of real estate assets and their corresponding investment techniques. The chapter on modern alternatives, Chapter 4, covers a broad range of investments but without the same level of detail since many of these assets are relatively new, such as cryptocurrency and asset-backed tokens, and less broadly adopted by institutional investors. Finally, Chapter 5 provides background information on the process of portfolio management and explains the important contribution that alternative investments can provide, for both institutions and individuals. The Appendix continues the topic of Chapter 3, real estate, in more detail.

It is important to acknowledge that since human creativity has resulted in a wide variety of investments around the world, this book is not intended to cover an exhaustive list of assets. For example, many readers will have heard of SPACs, or Special Purpose Acquisition Companies, which became a sensation among retail traders during the Covid-19 lockdowns of 2020–2021. The authors do not address SPACs separately, believing that they represent an alternative form of initial public offering and, as such, are more properly considered a subset of public equity investing. The long list of niche or country-specific opportunities that are not addressed here includes:

- tax lien investing, billboards, etc. (United States)
- favorable tax treatment for treasure hunting (UK)

- reselling certain qualifying insurance policies (Singapore)
- favorable tax treatment for conversion/restoration of certain classes of property (Germany)

Despite these limitations, the authors believe that the material contained in this book will be of considerable interest to many different readers. Anyone who is curious about new and unusual investment opportunities will find much to learn, as will individuals or families with financial means, risk appetite, and illiquidity tolerance to consider something new and different. Advisors to qualified investors who want to be knowledgeable about up-and-coming opportunities will similarly find new ideas here. Finally, this book may be a useful supplementary text for students in courses on alternative investments, or for anyone preparing for the Chartered Alternative Investment Analyst exam and other industry exams.

Note

1. This book uses the terms "assets," "asset class," and "investments" interchangeably as is common in industry practice.

1

Introduction to Alternatives

This chapter provides background information on the world of alternative investments, beginning with a definition of alternatives and some common characteristics that distinguish these assets from traditional investments in stocks, bonds, or cash.

Next, this chapter reviews the structure of alternative investment firms and funds, highlighting several important differences compared to traditional assets. We also discuss important techniques and attributes of alternative strategies, including leverage, short selling, hedging, and fees.

With that foundational understanding in place, we present a due diligence framework. Much as institutional investors conduct due diligence on potential investments, we will refer to different elements of this framework throughout the book to help the reader understand the various alternative strategies and the role they may play in investor portfolios.

Finally, we discuss in brief two issues of more than passing interest to investors in alternatives: regulations and performance measurement. Both of these topics are more complex than can be addressed in this book, so we will limit our material to a few of the most important differences between alternatives and traditional investment products.

1.1 What Are Alternatives?

Ask someone on the street about investing and the answer will likely refer to stocks or maybe bonds. Together with cash, these constitute the "traditional" financial assets and are accessible to individuals through direct purchase (buying shares of stock) or through funds (i.e., mutual funds in the United States, unit trusts in Europe). In many countries these assets are closely regulated to provide individual investors with certain protections against fraud and bad actors. Typical regulations require standardized disclosure of financial and other information, transparent pricing, and trading through regulated securities exchanges.

If stocks, bonds, and cash are "traditional investments," what does the term "alternative investments" mean? The first word is the most important, "alternative"—somewhat obviously it means any investment that is not stocks, bonds, or cash—anything else is considered an alternative investment. Note that IPOs (initial public offerings) and SPACs (Special Purpose Acquisition Companies) are considered specialized examples of stocks in this book, as are nearly all ETFs (exchange-traded funds).

Although some alternative investment strategies trade in exchange-listed public assets—hedge funds being one example—many alternative asset classes involve investments in entities that are not traded on an exchange ("unlisted"); these are often referred to as belonging to the "private markets." Private markets assets include ownership stakes in private companies (most commonly Venture Capital and Private Equity), some Real Estate and Infrastructure investments, and Impact Funds as examples. Beyond these investments in companies and projects, alternative investments also include commodities, collectibles, and a wide range of other assets that are not stocks, bonds, or cash.

Alternative investments often share other characteristics that may cause the investment to be riskier (or more expensive) than traditional investments, and as a result, the investor should do more due diligence before investing.

Table 1.1 presents the common features of alternative investments.

To aid understanding of why these features of alternative investments are important, let us describe a few of these characteristics, starting with "Liquidity restrictions." The ability to buy or sell an asset

TABLE 1.1. Common features of alternative
investments

- Narrow manager specialization and potentially unconventional investment strategies
- Concentrated portfolios, potentially higher risk due to lower diversification
- Limited and potentially problematic historical risk and return data, making performance measurement more difficult
- Relatively low correlation of returns with those of traditional investments
- Absolute return targets
- High fees and/or performance-based fees ("2 and 20")
- Restrictions on redemptions (i.e., "lockups" and "gates")
- Liquidity restrictions, often associated with a return premium as compensation
- Unique legal and tax considerations
- Less regulation and less transparency than traditional investments
- Not generally publicly traded—these are private investment vehicles
- High due diligence costs, and available for "sophisticated investors" only

without significantly influencing the price of the asset is referred to as "liquidity." Investments in cash, stocks, or bonds, or even mutual funds or unit trusts, are straightforward to trade through a brokerage account. Many of these investments are relatively liquid. In contrast, most alternative investments do not trade on public exchanges, making them harder to buy and sell, and therefore they are described as being less liquid.

Furthermore, many alternatives place restrictions on redemptions (sales), requiring a minimum holding period (also called a lockup) followed by a notice period before it is possible to redeem them. For example, private equity funds invest in unlisted companies that take considerable time to buy and sell, and typically require investors to commit to minimum holding periods of 7–10 years. Some managers investing in less liquid assets may also place "gates" on funds to control the pace of redemptions, or halt redemptions altogether in an extreme case like the Global Financial Crisis. One example of a gate could be a fund that only allows investors to sell one quarter of their holdings at any one time. Investors in alternatives should carefully consider the impact of these additional restrictions on liquidity from lockups and gates when deciding whether (and how much) to invest.

"Limited and potentially problematic historical risk and return data" is another common and important characteristic of alternative assets. Stocks and mutual funds trade on exchanges, creating a very detailed record of historical price information. Alternative investments, on the other hand, typically don't trade on exchanges, and, as a result, historical data may be limited in scope and detail (e.g., monthly or quarterly data only). In addition, price and performance data are often self-reported by the manager—this is potentially problematic because you must trust that the manager is reporting the correct figures.

1.2 Investing in Alternatives

For reasons which will be explained throughout the book, institutions and wealthy individuals account for the majority of investments in alternative assets. These investors may have direct contact with alternative investment managers, or they may access and invest in these assets through intermediaries like private banks.

From the fund manager's perspective, raising money is one of the most important challenges to building a successful business. Like entrepreneurs in other industries, fund managers therefore tap into different distribution channels to find suitable investors for their fund. Institutions are often large enough to be able to make significant investments, and fund managers attend conferences and hire dedicated staff to reach these investors. Wealthy individuals, on the other hand, have relatively less capital to invest, so it can be more efficient to raise capital from wealthy individuals by partnering with a private bank.

From an investor's perspective, large institutional allocators may enjoy direct relationships with fund managers, which also means avoiding the additional layer of fees charged by intermediaries like private banks. The intermediaries provide benefits such as access to funds and additional due diligence on managers that may justify the additional fees for individual investors who would otherwise find it difficult to invest in these alternative funds.

1.2.1 The Market for Alternatives

One way that investors evaluate the attractiveness of different investments is through the relationship between return and risk. A 2021 study of private markets funds by Morgan Stanley shows historical return and risk for many major asset classes. Venture Capital and Buyout Funds (two of the major Private Equity strategies that will be described further in Chapter 2) stand out for their superior returns per unit of risk (Figure 1.1).

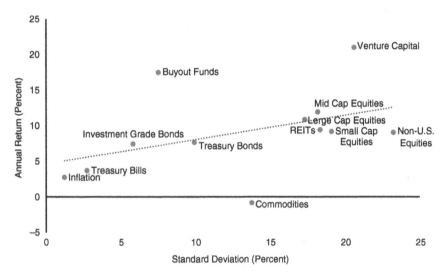

FIGURE 1.1. Performance of major asset classes, 1984–2015.
Source: Mauboussin and Callahan, 2020, Morgan Stanley.

Given this historically strong performance, perhaps it shouldn't be surprising that assets in alternative strategies have been growing faster than public markets. The industry uses "assets under management" (AUM) as a measure of the amount of capital being managed by investment firms. Looking back over the past 40 years of US data, the same Morgan Stanley report documents a tremendous rise in allocations to US Buyout funds.

When viewed in the context of the broader asset management industry, we see that investments in alternative assets are growing more quickly than the industry as a whole: a recent report by the Boston Consulting Group finds that between 2009 and 2020, alternative assets increased their share of total assets from 13% to 15%. (Figure 1.2).

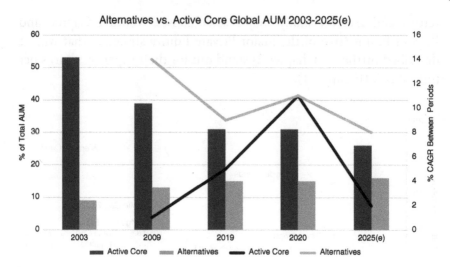

FIGURE 1.2. Comparison of AUM and CAGR, Alternatives vs. Active Core, 2003–2025(e)

The growth in alternative assets is not uniform across asset classes. For example, other studies have shown Private Equity AUM growing faster than other large alternative asset classes like real estate and hedge funds.[1]

1.2.2 Managing Alternative Investment Funds

As explained above, alternative investment strategies are characterized by important differences from the "plain vanilla" investments (stocks and bonds) that are familiar to most individual investors. This section explores some of these differences in greater detail.

1.2.2.1 Illiquid Structures

There are two types of entities involved in most alternative investment funds: the firm responsible for running the fund and the investors in the fund. The firm running the fund is generically called the General Partner (GP). As shown in Figure 1.3, what practitioners call the GP is more properly called a "financial sponsor," which for liability purposes maintains two separate legal entities: the GP which legally runs the fund and assumes liability, and the management company that employs the people making the investment decisions for the fund.

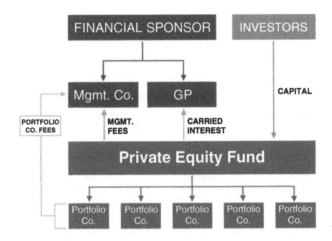

FIGURE 1.3. Roles of financial sponsor and investor.

Source: A Simple Model, https://www.asimplemodel.com/insights/private-equity-fund-structure, last accessed December 14, 2022.

Investors in the fund are called Limited Partners (LPs). As the term suggests, LPs' interests are limited to a financial investment in the fund; they have no other involvement or economic interest. The fund is a separate entity as well, which means it is important to be clear whether something refers to the manager of the fund (GP) or the fund itself. The fund holds the investments that are made, which can include ownership stakes in private companies, shares in company stocks, bonds, or other types of assets. Prior to the collapse of Lehman Brothers during the Global Financial Crisis (GFC) of 2008–2009, LPs were often content to make their investments in a single, shared entity for the fund. These so-called "co-mingled" vehicles offer several conveniences for manager and investor alike, including economies of scale with respect to operational activities such as trading, accounting, and reporting. When Lehman Brothers collapsed, however, many LPs were burned by an important shortcoming of co-mingled vehicles: because the investments from different investors were held in a single fund, it was difficult to settle competing claims on the remaining assets during bankruptcy proceedings. In fact, as of mid-2022, lawsuits are still pending in New York and London—nearly 14 years later.[2]

In the years following the GFC, institutional LPs have become more likely to invest via a "separately managed account" (SMA), a different structure that ensures that each investor's assets are kept legally separate from other LPs in a fund. The downside for fund managers is that SMAs are operationally more expensive to set up and maintain, so GPs typically require larger minimum investments (on the order of $50 million or more for larger managers) to justify the additional expense.

1.2.2.2 ETFs, Liquid Alternatives, and Interval Funds

Adherents to the "efficient markets hypothesis" believe that all relevant information about a security is already (or immediately) incorporated into its price, meaning that it would be pointless for investors to try to beat the market.[3] Therefore, to capture market returns, or beta, many investors use "passive" strategies designed to mimic the returns of the market index (e.g., S&P 500) as closely as possible with the lowest possible fees. The first products to offer this strategy were index mutual funds; over time the mutual fund design has been eclipsed in popularity by exchange traded funds, or ETFs. In addition to the low fees associated with passive investing in general (because the manager is only trying to mimic the index returns as closely as possible), investors also prefer that ETFs trade during the day like stocks. To capitalize on increasing investor demand, index providers and fund managers alike have developed a wide range of indices and ETFs to track those indices.[4] BlackRock has become the world's largest asset manager in large part due to the success of its passive investing products, iShares.

Despite the attractive components of ETFs, they do have their inherent risks as well. Investors should note that it is often difficult to track market indices closely because it is not possible to purchase each security in the same proportion as a basket of stocks tracked by the indices. The portfolios of stocks in an index are often weighted by market capitalization, which can lead ETFs to overweight stocks that are trading at a premium and underweight stocks that are trading at a discount.

A small subset of the ETF market is referred to as "liquid alternatives." As the term suggests, these products transform otherwise illiquid alternative assets like hedge funds and private equity into liquid versions that trade like mutual funds (daily liquidity) or even stocks (intraday liquidity). As opposed to private investment vehicles available only to accredited investors (see Section 1.4.1), liquid alternative funds are designed for retail investors and are subject to the same regulations that provide limits and protections to investors in mutual funds, for example. As of August 2022, ETF information provider VettaFi lists 23 ETFs totaling over $4.5 billion AUM under the category "Long/Short."[5] An excerpt from the VettaFi database showing the 10 largest long-short ETFs (Table 1.2) reveals a wide range of strategies and performance, many of which are available to individual investors without accreditation or qualification (see Section 1.3).

TABLE 1.2. The 10 largest long-short ETFs in the VettaFi database

Symbol	ETF Name	Total assets ($)	YTD (%)	Avg volume	Previous closing price	1-day change (%)
XYLD	Global X S&P 500 Covered Call ETF	2,226,690	2.36	561,444	$40.30	0.02
QAI	IQ Hedge Multi-Strategy Tracker ETF	634,859	2.39	238,967	$29.14	−0.07
FTLS	First Trust Long/Short Equity ETF	618,011	2.11	99,481	$49.90	0.26
BTAL	AGFiQ US Market Neutral Anti-Beta Fund	441,962	−4.90	598,635	$20.17	−1.27
CSM	Proshares Large Cap Core Plus	430,795	4.67	15,784	$47.01	−0.15
KMLM	KFA Mount Lucas Managed Futures Index Strategy ETF	248,836	−4.51	228,759	$29.17	−0.41
CTA	Simplify Managed Futures Strategy ETF	145,975	−4.38	269,216	$24.87	−1.50
MARB	First Trust Merger Arbitrage ETF	98,605	−0.31	51,479	$20.11	0.10
LBAY	Leatherback Long/Short Alternative Yield ETF	97,676	0.72	44,037	$29.57	−0.94
FLSP	Franklin Systematic Style Premia ETF	92,928	−1.08	10,103	$21.01	−0.19

Source: Adapted from ETF Database / https://etfdb.com/etfdb-category/long-short/.

Another structure known as "interval funds" offers a partial solution to the issue of liquidity for alternative investments. These funds provide periodic (often quarterly) opportunities for investors to redeem a portion of their holdings. As opposed to liquid alternative ETFs with daily liquidity, interval funds are more suitable for strategies that require longer holding periods such as private investments. For example, US-based advisor Stone Ridge (www.stoneridgeam.com) manages an interval fund that invests in reinsurance-based securities (to be discussed further in Chapter 4, Section 4.2.1). This fund provides better liquidity than a 7- to 10-year lockup, to be sure, but the minimum investment is $15 million[6] and likely out of reach for many otherwise qualified and accredited investors.

1.2.2.3 Funding and Capital Calls

The private markets GPs described above typically raise money for multiple funds over time. Each fund is usually expected to have a lifespan of 7–10 years as measured from the "closing" of the fund and first investments to the sale or disposal of the last remaining assets—some may live as long as 15 years or more. Funds are raised and then closed to new investors; the LPs in the fund commit to invest a certain amount of capital over the life of the fund. Rather than making the full investment when the fund is launched, LPs are expected to deliver their capital to the fund when "called" by the manager (GP) over time, usually driven by the timing of potential investment opportunities for the fund. One common practice is for the initial investment to be 10–20% of the total commitment at closing. The year in which the fund is closed and the first capital is referred to as the "vintage" of the fund.

Consider the following (oversimplified) example. The GP raises a $1 billion fund to invest in private companies around the world. An LP commits to invest $50 million, and at closing delivers $10 million, or 20% of its commitment, to the fund. The GP uses the initial capital (20% of $1 billion, or $200 million) to buy three mid-sized companies it has already identified. Nine months later, the GP has found another two companies to buy for a total of $100 million. The GP calls capital from the LPs in proportion to each commitment; in our case, the LP represents 5% of the total fund ($50 million out of $1 billion) and so is expected to deliver another $5 million to the fund—usually within a week of receiving the capital call.

By timing capital calls in this way, investors' capital spends the least amount of time sitting idle in a low-return riskless account waiting to be invested. This allows GPs to put the capital to work as quickly as possible and maximize their reported performance for their LPs (see the discussion on internal rate of return in Section 1.2.4).

In public markets alternative funds—typically hedge funds and commodity trading advisors (CTAs)—the underlying investments (e.g., stocks) are more liquid than the underlying investments held by private markets funds (e.g., ownership of private companies). The underlying investments are liquid, however, the funds are not. For public markets funds there are no capital calls, but there may be restrictions related to redemptions.

1.2.2.4 Fees

Different alternative assets use slightly different terms, but fee structures usually contain three major components: (1) a management fee that gets paid regardless of performance; (2) an incentive fee that gets paid only if performance exceeds a predetermined level; and (3) any conditions on either of the first two.

Management fees, often 1–2% of assets, compensate the manager for the expenses of running the fund, especially staff salaries. Note that these fees are significantly higher than the fees for either ETFs or mutual funds, even if those funds were to focus on the same investment universe (e.g., S&P 500 stocks). Some very successful hedge funds are in such high demand by investors that instead of charging a fixed percentage management fee, they pass actual expenses through to their investors ("expenses-and-20"). Unsuspecting investors in these funds may end up paying 3% or higher in management fees.

Incentive fees, typically a percentage of any net profits generated by the fund, are designed to align the interests of the manager with the investors (i.e., for the fund to generate strong performance). Regulators often take a dim view of performance-based incentive fees, however, since they might encourage unnecessarily aggressive risk-taking by the manager.

The mechanics of incentive fees differ depending on the type of alternative investment. Hedge funds and CTAs usually refer to this incentive fee as a performance fee; it may be as much as 10–20% of the profits (or more). These funds tend to invest in public markets assets and the performance during any given measurement period includes a mix of realized (where stocks have been sold) and unrealized (where stocks have appreciated but have not yet been sold) gains. Consequently, the calculation of performance fees is complicated by variability of fund performance over time. For example, a fund that is +10% in year 1 may be –20% in year 2. Naturally the manager would have received performance fees in year 1 and none in year 2 (no profits), but what about year 3? If the fund returns +10% in year 3, theoretically the manager should earn performance fees, but the fact remains that investors would still be losing money over the three-year period, as illustrated in Exhibit 1.1.

EXHIBIT 1.1. Fund performance and fee calculation

	Year 1	Year 2	Year 3
Fund size Jan. 1	$100 million	$108 million	$86.4 million
Fund performance	+10%	–20%	+10%
Gain (loss)	$10 million	($21.6 million)	$8.64 million
Performance fees	($2 million)	$0	($1.728 million)
Fund size Dec. 31	$108 million	$86.4 million	$93.312 million

Note: This illustration assumes no additional investments are made in the fund during the period and ignores all other fees (including management fees) and expenses. For a more detailed exploration of performance fee calculations, see https://www.preqin.com/academy/lesson-3-hedge-funds/hedge-fund-fees-types-and-structures.

To address this issue, investors in hedge funds and CTAs typically expect the performance fee calculation to be based on what is called the "high water mark" (HWM). The high water mark states that if a fund loses money during a measurement period, then it must recover those losses first before the manager earns performance fees again. In our example above, the manager will not be eligible for performance fees until the value of the fund closes the year above the HWM of $108 million established at the end of year 1. More generally, the impact of HWMs on performance fees can be illustrated, as in Figure 1.4.

Private markets funds like venture capital and private equity have a slightly different approach to fees. Management fees are based on the estimated value of the portfolio instead of market prices since private assets do not trade on an exchange like stocks or bonds do. Performance

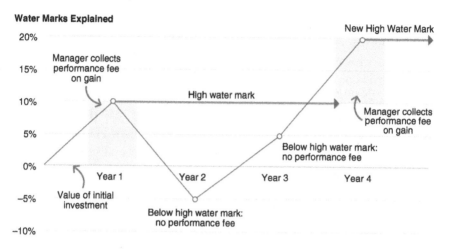

FIGURE 1.4. Explanation of high water mark.

Source: Preqin, https://www.managedfunds.org/wp-content/uploads/2016/06/
06.09.16-How-HFs-are-Structured.pdf, last accessed December 14, 2022.

fees, which in this case are referred to as "carried interest," are earned when deals are exited (realized gains). Carried interest may only be earned if performance exceeds a "hurdle rate," often 6–12%. Finally, if a private equity fund pays carried interest fees early in its life but the performance is lower when the fund is finally closed, LPs may receive "claw-back" payments so that the final carried interest paid to the GP ties up to the final performance figure.

One common critique of the fee model common to alternative investing is that many fund managers appear to be getting rich off fees while their investors do not. Investing is a scale-sensitive business, such that a team managing $500 million might be able to invest $2 billion without a proportionate increase in headcount and expenses. Therefore, as fund managers have gotten bigger, the management fees alone can create significant wealth, reducing the incentive for managers to deliver superior investment performance. There is some debate about the robustness of these findings, but studies have shown that smaller and/or first funds tend to outperform their larger or more established competitors. See Chapter 2, Section 2.3 for further elaboration on this topic.

Readers may well wonder what happens to managers of funds with these fee arrangements—especially hedge funds investing in more liquid assets—when their performance is poor. One natural reaction might be for the manager to increase risk-taking in an attempt to recoup any losses and generate performance fees. If the manager is successful, this could appear to be a favorable outcome for the investor as well, but this risk-seeking behavior could also lead to further, larger losses; *ex ante*, investors in poor performing funds may prefer to avoid this tactic. When fund managers are so far below their HWM that they cannot foresee generating performance fees for several years, it is very common for the manager to attempt to renegotiate the HWM with investors, or failing that, close the fund and then attempt to launch another fund with fresh capital and establish a new HWM.

1.2.3 Alternative Techniques

Leverage, short selling, and hedging are common techniques in some of the most popular alternative asset classes. Hedge funds typically make use of all three, while leverage is also an important component of some private equity strategies. The following section provides a brief introduction to these concepts.

1.2.3.1 Leverage

What happens if instead of using its own money to make an investment, an investor borrowed some money instead? Borrowing money reduces the amount of capital the investor has to contribute for a given investment (e.g., a $1,000 investment could be made using only the investor's capital, or the investor could borrow $500 and only use $500 of its own capital). Use of borrowed capital to amplify returns is called "leverage."[7] The general calculation of investment returns when using leverage can be expressed as:

$$ROE = ROI + \left[L \times (ROI - d) \right]$$

where

ROE = (levered) return on equity

ROI = (unlevered) return on investment

L = D / E = leverage factor, or ratio of debt (D) to equity (E) invested

d = cost of debt financing

Expanding on the example above, consider the case when an investor buys one hundred shares of a stock at \$10.00 per share, and one year later sells that stock for \$11.00 per share, a return of 10%. Without leverage, the investor's return is still 10%:

$$ROE = 10\% + \left[0 \times (10\% - 0\%) \right] = 10\% + 0\% = 10\%$$

If instead of investing \$1000 of her own capital, the investor borrows \$500 at an annual interest rate of 5%, the leverage ratio L = (\$500/\$500) = 1 and the levered return on equity is:

$$ROE = 10\% + 1^* \left[10\% - 2\% \right] = 10\% + 8\% = 18\%$$

In this case, the investor has increased her returns because she borrowed half of the money she invested; note that in this example she doubles her returns (less the 2% interest payment) by using half the amount of her own money. Of course, leverage has a similar effect on losses. If instead our investor lost –10% on the investment, after leverage, the ROE would be:

$$ROE = -10\% + 1^* \left[-10\% - 2\% \right] = -10\% - 12\% = -22\%$$

Many alternative investments involve leverage, and investors would do well to be mindful of this when evaluating funds.

1.2.3.2 Short Selling

Short selling is a way to profit when the price of a stock goes down. As an example, let's look at the case of Tencent Holdings (HKG: 0700).[8] From October 11, 2021 to October 10, 2022, Tencent stock declined by –46.81% (Figure 1.5).

If our investor had decided to short Tencent for that one year period—opening the short on October 11, 2021 and covering (or closing) on October 10, 2022—what kind of return would she have achieved? The calculation appears as:

$$ROI = (496.00 - 263.80) / 496.00 = 232.20 / 496.00 = 46.81\%$$

Note that this is the same figure as the price decline shown in the price chart. By selling high (shorting) and then buying lower later (called "covering" the short), our investor has profited from the price of a stock going down instead of up.[9]

FIGURE 1.5. Tencent stock performance, October 11, 2021 to October 10, 2022.
Source: Google, "Tencent stock price," retrieved October 10, 2022.

There are (at least) three different motivations for short selling. Our hypothetical Tencent short above is an example of the first and most basic motivation, a bet that a stock will decline in price—often referred to as a directional, single-stock short. We highlight the fact that it is a single-stock short (a bet on the individual stock) to differentiate it from the next kind of short sale: a pair trade.

As the name suggests, pair trades involve two securities. A common type of pair trade is to bet that one competitor in an industry will outperform another in the same industry (e.g., UPS and Fedex). The historical price graph of FDX (white) and UPS (grey) shows how these stocks have performed relative to each other over the past five years (Figure 1.6).

Another way to look at this chart is to look at the area between the white and grey lines, called "the spread." Professional investors using an information service such as Bloomberg will be able to graph the spread by itself as shown in Figure 1.7.

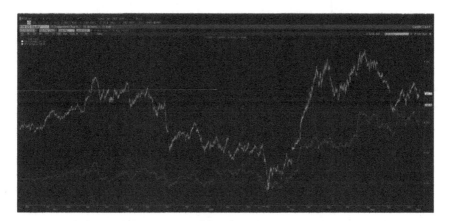

FIGURE 1.6. Five-year price history of FedEx and UPS.
Source: Bloomberg L.P.

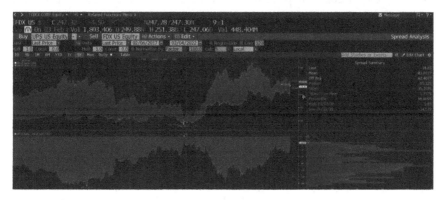

FIGURE 1.7. Historical "spread", long UPS / short FedEx.
Source: Bloomberg L.P.

In Figure 1.7, the top left quadrant shows the spread—notice how it looks like the previous stock price chart. On the right-hand side are some descriptive statistics about the spread today and how the spread has changed over time. On the bottom right quadrant the frequency histogram shows that the spread today is about as narrow as it has been during the past five years—note the value highlighted in a different color at the top part of the distribution. If our investor wanted to trade the spread, she could use a pair trade, long FDX and short UPS. In this way she doesn't care if the stock market goes up or down, because as long as FDX outperforms UPS, she would make money.

1.2.3.3 Hedging

The third and final motivation for short selling is risk management, in this case referred to as "hedging." A hedge is a position that is designed to make money (or reduce risk) when other positions are losing money (contributing risk). Long-only managers can't sell short, so they manage risk by looking for assets with low-to-negative correlation with the other positions in their portfolio. Hedge funds, on the other hand, can sell short, and therefore have two additional motivations for short selling.

The first opportunity is to hedge a single-stock position. For example, our investor might love Microsoft (NASDAQ: MSFT) stock but not be comfortable with all the risk, so she could sell short shares of another software company, Oracle (NASDAQ: ORCL), as a hedge. Note that this is not considered a pair trade; the short ORCL is designed to cushion potential losses from the long MSFT position rather than expressing a view on the relative spread between Microsoft and Oracle. As long as MSFT outperforms ORCL, this hedged position will make money.

The second application of hedging occurs at the portfolio level. To begin, let us consider the amount of capital in both longs and shorts in a portfolio. If our manager's portfolio has the same amount of money long and short (e.g., $100 million on each side), that is called "market neutral." In theory, the equal amounts of capital long and short mean her portfolio has no exposure to the market because if the market goes up or down the longs and shorts will cancel each other out. The short portfolio in aggregate acts as a hedge for the long portfolio. This type of portfolio is illustrated in Table 1.3. Note that the sum of the weights on the long and short portfolios are both equal to 1 (100%), and longs and short both sum to $100 million.

But it turns out that even though this is a hedged, market-neutral portfolio, there is another kind of unwanted risk remaining: beta. Beta (represented by the Greek letter, β) is defined as the exposure to market risk. A stock has a beta of 1.0 if it moves in line with the market; if the market increases 1.2%, the 1-beta stock should also increase by 1.2%. "High-beta" stocks move significantly more than the market, both up and down, while "low-beta" stocks don't move as much as the market in either direction. A hot tech IPO could be an example of a high-beta stock, while a conservatively managed utility company might be a low-beta stock.

TABLE 1.3. Sample long and short portfolios.

Long Portfolio

Ticker	Weight	β	Position Size ($)	Share Price ($)	# Shares
AES	0.151	2.39	15,100,000	9.440	1,599,576
WMB	0.132	2.2	13,200,000	0.982	13,441,955
DYN	0.129	2.51	12,900,000	4.280	3,014,019
FCX	0.108	1.11	10,800,000	42.130	256,349
NOVL	0.103	2.84	10,300,000	10.530	978,158
GLW	0.098	3.5	9,800,000	10.430	939,597
SANM	0.096	3.73	9,600,000	12.600	761,905
PMCS	0.094	4.5	9,400,000	20.100	467,662
YHOO	0.089	3.04	8,900,000	22.515	395,292
Total	1	2.78	100,000,000		

Short Portfolio

Ticker	Weight	β	Position Size ($)	Share Price ($)	# Shares
Q	0.108	2.9	10,800,000	4.320	2,500,000
NWL	0.114	0.85	11,400,000	22.770	500,659
MRK	0.115	0.39	11,500,000	46.200	248,918
SGP	0.118	0.35	11,800,000	17.390	678,551
T	0.118	0.72	11,800,000	20.300	581,281
KSS	0.134	0.81	13,400,000	44.940	298,175
EK	0.145	1.21	14,500,000	25.670	564,862
KG	0.148	0.59	14,800,000	15.260	969,856
Total	1	0.95	100,000,000		

Even when a portfolio is market-neutral, beta can have an unintended impact on performance. If our investor's portfolio is long higher beta stocks compared to the beta of the short positions, then in a market selloff the longs will decrease more than the shorts and what seemed like a market-neutral portfolio still loses money. Take another look at our example portfolio and you'll see that we have this problem: the weighted-average beta of the long portfolio is 2.78, while that for the short portfolio is 0.95.

Some hedge funds try to control risk so that their portfolios are both dollar-neutral and beta-neutral. Without completely changing her portfolio, our investor can use professional portfolio management tools (or a spreadsheet if the portfolio is relatively simple) to adjust the weights of the positions so that she can achieve both objectives at the same time. Portfolio construction and risk management are a rich, quantitative field with a deep literature available for those with an interest in delving deeper into these topics.

1.2.4 Performance Measurement[10]

Throughout this book we will talk about the performance of alternative investments. When investing in publicly traded assets, such as stocks, bonds, currencies, and commodities, performance measurement is relatively straightforward because there is a market price to use as a reference point. Private market assets, such as private companies, however, do not have a readily available market price, which makes performance measurement more complicated.

1.2.4.1 Liquid Assets

Performance measurement is relatively straightforward for individual liquid assets, such as stocks and bonds: the change in price or value during a time period, expressed as a percentage. For example, when performing an internet search for the stock price of Itau Unibanco in Brazil (BVMF: ITUB4), the results in Figure 1.8 show the price change of +1.01%, calculated as the 1-day price change divided by yesterday's price, or 0.26/25.74. The same calculation can be applied for any time period of interest; common measurement periods of returns are daily, monthly, quarterly, annual, year-to-date (YTD), and longer time frames such as 3-year, 5-year, and 10-year returns. Other statistical measures can be calculated based on the time series of returns, the most important of which are measures of *risk*, or "volatility." There are many available risk metrics but the simplest and most common is the standard deviation of daily returns, known by its Greek letter σ.

For investments in *portfolios* of liquid assets, the investment return is calculated as the weighted average of the changes in price of the individual assets. Selecting a corresponding measure of risk is more complicated. Depending on the type of portfolio being analyzed and

Market Summary > Itau Unibanco Holding SA Preference Shares

26.00 BRL

+0.26 (1.01%) ↑ today

30 Nov, 6:12 pm GMT-3 · Disclaimer

Open	25.80	Mkt cap	237.18B	CDP score	B
High	26.04	P/E ratio	8.89	52-wk high	31.29
Low	25.43	Div yield	1.74%	52-wk low	20.57

FIGURE 1.8. One-day stock price chart of Itau Unibanco in Brazil.
Source: Google, "banco itau stock price", retrieved December 1, 2022.

the objectives of the investor, several different metrics can be used to assess the performance relative to the amount of risk being taken:

1. the information ratio
2. the Sharpe ratio
3. the Sortino ratio
4. Capture ratios

1. **The information ratio** (abbreviated IR) is an appropriate measure for funds that have a clear benchmark (e.g., a European large cap growth fund). IR captures the amount of additional return delivered by a portfolio in excess of its benchmark, relative to the degree to which the return of the portfolio on average differs from the return of its benchmark:

$$\frac{E\left(R_p\right) - R_{benchmark}}{TE}$$

where $E(R_p)$ is the historical or average return of portfolio p; $R_{benchmark}$ is the historical or average return of the portfolio's benchmark; and TE is the tracking error of the portfolio (the standard deviation of the difference between the portfolio and the benchmark return, over time). Funds with a high IR have low tracking error and outperform the benchmark on a consistent basis.

2. **The Sharpe ratio** is a measure of risk-adjusted performance (i.e., the amount of performance generated per unit of risk). The formula divides excess or expected returns by the volatility (standard deviation) of returns:

$$\frac{E(R_i) - R_f}{\sigma_i}$$

where $E(R_i)$ is the historical, or expected, return of asset i; R_f is the risk-free rate, often represented by the interest rate on short-term US treasury bills; and σ_i is the standard deviation (volatility) of the returns for asset i. Although valuable as a measure of risk-adjusted performance, there are some important limitations to this measure. First, it is a standalone measure and does not capture the incremental effect of adding an asset to a portfolio. Second, it is less valuable when returns for an asset are non-normally distributed (e.g., when the probability of a large positive or negative result is more likely than accounted for by the normal distribution [so-called "fat tails"]). Third, the formula is sensitive to the time period being used—annual (or annualized) data are assumed and calculating a Sharpe ratio using non-annualized quarterly or monthly data will generate a measure with a very different magnitude.

3. **The Sortino ratio** measures the return relative to the amount of *downside* risk instead of the full, two-sided risk, a reflection of investors' greater concern with the risk of losses instead of the "risk" of profits. This ratio is particularly useful for assets such as insurance or bank loans where the distribution of historical returns is asymmetrical (skewed), with high

probabilities of small profits and very low probabilities of large losses. To calculate the Sortino ratio, investors replace the two-sided standard deviation σ_i in the Sharpe ratio with a one-sided measure of downside volatility and replace the risk-free rate with a target return.

4. **Capture ratios** measure the performance of a fund manager during periods of positive or negative market returns. *Upside capture* is the ratio between the performance of the fund and the performance of the market during a rising market. A value of 1.0 indicates that the manager performs in line with the market, while upside capture of less than 1.0 means the manager does not completely track the market when moving higher. For example, if the market increases by 10% over a period and a fund increases 8%, then the upside capture would be 0.8 to reflect the fact that the fund only captured 80% of the positive market performance. A similar logic applies to the opposite measure, *downside capture*.

1.2.4.2 Illiquid Assets

Many investors in illiquid, private markets assets—private equity, in particular—measure their performance using internal rate of return (IRR), a financial metric used to measure the profitability of an investment while accounting for the time value of money. Many readers will be familiar with the concept of NPV, or net present value; IRR is the annual return (or discount rate in NPV calculations) that makes the NPV of cash flows in a discounted cash flow analysis equal to zero.[11]

There are a few problems with IRR, including inconsistent definitions across managers and no reference to a benchmark. In some instances, private equity managers draw on lines of credit before issuing a capital call, shortening the amount of time that investors have their capital in the fund and therefore "increasing" IRR. The IRR calculation also assumes investors can reinvest interim cash flows at the IRR, which is unlikely to be the case.

Separate from or in addition to IRR, some private markets funds prefer to use a measure of return on capital without accounting for time. These measures can be called either "multiple on invested capital"

(MOIC) or "total value to paid-in" ratio (TVPI, or sometimes just TPI). These measures are expressed as follows:

$$TVPI(or\ MOIC) = (D + RV)/PIC$$

where

- D = distributions (any money returned to investors after selling a portfolio holding)
- RV = residual value (the estimated value of positions remaining in the portfolio)
- PIC = paid-in capital (the amount of funds delivered by the investor, which is not the same [always less than or equal to] as committed capital)

MOIC and TVPI are absolute measures of return, rather than percentages. To illustrate, let us revisit the example in Section 1.2.2.3:

> The GP raises a $1 billion fund to invest in private companies around the world. An LP commits to invest $50 million, and at closing delivers $10 million, or 20% of its commitment, to the fund. The GP uses the initial capital (20% of $1 billion, or $200 million) to buy three mid-sized companies it has already identified.

In this example, the committed capital is $50 million and the paid-in capital is $10 million. If the following year the fund sells one of the companies for a profit of $50 million, the fund could distribute that capital back to its LP investors. In our example, because the investor represents 5% of the fund, it would receive a distribution of 5% * $50 million = $2.5 million. If the residual value of the remaining two positions is $200 million, then our investor's share of that value is 5% * $200 million = $10 million. It follows that:

$$TVPI(or\ MOIC) = (D + RV)/PIC = (\$2.5 + \$10)/\$10$$
$$= \$12.5/\$10 = 1.25x$$

Because these measures of return on capital ignore the timing of cash flows, comparison across funds and time frames is challenging.

To address some of the shortcomings of IRR and MOIC (TVPI), some research and publications refer to "public market equivalent" (PME) returns. PME is expressed as a ratio between the private fund and public market returns, such that a ratio above 1.0 reveals relative outperformance and below 1.0 means underperformance. To illustrate, consider a fund that drew $200 million from an investor on January 1, 2013 and paid out $500 million on December 31, 2017. Alternatively, an investor could have invested the $200 million in the S&P 500, which would have returned $416 million over the same period.[12] The PME would be as shown in Exhibit 1.2.

EXHIBIT 1.2. Calculation of public market equivalent return ($ million)

	Private equity fund	*S&P 500*
January 1, 2013	200	200
December 31, 2017	500	416
PME		500 / 416 = 1.2x

In addition to the methodological problems described above, there is another, structural issue that complicates the measurement of performance for private markets investments. Unlike publicly traded assets, such as stocks and bonds, there is no generally accepted daily price that values a private company, for example, and only when the investor exits the position will the final value be known. Between the purchase and sale of a private asset, therefore, private markets investors use "mark-to-market" valuations for their portfolio holdings.

For the reasons described above, readers whose investing experience is limited to stocks, bonds, or mutual funds/unit trusts may find it difficult to evaluate the performance of private markets investments like venture capital and private equity funds.

1.2.5 Due Diligence

The process of evaluating investment opportunities is referred to as "due diligence." Some readers will be aware that this term is used in other settings as well (e.g., in mergers and acquisitions the buyer performs "due diligence" on the firm it wants to purchase). Depending on the type of investment being made, investors may perform due diligence at the individual asset level or at the fund level. The set of issues to be examined varies widely between the two levels and across different asset classes as will be explained in the following sections.

1.2.5.1 Individual Assets

- **Financial:** Financial due diligence may take different forms depending on the asset itself. For a real estate property, investors should check the validity of the financial statements provided by the sellers, reviewing a building's rental collections from each of the tenants, checking that the bank accounts tally with the items in accounting ledgers, and monitoring outstanding expenses, such as unpaid utilities, government taxes, bank loans, salaries, and other liabilities. A debt or equity investment in a private company will likely require similar analysis of financial statements and other information. For assets, such as collectibles, however, this step may not be required.

- **Legal:** Legal due diligence sets out to confirm that the ownership of the property, land titles, building permits, and the use of the building are in order and in accordance with what was represented by the seller. In addition, all the tenancy contracts, loan documents, security and maintenance services agreements from suppliers, among other things, need to be reviewed. Given the complexity and volume of work, investors typically hire lawyers to perform this task. While performing the legal due diligence, investors should also consider if potential legal or compliance issues might arise after the transaction is completed.

- **Physical condition:** Tangible assets, such as collectibles or real estate, require due diligence on the physical condition of the asset. This task is usually outsourced to a qualified person, e.g., a licensed engineer, who can properly assess the condition, the quality, and sufficiency of maintenance and upkeep. In a real estate setting, if there were defects in the plumbing, or glitches in the air-conditioning compressor, or deficiencies with the filtration system of the swimming pool, the qualified person will estimate the cost of rectifying the faults so that the investor can renegotiate the purchase price or make provisions for capital expenditure in their cash flow analysis.

- **Provenance:** For some assets the ownership history, or "provenance," is extremely important. For example, artwork with well-documented provenance will be more valuable since an unbroken trail of verifiable ownership reduces the risk that the artwork could be counterfeit. If an asset was owned or used by someone famous (a house someone famous once lived in, or a football jersey worn in a World Cup match and signed by the famous player), that too can make an asset more valuable.

1.2.5.2 Third-Party Funds

Performing due diligence on third-party managed funds involves a different set of issues; the fund manager performs due diligence on the individual assets as part of its investment process, so the investor needs to investigate the manager of individual assets. Some of the important concepts are described in Table 1.4.

The framework described in Table 1.4 is a highly simplified checklist of some of the more important investment due diligence issues. Professional investors often have teams dedicated to performing due diligence on managers or outsource that function to specialized investment consultants. The following paragraphs provide examples for investors who may not be familiar with these concepts.

First, the investor should review the fund mandate, which is a high-level description of the objectives of the fund, the expected level of risk, and the types of assets allowed in the portfolio. At the same time the investor should review the strategy which describes how the manager intends to invest the funds and generate performance. Since each fund defines its own investment mandate and its own strategy, funds within a given asset class may vary greatly in style and approach. With this information at hand, the investor can make an informed judgment about the suitability of the fund and watch for signs that the manager may be deviating from the mandate or strategy. For example, a manager might have a mandate to deliver consistent but lower risk returns and follow a strategy that includes stocks with high dividends and up to 20% corporate debt. If the investor reviews a newsletter or

TABLE 1.4.   Performance of due diligence on third-party managed funds

Concept	Comments	Example
Mandate	What the manager is authorized to do; may also be called "Objectives"	The income mandate seeks to provide stable and regular income using mainly money-market and other cash investments, government bonds, corporate bonds, and, to a lesser extent, high-dividend equities (to a maximum of 25%)[†]
Strategy	How the manager describes how the fund will generate performance	To invest in under-covered companies with strong products and local brands, poised to benefit from the growth in domestic consumption in emerging economies
Investment universe	The target set of securities or companies for investment	Stocks included in the MSCI Emerging Markets Index
Investment process	Describe the process from idea generation to asset selection	Screen for liquid stocks trading below their average historical valuation, then fundamental analysis to identify solid companies trading at a discount to fair value
Historical performance	1-, 3-, 5-, 10+-year performance, both absolute and relative to benchmark	Performance disclosures are often highly regulated for public funds and will usually show a table with the fund's performance and the benchmark performance over the same time period for easy comparison
Number of positions, position sizing	How many positions are typically in the fund? How is position size determined? Is there a maximum position size?	50–70 positions, with a maximum position size of 5%
Capacity	The amount of capital a fund could invest without making it too difficult to generate returns. For public markets, this may be approximated by (# positions * average position size) relative to the average daily value traded in the target securities.	Estimated capacity of $1 billion, assuming most positions could be sold in one week and all capital could be returned in one month

TABLE 1.4. (Continued)

Concept	Comments	Example
Leverage	How much leverage is used? What is the source of financing?	Maximum leverage of 150%
Team/Structure	Experience and size of team, separation of responsibilities (checks and balances). Does it match with the fund strategy?	One portfolio manager and team of four research analysts
Fees	What fees are charged (management fees, incentive fees) and how do they compare with averages for the strategy?	1.5% management fee, 15% performance fee for private funds, or 0.89% expense ratio for public funds
Liquidity	Minimum investment size, restrictions on redemptions (e.g., lockup period)	Quarterly redemptions with 3-month notice period
Transparency	How often is performance reported? What information is provided?	Quarterly letter to investors

†https://www.purecapital.eu/en/wealth-management/our-solutions/personalised-discretionary-management/income-mandate.html

report from the manager and notices the fund has large positions in risky technology growth stocks, that could raise a red flag due to inconsistency with the stated mandate and strategy.

The investment universe, number of positions, and average position size are interrelated and should be analyzed together. The investment universe defines the set of assets that the manager can draw from when building the fund; the universe might be expressed as "stocks in the MSCI Emerging Markets Index." The number of positions is usually given as a range; fundamental research is difficult and time-consuming, so the number of positions is generally smaller than portfolios managed using quantitative techniques that are more easily applied to longer lists of stocks. Average position size is useful when evaluating the size of the positions disclosed by the manager in the context of the strategy. For example, emerging markets stocks may not be very easy to trade, so an emerging markets fund with less than 40 positions and large ("concentrated") positions can pose significant risk. On the other hand, a large-cap growth fund that holds 400 small positions would be inconsistent with a stated fundamental investment process due to the amount of effort required to identify 400 attractive assets.

Finally, investors need to consider the team responsible for managing the fund. This step is crucial, as the success of a fund is dependent on its manager's ability manage the investments, maximize revenue opportunities, and ensure that the objectives of the fund are met. Due diligence should consider different attributes of the team, including

- the experience the manager has both running that specific fund and in aggregate, e.g., "John Doe has been portfolio manager for the fund since 2016 and has 28 years total investment experience."
- the total size of the research team relative to the size of the portfolio—a team of two people would have a difficult time managing a portfolio of 125 stocks if they are the only ones doing all the fundamental analysis as well.
- separation of responsibilities—the portfolio manager ("PM") could be distracted if he manages other portfolios at the same time, or there may be conflicts of interest in a small firm where the PMs may also hold a compliance or management role.

Due diligence is a difficult and important part of making any investment decision. Especially when investing in private assets or funds which make those kinds of investments, the information required for a thorough analysis may not be available. With experience, however, even individual investors can make better informed investment decisions that minimize some undesirable risks.

1.3 Diversification[13]

One reason investors allocate capital to alternative investments is to diversify their portfolios. Readers familiar with finance and statistics will recall the concept of correlation (or more accurately, covariance), a measure of how two things move relative to each other over time.

To better understand how this relates to investing, imagine a portfolio comprised entirely of shares in restaurant companies. When the Covid-19 pandemic hit and most of the world entered some sort of lockdown, dining at restaurants was severely restricted and all those stocks would have done poorly at the same time, bad news for the *undiversified* portfolio of restaurant stocks. At the same time, however, shares in "work from home" or "lockdown" companies like Zoom and Netflix did very well. Those stocks had a *low correlation* to the restaurant stocks, and so adding Zoom or Netflix would have helped *diversify* the portfolio.

Implicit in that example are several important characteristics of diversification. To begin with, diversification helps reduce risk, in this case, the risk that the entire portfolio reacts the same way to an external event. However, diversification can be costly. It may take more work (analysis) to build a diversified portfolio, since one of the objectives will be to actively search for investments that are low correlation with the rest of the portfolio. Additionally, a diversified portfolio will never perform as well as the strongest of its investments, so investors may regret not having more capital allocated to the riskier assets. However, research shows that diversification is a powerful tool that investors can use to generate long-term performance while simultaneously lowering risk.

Alternative investments are an attractive option for long-term investing in part because they tend to have lower correlation to stocks and bonds. Investment professionals often speak of portfolios in terms of the "efficient frontier," a way of understanding the return (y-axis) and risk (x-axis) of different portfolios formed by combinations of different assets. In Figure 1.9, the dark line represents portfolios formed only from stocks and/or bonds in different proportions.

Portfolios on the light line may also include an allocation to alternatives. The light line is always to the left of the dark line, meaning that for a given value of return (y-axis), the portfolio with an allocation to alternatives will have lower risk than the portfolio that only holds stocks and/or bonds. The alternative assets described in Chapters 2–4 offer investors many options to diversify their portfolios. Chapter 5 describes several techniques investors use to build portfolios of traditional and alternative assets to satisfy different objectives for risk and return.

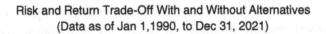

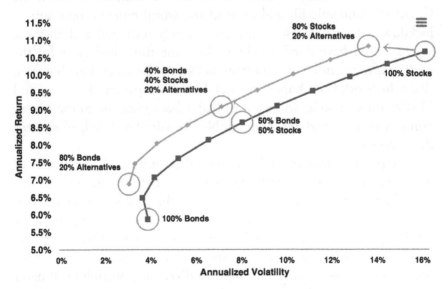

FIGURE 1.9. Risk and return trade-off with and without alternatives.

Source: Morgan Stanley, https://www.morganstanley.com/ideas/alternative-investments-portfolio-diversification, last accessed 28th January 2023.

Finally, it is worth noting that the diversification benefits associated with alternatives apply not only between traditional assets and alternatives but also *within* the set of alternative investments. Just as the portfolio holding only restaurant stocks is undiversified, so too would be a portfolio consisting of only equity long-short hedge funds, or only global private equity funds. This places an incremental burden of manager research and due diligence on the would-be investor in alternative assets; just as mutual funds offer diversified portfolios of stocks and bonds, Chapter 2, Section 2.6 describes a similar product ("funds of funds") for alternative investments.

1.4 Regulation

Securities regulation is a rich, complex, and technical subject well beyond the scope of this book; however, two aspects of regulation are important for the chapters that follow and merit a high-level explanation: (1) protections for investors; and (2) certain regulations for investment managers.

1.4.1 Regulatory Protections for Investors

Regulatory agencies such as the Securities and Exchange Commission (SEC) in the United States and the Monetary Authority of Singapore (MAS) have a mandate to provide some level of consumer protection when it comes to investments. One of the most common ways in which regulators protect consumers is to restrict who is permitted to invest in unregulated alternative investments such as hedge funds and private equity. The reasoning being applied is that the average retail investor may not be able to properly assess the risks involved in alternative investments, so only "sophisticated" investors are permitted to make such investments. Countries may define "sophisticated" in different ways, but the basic principle is to use either income or wealth as a proxy for investment knowledge as described in Table 1.5.

Even with such consumer protections in place, fraud (and theft) is still a part of modern financial markets, and investors still lose money. This has been a noticeable problem in the unregulated market for cryptocurrencies and tokens (see Chapter 4, Section 4.4), but even well-known businesses are vulnerable to unintentional and intentional risks such as those described below.

1.4.1.1 Accounting Fraud

One of the largest (known) cases of accounting fraud concerned the US energy company Enron.[14] In the wake of the deregulation of energy markets, by 1990 Enron was established as an energy trading company and supplier. Enron executives used a mark-to-market accounting policy and off-balance sheet special purpose vehicles (SPVs) to hide losses from investors. The prestigious audit firm Arthur Andersen was complicit in this fraud, instructing Enron to shred documents; Arthur Andersen was disgraced and essentially dissolved. Enron filed for bankruptcy on December 2, 2001, and its top executives were variously convicted of fraud, conspiracy, and insider trading.

TABLE 1.5. Accredited investor equivalents in different countries

Country	Accredited investor equivalent
United States	Accredited Investor • An individual whose income exceeds $200,000 in each of the two most recent years (or $300,000 in joint income with a person's spouse) and who reasonably expects to reach the same income level in the current year • An individual whose net wealth exceeds $1 million, excluding value of primary residence
Canada	Accredited Investor • An individual who, alone or together with a spouse, owns financial assets worth more than $1 million before taxes but net of related liabilities • An individual who, alone or together with a spouse, has net assets of at least $5,000,000 • An individual whose net income before taxes exceeded $200,000 (or $300,000 in joint income with a spouse) in both of the last two years and who expects to maintain at least the same level of income this year • An individual who currently is, or once was, a registered adviser or dealer, other than a limited market dealer

The EU and Norway	Elective Professional Client
	• The "Qualitative Test": The firm undertakes an adequate assessment of the expertise, experience, and knowledge of the client that gives reasonable assurance that the client is capable of making their own investment decisions
	• The "Quantitative Test": Client meets at least two of the following:
	  • has carried out transactions of significant size on the relevant market at an average frequency of 10 per quarter over the previous four quarters
	  • has a financial portfolio exceeding EUR 500,000
	  • works or has worked in the financial sector for at least one year
	• The client must state in writing that it wishes to be treated as a professional client and the firm must give the clear warning of the protections that client may lose

Singapore	Accredited Investor • An individual whose net personal assets exceed S$2 million • An individual whose income in the preceding 12 months exceeds S$300,000
Hong Kong	Professional Investor • Individuals, either alone or with any associates on a joint account, having a portfolio of not less than HK$8 million or its equivalent in foreign currency
Australia	Sophisticated Investor • A person who has net assets of at least A$2.5 million; or • A person who has a gross income of A$250,000 for each of the last two financial years

Source: https://toniic.com/accredited-investor-equivalents/.

1.4.1.2 Ponzi Scheme

Bernie Madoff ran one of the largest known Ponzi investment schemes before confessing in 2008 as a result of the Global Financial Crisis.[15] Starting from modest origins in the 1960s, Madoff formed a broker-dealer called Madoff Securities. Afterwards his firm began to offer investment funds that were described as following a derivatives strategy called "split-strike conversion"—and clients, most of them retail, only understood that the track record was consistently positive year after year. Regardless of whether the markets moved up or down, Madoff continued to post positive returns until the market went sharply negative at the beginning of the Global Financial Crisis in 2008. At that point, as investors clamored to redeem their holdings in the fund, it was revealed that Madoff had not actually been running a special proprietary investment strategy, but rather he had been running a Ponzi scheme.

1.4.1.3 Mismanagement

Long-Term Capital Management (LTCM), founded by John Meriwether and colleagues from Salomon Brothers in 1994, specialized in fixed income arbitrage. In this strategy, LTCM tried to identify assets that were relatively mispriced based on a modeled fair value, going long on the underpriced assets and short on the overpriced assets. If its models were correct, LTCM could realize a profit when the assets converged to their theoretical values. Because the absolute price differentials were quite small, fixed income arbitrageurs like LTCM typically used a lot of leverage to transform small returns into larger returns of greater interest to investors. Unfortunately for LTCM, just because the models flagged assets as relatively mispriced, that didn't mean that the mispricing would correct itself straightaway. During one period in 1998, prices for assets in LTCM's portfolio were mispriced *and continued to become even more mispriced*; with leverage, the losses quickly reached a point where the firm could no longer afford to stay in business and the fund was liquidated.

1.4.2 Regulations for Fund Managers

As a rule, investments in stocks or bonds that trade on an exchange enjoy some level of protection as a result of regulatory restrictions placed on the companies that issue stocks or bonds to the public. For example, companies with public securities may be required to disclose audited financial information on a regular basis and hold annual shareholder meetings where owners of the stock may vote on certain company matters. In the United States, an important regulation is the Sarbanes-Oxley Act of 2002. Passed in response to the bursting of the "internet bubble" in 2001 as well as the cases of accounting fraud at Enron, described above, and WorldCom, the "SOX" or "Sarbox" Act strengthened rules for accounting and external audit firms, enhanced requirements for corporate financial disclosures, and addressed conflicts of interest for securities analysts, investment banks, and other securities firms.

Investors in stocks and bonds, including institutional investors managing mutual funds and hedge funds, benefit from the improved oversight enabled by Sarbanes-Oxley. To protect the ultimate investors in commingled funds, another layer of regulatory protection covers certain investment products in different jurisdictions.

- **United States:** Mutual funds in the United States are subject to the terms of the Investment Company Act of 1940. Under the terms of the so-called '40 Act, covered funds are subject to restrictions in concentration of holdings (limits on the amount of capital allocated to any one issuer or industry); limitations on the percentage ownership of any one security without disclosure (10% of shares outstanding); must provide regular (commonly implemented as daily) liquidity; implement symmetrical performance fees that reward profits and givebacks on losses; and disclose information such as fund holdings on a regular basis. To this last point, for example, investment managers with more than $100 million AUM must submit 13F filings to the SEC that report holdings as of the end of the previous calendar quarter within 45 days of the quarter-end.
- **Europe**. Member states of the European Union have attempted to harmonize their securities regulations under the Markets in Financial Instruments Directive (abbreviated MiFID). More specifically for investment funds, the Undertakings for Collective Investment in Transferable Securities (UCITS) directives impose restrictions on liquidity, diversification, and transparency in a similar vein to the US '40 Act.

Alternative investment managers may be subject to less restrictive regulations or may be entirely unregulated, depending on the type of investments being made, the size of the manager, and the jurisdiction in which the fund is managed. In the United States, for example, there are exemptions available under the '40 Act that remove many of the requirements (e.g., allowing performance fees that do not allow for givebacks if performance is negative). Because managers of exempted funds are not subject to the same level of regulation, as a consequence they may only accept investments from accredited investors as described in Section 1.4.1.

The relationship between investor "sophistication" and the "lighter" regulation of alternative investment managers is the most relevant aspect of regulation for readers of this book. In the chapters that follow, we describe a wide range of alternative investments that are available to institutional or accredited investors but may not be available to (or appropriate for) the general public. Where different structures exist to provide regulated access to alternative strategies for retail investors, we highlight those structures appropriately.

1.5 Summary

This chapter introduces readers to the exciting and complex world of alternative investments, beginning with the definition of alternatives (not stocks, bonds, or cash) and continuing on to an overview of the market and some important characteristics of funds, such as structures, funding mechanisms, and fees. Common techniques, such as leverage and short selling, were described next, followed by a review of issues associated with performance measurement for alternatives. Additional issues and characteristics of investments in individual assets and funds were covered in Section 1.2.5, on due diligence, preparing readers for the long list of potential questions to ask when considering an investment in alternatives. The case for making such investments is supported by the benefits of portfolio diversification, and the low(er) correlation that alternative investments may have with traditional investment portfolios. Finally, the chapter concluded with a brief overview of regulation and the relationship with both investors and fund managers.

After reading this foundational information, readers will be better prepared for the remainder of the book which explores and explains the different types of alternative investments, starting in Chapter 2 with the most common "traditional" alternative investments: venture capital, private equity, hedge funds, infrastructure, and commodities. Real estate is conspicuously absent from that list, but only because it merits a separate discussion in Chapter 3. Finally, Chapter 4 presents a list of "modern alternatives" in various stages of maturity and accessibility to different types of investors.

Notes

1. Note the unequal time periods: 2003, 2009, 2019, 2020, and 2025(e). The CAGR refers to the compound annual growth rate between two time periods, even though they may be of very different length.
2. https://www.bloomberg.com/features/2022-lehman-brothers-collapse-plan-repay-after-bankruptcy/.
3. For more information on the efficient market hypothesis, see https://www.investopedia.com/terms/e/efficientmarkethypothesis.asp.
4. Academic research has identified a whole host of different "factors"— "any characteristic relating a group of securities that is important in explaining their return and risk" (https://www.msci.com/documents/1296102/1336482/Foundations_of_Factor_Investing.pdf/004e02ad-6f98-4730-90e0-ea14515ff3dc). A type of ETF called a "smart beta" product allows investors to allocate capital to these factors. As an example, the size factor states that over time, small stocks should outperform large stocks. Most equity indices are market cap-weighted, meaning that the constituent weight of any one stock in the index is based on its market cap, and larger stocks have larger weights in the index. An investor looking to capture the size factor could buy an ETF where the constituents of the S&P 500 are equal-weighted instead of market cap-weighted like the S&P 500 index. The difference in performance between this equal-weighted ETF and the traditional, market cap-weighted ETF, represents the performance of the size factor.
5. https://etfdb.com/etfdb-category/long-short/.
6. https://www.stoneridgefunds.com/documents/Stone_Ridge_Interval_Fund_Prospectus.pdf?v=7.

7. Real estate owners will be familiar with one common type of leverage: a mortgage. The use of leverage in real estate investing is explained in detail in Chapter 3 and the Appendix.

8. This example uses the Hong Kong (Hang Seng) listing for Tencent for illustrative purposes only; some investors may not be able to short stocks listed on certain exchanges.

9. For simplicity, we have ignored the financing cost in this example. When hedge funds borrow the stock to sell it short, they pay fees that would be subtracted from the return, similar to the financing cost of leverage explained in Section 1.2.3.1. If the stock pays a dividend while the hedge fund is short, the fund must pay those dividends as well because the owner of the stock would have received dividends had it not lent the stock to the hedge fund.

10. Readers looking for more information on this topic may refer to https://www.morganstanley.com/im/publication/insights/articles/articles_publictoprivateequityintheusalongtermlook_us.pdf.

11. Calculating IRR (or NPV) is best done with a financial calculator or spreadsheet. The material here is drawn from https://www.investopedia.com/terms/i/irr.asp and mirrors that which can be found in any number of corporate finance textbooks.

12. The value of an equivalent $200 million investment in the S&P 500 over the same period would be calculated based on the change in the closing price from the beginning to the end of the period.

13. See https://www.investopedia.com/investing/importance-diversification/ for a non-technical description of diversification.

14. See https://www.investopedia.com/updates/enron-scandal-summary/.

15. Interested readers may wish to refer to https://en.wikipedia.org/wiki/Madoff_investment_scandal or one of the many articles and videos available on the topic.

Chapter 2

Traditional Alternatives

The world of alternative investments can seem overwhelming at first due to the number of different asset classes that are considered "alternatives." The newest of these traditional alternatives are venture capital and hedge funds, both of which trace their origins to the 1940s. Investments in companies, infrastructure, and commodities, however, date back hundreds of years or more. With the exception of most hedge funds, these alternative investments are made in private rather than public entities (i.e., ownership in a private company rather than shares of stock in a public company listed on a securities exchange).

Collectively, these assets are often referred to as "private markets" and represent an important and growing subset of investment products, especially for larger institutional investors. One reason for the growth is that risk-adjusted returns from private markets strategies have been attractive (see Table 2.1, on p. 48, for recent data). As described in the sections that follow, modern iterations of these investments are subject to the same structures and regulatory oversight described in Chapter 1.

2.1 Venture Capital

Venture capital (VC) is a type of investment in private companies where the firms are young, small, and hopefully attractive prospects for an initial public offering or sale to a bigger industry player. The venture capital industry originated in the United States in 1946 when Boston-based American Research and Development was formed to commercialize technologies developed in WWII by investing in early-stage startups. General Georges F. Doriot from Harvard Business School, considered the father of VC, focused on adding value beyond just supplying capital, including more "hands-on" help through industry expertise and management experience. In 1957, an extremely successful investment in Digital Equipment Company (DEC) was described as a "home run"[1] due to its outsized positive performance. From that point forward, venture capital grew around the dual concepts of "hands-on" investing and the search for "home runs," especially those with valuations over $1 billion which are called "unicorns."

Since its relatively modest beginnings more than half a century ago, venture capital has evolved into a dynamic, global industry. According to consultancy KPMG, 2021 was another very active year for venture capital even when compared to a recent string of years with strong activity. Since 2014, global VC investments have exceeded $671 billion in capital across 38,644 deals (Figure 2.1).

Furthermore, since 2015, the global VC market has received new capital allocations of US$100–200 billion per year flowing into 1,400–1,700 funds (Figure 2.2).

Such strong flows of new capital imply that performance must be attractive, otherwise why would investors allocate so much money to VC? A recent report by financial data provider PitchBook uses short-term IRRs[2] to describe the strong performance for the period 2012–2021; in every category, venture capital has the highest reported return (Table 2.1).

As important contributors to the maturation and success of the VC market, some prominent investors like the ones listed in Table 2.2 have achieved near-legendary status among entrepreneurs and allocators alike.

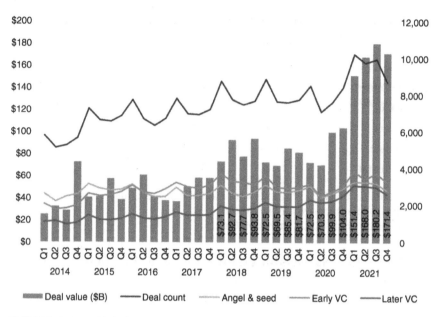

FIGURE 2.1. Global venture financing activity, 2014–2021.
Source: Lavender and Moore, 2022, KPMG International.

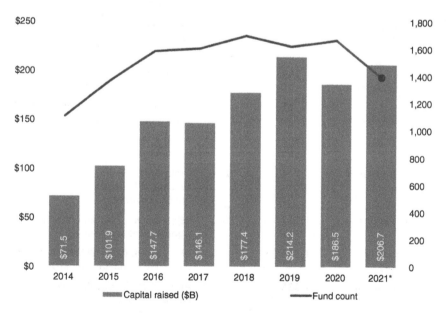

FIGURE 2.2. Global venture fundraising, 2014–2021.
Source: Lavender and Moore, 2022, KPMG International.

TABLE 2.1. Rolling one-year horizon IRR by strategy (%)

	1-year	3-year	5-year	10-year
Private equity	46.6	27.4	22.5	17.6
Venture capital	50.5	33.7	25.3	17.8
Real estate	24.8	11.8	11.2	12.4
Real assets	20.7	6.4	7.4	6.6
Private debt	14.9	8.7	8.3	9.5
Private capital	37.6	20.9	17.8	14.9

Notes: Data as of 12/31/2021. Private Capital totals include Funds of funds and Secondaries, omitted here for simplification.
Source: Hilary et al., 2022, PitchBook Data.

TABLE 2.2. Successful VC investors and their investments

Firm	# Investments	Total funds ($ billion)	Key investments/exits
Accel	1,424	12.3	Facebook, Groupon, Dropbox, Spotify, Etsy, Baidu, Hootsuite, Slack
Andreessen Horowitz	806	4.2	Facebook, Groupon, Zynga, Jawbone, Skype, Pinterest, Slack
Benchmark Capital	598	3	eBay, Twitter, Ariba, Juniper Networks, Red Hat, Tropos Networks
Bessemer Venture Partners	949	6	Skype, VeriSign, Yelp, LinkedIn, Zoosk, LifeLock, Twilio, DocuSign
Draper Fisher Jurvetson	83	7	Baidu, Skype, Overture, Hotmail, Tesla Motors, SpaceX
GGV Capital	602	6.2	Alibaba, Airbnb, Grab, Peloton Interactive, Slack
Greylock Partners	704	2	Groupon, LinkedIn, Pandora, Facebook, Dropbox, tumblr, Payoneer
Kleiner Perkins	1,168	9	Beyond Meat, Twitter, Uber, Slack, Google, Amazon.com
New Enterprise Associates	1,589	11	Uber, 3com, CareerBuilder, Diapers.com, TiVo, Vonage, WebMD
Sequoia Capital	1,335	4	Apple, Google, Kayak, LinkedIn, PayPal, Yahoo!, YouTube

Source: Based on Sarath, "Best 100 Active Venture Capitalist Firms for Startup Funding," *Eqvista,* July 20, 2020, https://eqvista.com/best-100-active-venture-capitalist-firms-for-startup-funding/, October 2021.

2.2.1 How Venture Capital Works[3]

Venture capital firms are typically structured with the GP/LP structure described in Chapter 1, Section 1.2.2.1. The VC firm is the general partner (GP) and is responsible for managing one or more funds. GPs receive compensation from the fund, typically a management fee and a share of any profits generated, in return for managing the investments. External investors invest in a specific fund rather than the VC firm itself; these investors are referred to as limited partners (LPs) since their interests in the fund are only financial. The funds in turn invest in companies, often younger startups, which are then referred to as portfolio companies.

Venture capital funds often invest in startups that have reached a specific "stage" of evolution. The lines between stages are not entirely black and white, but generally refer to something like what is shown in Table 2.3.

TABLE 2.3. Stages in startup development and typical investors

Funding stage	State of the company	Investors
Friends and family	Founders are exploring the idea	Founders tap into their networks to raise initial capital beyond their own personal investments
Angel	Developing initial prototype called the "minimum viable product" or MVP. Often "pre-revenue."	Often former entrepreneurs who are comfortable backing other entrepreneurs at this early stage of development
Seed	First product(s) and first paying customer(s). Need to expand the team to scale.	Typically when the company accepts the first "institutional" investments from venture capital
Series A Series B	Developing product-market fit and hopefully growing quickly and/or consistently	Referred to as "early stage" investments (early stage VC)
Series C Series D and beyond	Strong product-market fit and revenue growth. Starting to evaluate public capital (IPO) or strategic sales vs. remaining private.	Referred to as "growth stage" investments (growth VC)

Particularly for so-called "early stage" companies (i.e., up through Series B), VC investors have very limited "traditional" information such as financial statements to rely on because the companies are too young and under-developed. Instead, there is often said to be more "art" than "science" involved at this stage, and VC investors pay considerable attention to other, more qualitative inputs including:

- the backgrounds of the founders;
- the planned product or service and how it fits with a potential market;
- the size of that market (referred to as the total addressable market, or TAM);
- the business model, i.e., how the firm will make money.

While individual firms undoubtedly have their own versions, a typical venture capital investment process has four principal steps. The first step is sourcing and screening deals. VC firms may read through more than 100 proposals for every investment made, looking for the right set of founders with a great idea and a large addressable market. Once the startup is identified, screened, and the VC has conducted its due diligence, the next step is to structure the deal. Here the investor[4] and startup agree on the amount and type of financing, the timing of capital, board representation, and other variables that form the basis for the relationship between the two firms. After the investment is made, the third step is for the VC to help grow the startup through "hands-on" advice and know-how. Common examples include helping identify critical new hires and making introductions to potential customers or industry partners. Finally, the last step is to harvest the investment. When all goes well, this may take the form of a sale to another firm in the same or related industry, or, in some cases, an initial public offering (IPO).

Within "early" and "growth" stage investing, it's important to note that successful companies are usually growing quickly and may need to raise additional capital every 6–24 months. As the companies demonstrate their ability to grow and meet other operational milestones, these future rounds of fundraising take place at increasing valuations as well. The key concept here is "pre-money" and "post-money" valuations.

Pre-money valuation reflects the value of the company before any new fundraising; post-money valuation includes the next round of fundraising. While this may seem to be a trivial difference in terminology, it has important implications for early-stage investing as illustrated in the following example (Table 2.4). A startup wants to raise $1 million in a Series A round and meets with a VC investor who says she will invest at a $4 million valuation. Depending on whether the investor is referring to pre- or post-money valuations, the value of the company and the ownership stake for the founders can be quite different.

TABLE 2.4. Difference between pre-money and post-money valuations

	Pre-money valuation			Post-money valuation	
	$	%		$	%
Founders	4,000,000	80	Founders	3,000,000	75
Investor	1,000,000	20	Investor	1,000,000	25
TOTAL	5,000,000	100	TOTAL	4,000,000	100

In this example, the difference in language implies a difference in valuation of $1,000,000 and a 5% difference in the share of the firm remaining for the founders. If the company is successful, that 5% difference in ownership stake could be worth tens or hundreds of millions of dollars.

Venture capital investors must anticipate the impact of future fundraising and reserve capital to participate in follow-on investments if they want to maintain their ownership stake. In the above example, when the company raises $20 million in its Series B, if the VC doesn't invest at least $5 million, or 25% of the Series B round, its ownership stake will decrease. Therefore, a common rule of thumb is to reserve 66% of the fund for follow-on investments (i.e., a GP investing a $75 million fund might initially deploy $25 million and reserve $50 million for follow-on investments in the most promising portfolio companies).

2.1.2 Performance

Venture capital fund performance is often described as following a power law distribution, meaning that a small percentage of big winners deliver most of the performance—note how this follows directly from the original idea of seeking "home runs" described earlier in this chapter. Table 2.5 illustrates how this might work in practice. A given set of venture investments are ranked from top to bottom by performance and split into 10 equal groups, or deciles. The aggregate performance of the deals in each decile is plotted below as the percentage of total fund performance (i.e., the top decile of deals accounts for 90% of the performance of the fund). The success of just a small number of deals may account for all or nearly all of the fund performance, reinforcing the need for venture capitalists to seek out "home runs."

TABLE 2.5.   Representative performance of VC investments by decile

Decile	% deal count	% total fund performance
1	10	90
2	10	10
3	10	5
4	10	2
5	10	1
6	10	1
7	10	0
8	10	0
9	10	−2
10	10	−7
Total	100	100

When evaluating the financial returns from venture capital as an asset class, it is necessary to consider both the average *dispersion*[5] of returns and the average *persistence*[6] of returns. We turn first to the dispersion of returns.

Figure 2.3 presents 40 years of financial performance by asset class in a "box and whiskers" plot. The ends of the box represent the

75th and 25th percentiles, and the whiskers (the lines extending from the ends of the box) the 95th and 5th percentiles. To facilitate comparison across asset classes, the median of each box (50th percentile) is indexed to zero. Of the asset classes included in this analysis, venture capital has the greatest dispersion of returns, ranging from approximately +45% to –25%.

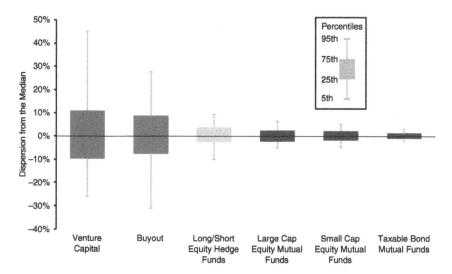

FIGURE 2.3. Dispersion of returns by asset class, 1980–2018.
Note: Returns for venture capital and buyout are based on net internal rates of return since inception for vintage years 1980–2018; returns for hedge funds and mutual funds are based on trailing 5-year annualized returns net of expenses with income reinvested through 12/31/2019.
Source: Mauboussin and Callahan, 2020, Morgan Stanley.

The implication is that an investment in venture capital could result in very attractive or very poor performance. So why are investors interested in venture capital? Aside from the attractive absolute levels of financial performance described earlier in Table 2.4, another reason may be the persistence of returns. Remembering that a GP typically manages multiple funds over time, Morgan Stanley looked at the persistence[7] of returns across funds from the same VC firm (Exhibit 2.1). Their findings show that VCs with a fund in the top quartile of performance are nearly 50% more likely to have their next fund also be in the top quartile; this holds true before and after the internet bubble in 2001.

EXHIBIT 2.1. Persistence for venture capital funds

Pre-2001	Subsequent Fund Quartile				Post-2000	Subsequent Fund Quartile			
	1	**2**	**3**	**4**		**1**	**2**	**3**	**4**
Previous Fund Quartile **1**	49%	14%	23%	14%	Previous Fund Quartile **1**	48%	20%	26%	6%
2	33%	27%	27%	13%	**2**	24%	43%	12%	22%
3	27%	36%	18%	20%	**3**	17%	23%	42%	19%
4	9%	20%	26%	46%	**4**	23%	14%	34%	29%

Source: Mauboussin and Callahan, 2020, Morgan Stanley.

This persistence in returns naturally leads investors in venture capital to want to invest in funds managed by the top GPs. Unfortunately, despite ever-larger funds, there is a finite amount of capacity available and everyone wants to invest with the same handful of firms.

2.1.3 Recent Developments

More recently, several developments are worth noting. First, two prominent investors have changed the size and speed of venture capital flows. A Japanese investor, Softbank, made huge investments in companies and encouraged the founders to think bigger than ever before. Some of these investments did relatively well (Uber) but others failed spectacularly (WeWork). As a result, the lasting legacy may be that investors no longer believe in the concept of "money moats" where huge bets can help startups become market leaders.[8]

Following nearly the opposite approach, a hedge fund called Tiger Global defied all convention with a very aggressive investment strategy: find deals early, close the deal quickly, offer very high valuations, and then stay hands-off.[9] Following this playbook, Tiger Global invested in many leading startups such as Peloton and Roblox at an early stage, generating billions of dollars in paper profits when those stocks went public. As of this writing, however, the venture market in 2022 has been far more challenging and the long-term performance of this aggressive strategy remains to be seen.

Third, Asia has become one of the strongest markets for venture investing since 2010. China in particular is home to many world-leading startups, though political and regulatory changes in 2020–2022 have the potential to negatively impact the local venture landscape. Beyond China, Southeast Asian VCs have generated strong performance through investments in local startups, such as Grab and Gojek, and the Japanese VC market is very active as well.

2.1.4 Summary

Venture capital is an attractive asset class for those who value startup stories and can access funds from the top firms. Without that kind of access, however, investors must recognize that investing in venture capital is very risky. For every hot IPO and Silicon Valley guru, there are many other companies and VCs that fail. First funds from new venture capitalists are especially difficult to assess, and inexperienced VC investors may do better by looking for ways to invest in subsequent funds.

2.2 Private Equity

Private equity (PE) generally refers to any strategy that makes equity investments in firms that are not publicly listed on a stock exchange. As opposed to venture capital which takes minority investments in young, smaller growth firms, private equity usually involves taking controlling stakes in larger, established firms to unlock embedded value through changes in strategy or structure. The firms in which private equity funds are investing (also referred to as "targets") may be private or, in a small number of cases, public and then "taken private." Modern private equity investing traces its origins to the 1970s and 1980s in the United States, a period when the likes of Michael Milken[10] encouraged junk-bond financing for leveraged buyouts, and the legendary buyout of RJR Nabisco by Kohlberg, Kravis, and Roberts (KKR) in 1988.

Since those early days, the number of private equity firms and deals has skyrocketed; a recent report by consultancy Bain & Co. (which has a shared history with PE firm Bain Capital) documents record levels of buyout activity in 2021, with over $1.1 trillion in total value—nearly double the level of 2020 and well above the previous record years of 2006 and 2007 (Figure 2.4).

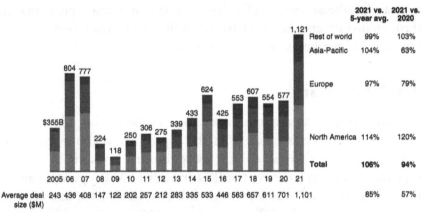

FIGURE 2.4.   Global buyout activity by region, 2005–2021 ($B)
Source: Bain Global Private Equity Report 2022.

Another measure of activity (and investor interest) is the amount of fresh capital raised for PE funds. Although 2021 was not a record year, Bain & Co. report that it was the second largest on record (Figure 2.5).

Like the earlier description of the venture capital industry, some of the early private equity investors have built global businesses that number among the largest and most influential investors in any asset class or region (Table 2.6).

2.2.1 How Private Equity Works

There are different flavors of private equity; the two most common strategies are called growth private equity and leveraged buyouts. In growth PE, investors look for mature companies with good products

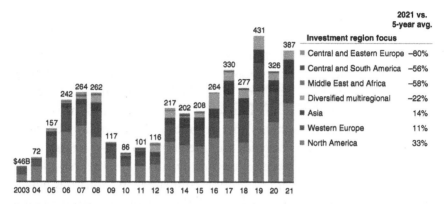

Notes: Buyout category includes buyout, balanced, coinvestment, and coinvestment multimanager funds; includes funds with final close and represents the year in which funds held their final close; excludes SoftBank Vision Fund

FIGURE 2.5. Global buyout capital raised by investment region, 2003–2021 ($B).

Source: Bain Global Private Equity Report 2022.

TABLE 2.6. Successful PE investors and their investments

Firm	HQ	Private equity assets *$ billion)	Notable investments
KKR	New York, NY	172	RJR Nabisco (1988), TXU (2007), Fiserv
Carlyle Group	Washington, DC	167	Supreme, Orion Breweries (JP)
Blackstone	New York, NY	131	Refinitiv, Ancestry, Bumble
Thoma Bravo	Chicago, IL	122	McAfee, FTX, QLIK, Solarwinds
Vista Equity Partners	Austin, TX	94	Klarna, PowerSchool
CVC Capital Partners	Luxembourg	87	Petco, Razer
Warburg Pincus	New York, NY	85	Ant Group, Inmarsat
TPG	San Francisco, CA	83	Airbnb, Viking Cruises
EQT	Sweden	75	Certara, Galderma

Source: Authors' selection of firms based on https://www.investopedia.com/articles/markets/011116/worlds-top-10-private-equity-firms-apo-bx.asp. AUM hand-retrieved from corporate websites, October 23, 2022.

and revenue growth, but which lack the capital to scale up their operations. Similarly, these firms are unlikely to have sufficient cash flow to finance their growth targets internally, which means that they are also unable to service the amount of debt that would be required for financing. Growth PE provides the capital to help these companies expand their operations; the PE investor typically executes the transaction via minority investments that require limited amounts of debt. Investments are usually held for the medium term (3–5 years) compared to the lifespan of a typical buyout PE fund (7–10 years). Ideally, growth PE investments are in leading companies in industries which are expected to grow more quickly than the overall economy, so that a tailwind is expected to support the continued growth of the company.

Buyouts are very different. Commonly referred to as LBOs or leveraged buyouts, that moniker correctly implies that these investments use a lot of leverage to acquire controlling stakes in the companies. In fact, because of the amount of leverage used—often 5–10 times the capital invested by the PE investor—target investments in buyout funds must have very strong cash flow and low existing debt to make the interest payments on the debt used for the leveraged buyout. Management is typically given very strong economic incentives to hit operational and financial targets every quarter, which might include cost cutting, changes in strategy, or smaller strategic acquisitions as part of the planned transformation of the company. Since buyouts are controlled or wholly owned, the exit process is a bit more complicated than for the minority investments used in growth investing. The biggest percentage of exits are through so-called industry sales to another company in the same industry.

Many buyouts follow one of four different strategies. The first is repackaging, where the investor buys a public company, makes some operational and/or financial changes, and then sells or IPOs the company. The second rationale is split-ups, where the investor sells different units of the company to unlock value—this is driven by a perception that the firm is trading below its sum-of-the-parts valuation. Third is a portfolio strategy, where the investor buys the company and then also buys a series of competitors in order to combine them into a single, larger company, sometimes called a "roll-up." Finally, there is the "savior deal," a management- or employee-led buyout to take control of a company and "save it" from bankruptcy or an unattractive sale.

Regardless of the strategy being used, company selection and leverage are important drivers of financial performance for investors. For deals where the private equity firm pursues operational changes at the firm, this "operational alpha" can be an equally important contributor to returns.

2.2.2 Valuation

Even though the holding period may be quite long, the basic principles of "buy low, sell high" still apply to private equity. At both ends of the investment, PE managers must use different valuation techniques to compensate for the lack of public stock prices to guide them. When buying private companies with predictable cash flows and sufficient operating history, private equity firms often apply one of two methods: either a discounted cash flow (DCF) analysis or earnings multiples. DCF analysis relies on the vast amount of data about the target company to forecast future cash flows, and then discounts those cash flows based on an appropriate cost of capital.[11] The earnings multiples valuation approach compares the target company to a set of public peer companies with similar scale and scope; common multiples used in private equity are Enterprise Value/EBITDA (EV/EBITDA), Enterprise Value/Sales, and Price/Earnings (P/E). Both approaches make assumptions about how different internal and external factors will affect valuation; more sophisticated investors will consider a mix of possible outcomes in a technique called scenario analysis, and then use the results of that analysis to calculate a valuation range for the target company. Making a better (or more realistic) estimate of valuation at the time of making the investment paves the way for more attractive returns when existing the investment.

Leveraged buyouts use some of the same information—especially the future cash flows—to estimate the maximum purchase price for the company while ensuring that the entities providing the financing will still be able to achieve their minimum expected returns. The difference between the value at purchase and at exit is called "value creation" and has three main components: earnings growth, multiple expansion, and debt restructuring/reduction. Organic growth is principally due to operational alpha described above, while inorganic growth may occur as a result of "tuck-in" acquisitions or roll-ups following a portfolio strategy. Debt restructuring and/or reduction is often part of the exit strategy for an investment.

The structure of a typical private equity firm is similar to venture capital investing (see Section 2.2.1 or Chapter 1, Section 1.2.2.1). Investors initially commit to invest a certain amount of money and deliver 10–20% of that "committed capital" when the fund is launched. After launch, when the GP identifies compelling investment opportunities it "calls" the capital from LPs. From the LP perspective, the maximum amount of capital to be invested is fixed in advance, but the timing is uncertain and depends on the GP. This creates a cash management challenge for private equity investors; satisfying potential capital calls may require a large cash balance that drags on fund performance. Remaining capital—either committed capital that hasn't been called yet, or capital that has been paid in but not yet invested—available for investment is called "dry powder" and reflects the potential buying power of the fund. Funds are expected to have a lifespan of 7–10 years from initial investments to exits, though some may last for 12–15 years or longer.

2.2.3 Other Important Terms

There are a few additional terms that investors in private equity funds (including venture capital) should expect to see while performing due diligence (Table 2.7).

2.2.4 Performance

One important concept in private equity investing is the "J-Curve"[12] (Figure 2.6). The first few years of a PE fund are often characterized by investment of capital without many positive realizations, as well as some fees and expenses, which combine to create a negative IRR. General partners may also choose to close some positions at a loss early in the life of the fund to focus capital and other resources on more promising investments, further contributing to negative IRRs. Over time, however, better performing funds will benefit from sales of companies with stronger performance, and the lifetime IRR for the fund will turn positive.

TABLE 2.7. Definitions of important terms for investors in private equity

Term	Definition
Target fund size	When raising a new fund, the GP sets a target fund size; if the GP is unable to close the fund at the targeted amount, it may indicate negative perceptions about the GP, the fund, or both and should be viewed as a cautionary signal
Vintage year	The year in which the fund was launched, an important part of performance analysis; funds of different vintages are not directly comparable due to the timing of investments and potential differences in economic conditions
Term	The term defines the expected duration of the fund, usually 10 years, and whether or not it can be extended with investor approval
Distribution waterfall	The term "waterfall" describes how distributions from portfolio exits flow from the LPs to the GP and therefore is used to calculate the GP's carried interest. In the US, distributions are typically made on a deal-by-deal basis subject to a claw-back (see Chapter 1, Section 1.2.2.4) at the end of the fund. Outside the US, a total return waterfall is more prevalent, and carried interest is calculated after the fund has returned all committed capital to investors or fund performance exceeds a predetermined level (e.g., 20%).
Co-investments	GPs occasionally offer the opportunity for LPs to invest directly in a deal outside the structure of the fund, termed a "co-investment." In these cases the fees and carried interest are likely to be much lower than the fund, or even zero, improving the economics for the LPs. For example, a GP plans to buy a company for $1 billion using $900 million from the fund (after leverage) and $100 million from co-investments. Upon exit, an LP with a $50 million co-investment makes money in two ways: from its share of the net profits that accrue to the fund and from its $50 million stake in the business with lower fees and profit sharing.

The characteristics of long-term performance are different for private equity compared to venture capital. According to the Morgan Stanley report cited above, the average median and weighted average IRRs for PE have both been slightly better than the market, and with far less volatility than VC, suggesting that investing in the "median PE fund" would be an attractive option if it existed. When it comes to persistence of performance from one fund to the next, however, private equity appears to be less attractive than venture capital, especially after the internet bubble (Exhibit 2.2).

The famous "J-Curve"

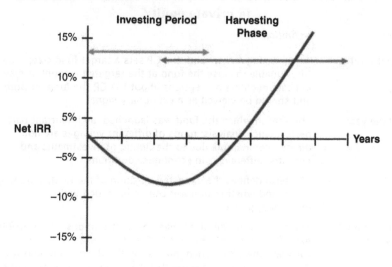

FIGURE 2.6. The private equity "J-Curve."

Source: Mercer LLC, https://www.mercer.com/our-thinking/wealth/the-flattening-of-the-private-equity-j-curve.html, last accessed December 14, 2022.

EXHIBIT 2.2. Persistence for buyout funds									
Pre-2001	Subsequent Fund Quartile				*Post-2000*	Subsequent Fund Quartile			
	1	**2**	**3**	**4**		**1**	**2**	**3**	**4**
Previous Fund Quartile **1**	38%	25%	19%	19%	*Previous Fund Quartile* **1**	24%	24%	27%	25%
2	30%	22%	30%	17%	**2**	23%	28%	29%	20%
3	21%	25%	32%	21%	**3**	17%	28%	32%	24%
4	17%	26%	30%	26%	**4**	27%	30%	21%	21%

Source: Mauboussin and Callahan, 2020, Morgan Stanley.

Prior to 2001, there was a slight persistence effect (i.e., the next fund from a manager where the previous fund was in the top quartile was 38% likely to also rank in the top quartile). After 2000, however, the effect disappears: the next fund from a PE manager of a top quartile fund has been roughly equally likely to be in any quartile, from top to bottom. Therefore, while in VC it is very important to be able to invest in the top managers, this may not be as important in private equity —more important is to maintain an allocation to private equity as an asset class, given its strong average risk-adjusted returns and diversification benefits.

2.2.5 Recent Developments

Among others, three recent developments in private equity are important to mention.[13] First, there is the rise of so-called "megafunds" that close with over $5 billion in committed capital. As highlighted in Figure 2.7, since 2017 megafunds have accounted for at least 40% of buyout capital raised, the highest level since the two years immediately preceding the Global Financial Crisis.[14]

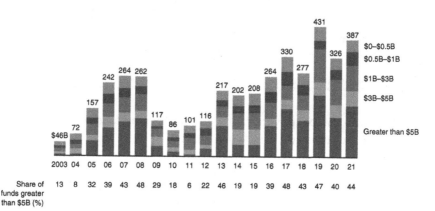

FIGURE 2.7. Global buyout capital raised by fund size ($B).
Source: Bain Global Private Equity Report 2022.

Because of their size, megafunds need to invest in larger companies than smaller funds in order to deploy all their capital. According to several consultants, since the Global Financial Crisis (GFC) of 2008–2009, larger PE funds have performed just as well as smaller funds. Especially against the recent backdrop of low or even negative real yields, asset owners value the ability to invest ever larger amounts of capital in megafunds without a tangibly negative impact on expected returns.

The second recent development to mention concerns dry powder and the implications for deal pricing. As mentioned earlier, the term dry powder refers to the amount of capital that is available for the fund manager to apply toward transactions, either because the capital has been committed but not yet called or paid in and not yet invested. Figure 2.8 shows how dry powder has reached over $3 trillion in 2020 and 2021, roughly triple the levels seen in the 2007–2009 bull market.

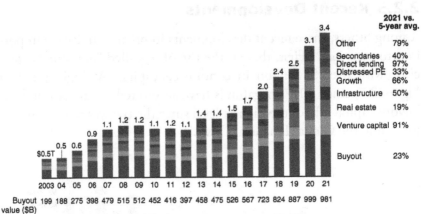

Buyout value ($B): 199 188 275 398 479 515 512 452 416 397 458 475 526 567 723 824 887 999 981

Notes: Other category includes fund-of-funds, natural resources, and mezzanine; buyout category includes buyout, balanced, coinvestment, and coinvestment multimanager funds; discrepancies in bar heights displaying the same value are due to rounding
Source: Preqin

FIGURE 2.8. Global private capital dry powder, by fund type ($T).
Source: Bain Global Private Equity Report 2022.

Similar to what happens to home prices when there are many buyers flush with cash, so too have prices paid for buyouts reached ever higher levels as measured by the average EBITDA purchase price multiples (see Figure 2.9). The implication is that when PE funds pay top-dollar prices for companies, it may become more difficult to sell those companies at even higher prices.

Finally, another development to highlight is the continued rise of Asian private equity. After a decade in which it grew 2.4x faster than the rest of the world, Asia has surpassed Europe as the second-largest region for private equity investing when all strategies are included (Figure 2.10).

Asia differs from other markets in that there are fewer mature, high cash flow companies that would traditionally be attractive LBO targets (though that is changing). Instead, Asian private equity historically has

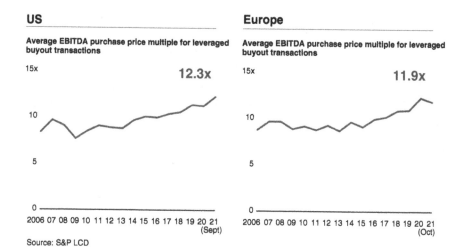

US

Average EBITDA purchase price multiple for leveraged buyout transactions

12.3x

Source: S&P LCD

Europe

Average EBITDA purchase price multiple for leveraged buyout transactions

11.9x

FIGURE 2.9. Average EBITDA purchase price for leveraged buyout transactions, the United States and Europe.

Source: Bain Global Private Equity Report 2022.

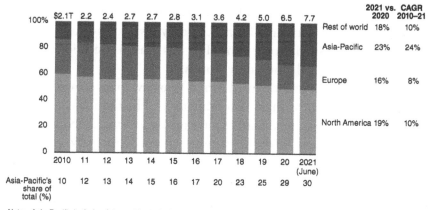

Notes: Asia-Pacific includes Asia and Australasia; rest of world includes Africa, Caribbean and South America, Middle East and Israel, and diversified multiregional funds

FIGURE 2.10. AUM by primary region, all PE asset classes ($T).

Source: Bain Global Private Equity Report 2022.

been skewed toward growth equity strategies. As the Asian markets continue to mature, however, so too will their capacity for the full range of private equity strategies.

2.2.6 Summary

Private equity is an attractive asset class for investors with the ability to lock up capital for 7–10 years or longer. Leading GPs, such as KKR, Carlyle, and others offer funds with a variety of strategies that can provide attractive returns and diversification for portfolios. Strong flows into PE have recently pushed deal prices up to all-time highs, however, which should serve as a reminder that all investments come with risks.

2.3 Hedge Funds

To better understand hedge funds, it is helpful to start with a recap of traditional equity investment products, such as mutual funds and unit trusts. Traditional equity managers face two related challenges when stocks decline. First, an investment thesis might have been correct on a *relative* basis, meaning that the stock did better than the market but still lost money because the market went down. Second, a manager may believe that a stock should go down but lacks a way to capitalize on that belief as a mutual fund can only own (or not own) stocks, expecting prices to rise over time. For this reason, traditional equity funds are often called "long-only" funds.

In 1949, an investor named Alfred Winslow Jones created the first hedge fund to address these two limitations. His fund tried to eliminate the impact of general market movements by simultaneously going long and short assets in the right proportions. Ultimately, combined with the use of leverage and a performance fee structure, Mr. Jones is credited with creating the first modern hedge fund. Over time, the term *hedge fund* has come to be associated with funds that share several important characteristics: organized as private investment vehicles for accredited or institutional investors, they impose incentive fees based on fund performance (see Chapter 1, Section 1.2.2.4), and have considerable flexibility in how they can invest, including short selling, use of leverage, and ability to trade derivatives and other non-cash assets. Although the additional flexibility enables hedge funds to create differentiated investment strategies, it makes due diligence more difficult for investors. Combinations of long and short positions in instruments such as derivatives with non-linear payoffs may require more complicated and active risk management, for example. Without the same regulatory restrictions on leverage that apply to mutual funds, some hedge funds meaningfully alter their risk and return profile through high-leverage strategies. Even sophisticated investors may find it difficult to properly assess the risks and opportunities associated with certain hedge fund strategies.

2.3.1 Classification

To provide some order to the hedge fund market, the CFA Institute[15] classifies hedge fund strategies into four major categories:

1. Event-Driven
2. Equity Hedge
3. Relative Value
4. Macro[16]

Event-driven strategies invest in companies expected to experience a corporate change. Sometimes the changes are structural in nature (i.e., a merger, spin-off, or other type of restructuring). Other events may be instigated by the investors themselves through a process called "shareholder activism." Event-driven investors profit when an event occurs as expected but usually lose money if the event is postponed, modified, or canceled. The return distribution for event-driven funds is decidedly non-normal, with relatively consistent generation of small profits punctuated by infrequent periods of larger negative returns.

The next category, *equity hedge*, is another bottom-up strategy. Equity hedge includes classic fundamental long/short strategies along the lines of what Mr. Jones envisioned so long ago. There are many flavors of equity hedge strategies, ranging from fundamental and quantitative to short-biased and sector-specific funds. Some funds are relatively "short-term," looking for near-term trade ideas, while others seek long-term fundamental investments. "Bottom-up" managers may be focused on factors that impact individual stocks or bonds rather than "top-down" factors, such as overall market movements or interest rates. Although not specifically included in the CFA classification, credit hedge funds apply a similar range of techniques to investing in loans to companies, called credit investing.

Relative value refers to another set of short-term and bottom-up strategies. Relative value investors look for discrepancies in the prices, or spread, between two assets based on their historical relationship. One very famous example of a hedge fund pursuing an arbitrage strategy was Long-Term Capital Management (LTCM). Based on its extensive quantitative analysis, LTCM believed that relative prices between assets ("the spread") would mean-revert to historical levels if the spread became wider than had traditionally been the case. The strategy worked very well for years until it failed in spectacular fashion in 1998, requiring a bailout by Wall Street firms that many believe prevented a much larger market crisis.[17]

The final category of strategy is *macro* investing, a top-down and multi-asset strategy. Macro funds usually start with fundamental macroeconomic analysis, often at the country level, and then drill down to identify the best asset or assets to implement an idea. These managers have the flexibility to trade stocks, bonds, interest rates, and currencies, long or short, and on a global basis. Many ideas are associated with changes in expected fund flows across countries and asset classes, for example, when a pegged currency is expected to devalue.[18] With such flexibility macro funds historically have delivered liquid, diversified, and financially attractive returns to investors—especially during times of market turbulence.

While this classification of hedge fund strategies seems logical, providers of hedge fund indices use their own, proprietary classifications. For example, the CFA Institute defines merger arbitrage—trading long/short positions around an announced merger—as event-driven, but index providers could create a separate merger arbitrage category or include it in a broader "relative value" category. Even when the classification system has been set, it may be difficult to determine how to classify any given manager. Compared to public mutual funds which tend to follow well-defined strategies (e.g., European Large Cap Value, or Greater China Growth), the considerable flexibility afforded hedge fund managers makes strategy buckets challenging to define and even harder to apply to individual funds.

Further complicating matters, several of the largest hedge funds include multiple strategies within the same fund vehicle in what is called a "multistrategy fund." Such funds house a variety of strategies within the same firm, manage allocations to strategies to create a single portfolio for clients, and charge a single layer of fees. In contrast, another approach to gaining exposure to multiple strategies in a single investment is through a fund that invests in other funds, called a "fund of funds" (FOF). Funds of funds (see Section 2.6) provide access to multiple strategies across multiple firms but charge an extra layer of fees for manager selection and due diligence, portfolio construction, and ongoing monitoring. Unfortunately for investors, the wide variety of hedge fund strategies means that there is no easy way to compare and analyze funds.

2.3.2 Structure

Irrespective of the strategy, most hedge funds are organized using a GP/LP structure similar to VC and PE but with two important differences. First, because hedge funds predominantly invest in more liquid public securities, investors typically provide the full amount of capital at the time of investment rather than waiting for capital calls over time. For this reason, performance measurement may be *relatively* straightforward for this subset of hedge funds. In addition, because public markets are more liquid, hedge funds usually have more generous redemption terms than private markets funds (e.g., quarterly with a quarter advance notice, instead of locking up investors' capital for 7–10 years or longer).

More so than venture capital and private equity firms, the largest hedge fund managers may be less well known to many readers. Some receive more public attention due to a combination of size, performance, and a high-profile founder like Ray Dalio (Bridgewater), Ken Griffin (Citadel), or Jim Simons (Renaissance Technologies), while others are far less well known or operate in near secrecy. For that reason the annual lists of the largest hedge fund managers is greeted both with interest and with a bit of skepticism given the difficulty in estimating assets under management for these firms. With that caveat in mind, one such list from *Pension & Investments Magazine* features many prominent funds within its top 10 (Table 2.8).

TABLE 2.8. Largest hedge fund managers and ranking, 2021–2022			
Manager	AUM (June 30, 2022) ($ billion)	Change (%)	2021 rank
Bridgewater Associates	126.4	19.6	1
Man Group	73.5	15.9	2
Renaissance Technologies	57.0	−1.7	3
Millennium Mgmt.	55.0	5.1	4
Citadel	53.0	40.8	9
D.E. Shaw Group	48.9	20.4	6
Two Sigma Investments/Advisers	41.0	3.6	7
Davidson Kempner Capital Mgmt.	37.5	0.3	10
Farallon Capital Mgmt.	37.4	−1.8	8
TCI Fund Mgmt.	36.2	−9.5	5

Source: https://www.pionline.com/largest-hedge-fund-managers/2022.

The remainder of this chapter takes a closer look at four specific strategies that readers may encounter in the financial press: fundamental long/short, quantitative long/short, merger arbitrage, and activism.

2.3.3 Fundamental Long/Short

Long/short investing is what many people associate with the term "hedge fund": buy stocks expected to outperform and sell short stocks expected to underperform, while using leverage to amplify potential returns. These strategies tend to be absolute return focused, prioritizing consistently positive returns with limited regard for a market benchmark (even though these funds tend to assume more market risk than other hedge fund strategies). Fundamental investing is the term used to describe a process which uses macroeconomic (e.g., inflation, unemployment) and company-specific (e.g., corporate financial statements) data to estimate a fair value for an asset.

As unregulated and relatively unconstrained managers, there are many different fundamental long/short strategies. First and perhaps foremost is the way in which the fund identifies its investment ideas, including by style (e.g., growth vs. value), pair trades, and "catalyst-driven" funds that specialize in short-duration ideas lasting from a few days to a few weeks. These and many others are included under the umbrella of "idea generation." Many hedge fund managers claim to derive most of their performance from security selection, so investors should pay careful attention to how the fund manager characterizes its process for idea generation.

While most fundamental long/short strategies generally assume a non-trivial amount of market risk, managers may vary widely in the risks they assume, particularly the components of leverage (see Chapter 1, Section 1.2.3.1), directionality, and beta and factor exposure. A key measure of leverage is "gross market exposure" (GME), calculated as the total invested capital divided by the total assets in a fund. As described earlier, higher leverage (which is equivalent to higher GME) increases risk. The second component, directionality, is measured as "net market exposure" (NME), which is the total capital in long positions minus the total capital in short positions. Table 2.9 shows how different hedge fund strategies may vary in the capital they employ, both long and short, as well as the amount of leverage being used. The fundamental strategy has GME of 200% and NME of 20% on a "gross basis"[19] (40M / 200M) (i.e., using the gross or levered capital as the denominator). This is risky but less so than the higher-risk version at 3.2x GME and 25% NME. In contrast, because quant managers use analytical techniques to hedge away most unwanted risks, they may use considerably higher leverage—in this example 8x—while maintaining an NME of zero percent.

TABLE 2.9. Hypothetical capital usage ($ million) by different types of hedge funds

	Fundamental Long/Short	"Higher-Risk" long/short	"Quant"
Capital	100	100	100
Longs	120	200	400
Shorts	−80	−120	−400
Gross	200	320	800
Net	40	80	0
Leverage	2:1	3.2:1	8:1

Finally, some funds differentiate themselves according to their exposure to other types of risks beyond exposure to the market. Two prominent examples are beta exposure (as explained in Chapter 1, Section 1.2.3.3) and factor exposure.[20] Funds typically make very deliberate decisions on whether and how to manage the types and amounts of risk in the portfolio. Some prominent funds commit to removing as much of these exposures as possible in a strategy called "beta-neutral" and "factor-neutral." Many of these funds achieve beta- and factor-neutrality through quantitative techniques, as will be explored in Section 2.3.4.

2.3.4 Quantitative Long/Short

Another popular hedge fund strategy, quantitative long/short, applies math and programming techniques to large amounts of data to identify variables that appear to predict future returns. Many firms say they use "AI"—artificial intelligence—as part of their investment process, though it is important that investors do not rely on such declarations as the basis for an investment decision. In today's environment of increasing computing power, machine learning, and abundant data, many "quant firms" are sophisticated enough that it requires highly specialized knowledge to evaluate these so-called "black box" strategies.

The output of the analyses performed by quant fund managers are variables that appear to be predictive of future returns; these variables are referred to as "signals." Many quantitative researchers prefer to look for signals grounded in economic or finance theory, such as valuation or solvency ratios, believing that such theoretical support may lead to a more durable signal. Another technique called technical analysis[21] involves signals such as momentum and support/resistance levels which are based on a combination of price and volume over time. Signals may also be based on information disseminated by the company or research analysts, as well as indicators of social media sentiment and geo-tagged measures of activity. Quantitative fund managers are incentivized to find as many investable signals as possible, both because more and better signals likely lead to better performance and also because competition from other managers erodes the value of many signals over time.

For an alpha signal to be tradable in a quant portfolio, it must include more than a list of stocks—it needs to include the size of each position as well. One simplistic approach is to equal-weight each position, but typically quant researchers look for ways to vary position sizing according to some other variable, such as the liquidity or volatility of the stock. Quant strategies are often managed so that they are market-, beta-, and even factor-neutral.

2.3.5 Merger Arbitrage

When one company ("the acquirer") announces that it will be merging with or acquiring another company ("the target"), their respective stock prices may move significantly higher or lower to reflect the prices paid and the potential value of the combined entity. For example, if the announced acquisition price is well above the last traded price for the target, the target company's stock will trade higher—but usually not all the way to the acquisition price. After the announcement, fundamental investors usually sell their shares in the target, realize their gains, and reallocate capital to another investment idea. In this way the target stock is left trading below the deal price, creating an opportunity for merger arbitrageurs to buy the stock and hold it until the deal closes in a few months or more.

Consider the following example of a corporate acquisition: shares in Company T (the "target") are trading at $12.00 per share when Company A (the "acquirer") announces a cash offer to buy Company T for $18.00 per share, a premium of 50%. The shares of Company T trade up to $17.00 where existing shareholders are likely to sell their shares to realize a profit. Investors following a strategy called merger arbitrage, however, might buy those shares in Company T, attempting to capture the $1.00 spread between the trading price today and the announced price that will be received when the deal closes. Instead, if the acquisition financing involved some or all stock from Company A, investors might structure a position that includes going long shares in Company T while simultaneously shorting shares in Company A to lock in a spread and hedge the risk of any price fluctuations between the announcement date and the date the deal closes.

Until the deal officially closes, merger arbitrageurs must also address risks that the deal will be delayed (reducing ROI as the position must be held longer than expected) or canceled. The biggest risk is that the deal doesn't complete as anticipated, perhaps because regulators block the deal on anti-trust grounds, or if shareholders believe the offer price undervalues the company. Merger arbitrage investors therefore must consider important questions before deciding to invest in the stock(s) involved in an announced deal:

1. How likely is it that the deal will close?
2. Is it a stock deal, a cash deal, or a mix? The investment strategy will depend on how the deal is going to be financed. When the acquirer is paying in stock or stock plus cash, merger arbitrage strategies often buy the target company stock and sell short the acquirer company stock
3. How long will it take for the deal to close?
4. If the deal closes as expected, what is the likely spread between the prices paid to open a position and the deal closing prices?
5. What will happen to the stocks if the deal "breaks" and does not take place?
6. What are the odds that another company might offer to buy the target at a higher price, creating a bidding war?

Although modern technology has reduced some of the inefficiencies that used to exist in merger arbitrage, as the questions above suggest, the strategy still requires significant—and specialized—expertise.

The best merger arbitrage funds consistently deliver small positive monthly returns, making them appear attractive to many investors. Their exposure to event risk, however, means that they will occasionally face large losses when deals break. Since deals involving public companies generally require regulatory (anti-trust) approval, assessing the risk that regulators block a transaction is a critical part of any merger arbitrage strategy. More generally, if the pipeline of M&A deals dries up or deals break as in during a market downturn, merger arbitrage funds will struggle. Investors considering an allocation to merger arbitrage should diversify across multiple managers, concentrating in different sectors or market cap bands to spread out the risk.

2.3.6 Activism

Shareholder activism occurs when shareholders disagree with the way that management is running the company. Some activism is socially motivated (e.g., calls for a drug company to halt animal testing). Activist investors are financially motivated. They look for companies that they believe are failing to maximize their share price and attempt to influence management to make changes. Three broad categories of potential improvement are common catalysts for activist investors (Table 2.10).

TABLE 2.10. Company improvements potentially targeted by activist investors

Area for improvement	Examples of potential activism
Capital structure	Debt restructuring; returning capital to shareholders through special dividend or share repurchases
Opposing announced deal	Argue against a deal, argue for more favorable deal terms (e.g., price)
Corporate structure and/or strategy	Spinning off parts of a business or splitting up a company; CEO compensation

Depending on the nature of the changes that an activist would like the company to make, activist investors may use different techniques to influence company management. Traditionally, activists start by quietly building a position in the company's stock, following the theory that management may be more likely to respond to shareholders (especially larger shareholders) than a non-shareholder. As described above, in the United States, investors accumulating 5% or more of a firm must file a Schedule 13D with the SEC within 10 days, at which point the position becomes public. Activist investors with a track record of success are watched closely by the market, and a stock may jump higher when filings[22] reveal that such an activist has filed a new position in that stock.

If an activist is "friendly," it may quietly engage corporate management to present its case for potential changes. For less cooperative activists (or when management rebuffs the friendly overtures), the next step is often to send management a formal letter detailing the issues that the investor would like to see addressed and suggested changes. Activists may hope that other shareholders will support their proposals, in which case the letter to management may be shared with (leaked?) to the press. If management agrees to make some or all of the changes, then the stock price may rise and activists may be satisfied. In the event that management dismisses or ignores the activist, however, the activist must then decide whether to "go hostile" in an attempt to force change upon the company. Hostile campaigns usually entail proxy vote contests and are expensive and difficult to implement successfully.

A 2021 activist campaign against ExxonMobil (NYSE: XOM) serves as an interesting example. The investor, a small firm called Engine No. 1, led a campaign to replace several board members at the company's annual shareholder vote. Its campaign was based on three issues:[23] (1) ExxonMobil share prices had underperformed its global peers (BP, Chevron, Shell, Total) for the past 1-, 3-, 5-, and 10-year periods; (2) during that time the board had awarded the CEO what Engine No. 1 believed to be grossly excessive compensation in light of the poor stock price performance; and (3) the campaign highlighted that the board lacked the relevant experience to address the critical issue of climate change and carbon transition. After an aggressive public campaign, candidates put forward by Engine No. 1 captured three board seats.

From a risk perspective, because activist investing is a high-effort strategy and requires highly concentrated positions, portfolios tend to be exposed to a meaningful amount of market and stock-specific risk. Some allocators may also be sensitive to potential reputational risk that could arise by being associated with funds leading public, confrontational activist campaigns.

2.3.7 Performance

Hedge fund investing rose to prominence in the United States following a period of noteworthy returns in the 1980s and 1990s. Some time in the 2000s, however, average hedge fund outperformance appears to have largely disappeared; several reasons are commonly cited in an attempt to explain this decline. Some studies attribute this effect to the growth in the number of hedge funds, believing that strategies that become more widely followed may lose their ability to deliver alpha, due to increased competition. Other studies have examined the impact on performance of fund age (number of years active), whether the fund is the first fund for the founder, or size. Some data suggest that funds run by "emerging managers" (smaller, younger funds) or first-time managers outperform their peers, perhaps because the managers haven't yet achieved the financial success to which they aspire and are therefore motivated to work harder. Studies also suggest an inverse relationship between size (AUM) and performance, citing the potential negative impact of larger funds attempting to follow the same strategy with increasing trade sizes and/or position counts.

The data used to analyze hedge fund performance must be interpreted with caution. Researchers typically try to account for these issues. Unlike mutual funds which are required by regulation to publish daily performance, hedge fund databases rely on managers to report their own data which is susceptible to several biases. Since data are self-reported, fund managers are only incentivized to report good performance. Additionally, funds closed to new investments may also stop reporting because they won't benefit from increased visibility. The combination of this reduced reporting creates "selection bias" and impairs the representativeness of hedge fund databases.

Another bias is referred to as "backfill bias." When a manager decides to report performance to a database for the first time, it has the option to provide historical performance data at the same time. Funds that choose to voluntarily provide their performance history are more likely to do so if their performance has been strong, meaning that databases may underrepresent weak performing funds that have decided not to provide their data. Finally, many funds close in the first several years of operation due to poor performance or lack of scale to cover fund expenses. Databases therefore may not include data from underperforming funds that have been shut down, resulting in "survivorship bias."

While researchers are aware of these potential problems with the data, readers should pay careful attention to how these biases are addressed when interpreting analyses of hedge fund performance. Selection bias, backfill bias, and survivorship bias are collectively likely to overstate historical performance; portfolios formed in the past are likely to underperform a benchmark portfolio built today from a database sample that does not effectively address these biases.

One nuance that is often missed in the financial press[24] is how the variety of hedge fund strategies makes it very difficult to evaluate performance for hedge funds in aggregate. As was described earlier, a single hedge fund category like fundamental long/short may include managers with very different strategies and risk appetites. Two funds with the same degree of leverage might have vastly different net market exposure, beta exposure, or factor exposure. Knowing that Fund A outperformed Fund B by 5% might just mean that Fund A took more risk. Proper performance evaluation is best done within strategies and should ideally focus on what is referred to as risk-adjusted performance (i.e., after adjusting for market, beta, and factor exposure).

2.3.8 Recent Developments

Despite, or perhaps because of, the recent performance challenges, many hedge funds are moving in two different directions. The first is often referred to as "alternative data," which generally means non-financial data that haven't traditionally been available for either fundamental or quantitative investors. Examples of alternative data include satellite images, social media sentiment analysis, and data derived from anonymized mobile phone tracking. Identifying the most promising data and developing the capabilities required to onboard the data for inclusion in an existing investment process are by no means an easy task, but one which better-resourced funds have pursued with dedication.

The second and more recent development is for hedge funds to expand into private markets investing. Many large hedge funds now have dedicated capital for venture-style investing, including blockchain and cryptocurrency projects; Tiger Global, described briefly in Section 2.1, is a good example. Hedge funds are also providing capital to alternative lending providers to access returns from lending to small and medium-sized businesses. These non-traditional alternative strategies will be covered in Chapter 4.

2.3.9 Summary

Investing in hedge funds presents a different set of challenges compared with venture capital and private equity. The range of strategies is wide and many will be difficult to understand without significant experience. Also, as opposed to private equity, size appears to have a negative effect on performance. All of this is to highlight the degree of difficulty associated with investing in hedge funds, and not to suggest that such investments are not worth pursuing. Many hedge funds deliver strong performance and play an important role in portfolio diversification.

Identifying those funds in advance and being able to make an investment, however, can be a challenge.

2.4 Infrastructure[25]

Theoretically, it may be more appropriate to speak of "real assets" as including land, structures built on land (which would include both real estate and infrastructure), commodities extracted from the land, commodities produced by the managed use of land, and intellectual property. Practically, investors usually treat these as different asset classes since they have markedly different investment characteristics. Hence this book covers real assets in multiple parts: infrastructure, land and commodities (Section 2.5), real estate (Chapter 3 and the Appendix), and intellectual property (Chapter 4, Section 4.7.1).

Infrastructure encompasses the man-made structures used to deliver services that support modern living, including utilities and related assets (e.g., electricity generation and transmission, water treatment), transportation assets (e.g., roads, ports, and airports), and communication infrastructure. The wide range of assets included within the infrastructure space share important characteristics:

- Most infrastructure assets are private rather than publicly listed (though exceptions exist).

- Assets are purpose-built and cannot be moved or repurposed, representing significant sunk costs.

- The scale of infrastructure investments is so large that the fixed costs of development and maintenance far outweigh the variable costs.

- Infrastructure assets are not a store of value and only have value to the extent that they are used.

- Since these assets are typically managed by government agencies, they are more susceptible to changes in administrative policy or regulatory issues.

- Infrastructure investing typically works well in an inflationary environment due to explicit contract language and regulated pricing.

These factors and associated risks are counterbalanced by a highly predictable return stream based on expected utilization of the asset over a long horizon (decades, not years), leading to generally attractive risk-adjusted returns for institutional investors. Investors can invest in new construction ("greenfield") or existing infrastructure ("brownfield") when the owner of the asset raises capital through a securitization.

Given the inherent differences between assets, investors use risk and return to classify infrastructure into super core (lowest risk and lowest return, e.g., regulated utilities), core, and core-plus (highest risk and return, similar to traditional private equity). Although valuation of private infrastructure assets is typically based on discounted future cash flows for each unique asset, systematic factors also have a strong relationship with valuation, including leverage (senior liabilities over total assets), size (total assets), profitability (return on assets before tax), investment (capex over total assets), and country risk (term spread). Understanding the common factors associated with the returns of private infrastructure enables investors to value these assets more accurately.

Different products are available to suit the needs of different types of investors, including private equity funds for institutions and qualified individuals, as well as mutual funds and ETFs for retail investors. For institutional investors, because the asset class is large and growing, asset owners are able to make meaningful allocations (often $200 million and up) with relative ease.

Similar to the other private markets asset classes, many readers may not be familiar with the names of the largest infrastructure investors (Table 2.11).

2.4.1 Performance

With the potential for low volatility and relatively high returns in this asset class, infrastructure fund performance has been strong relative to other private investments. As shown in Figure 2.11, the total return from Dec. 31, 2007 to Dec. 31, 2021 was 312% for infrastructure compared with 495% for traditional private equity, 174% for real estate, and 161% for natural resources.

TABLE 2.11. Largest infrastructure investors	
Manager	AUM (December 2021) (Euro billion)
Macquarie Asset Management	195
Brookfield Asset Management	122
Global Infrastructure Partners	60.7
IFM Investors	51.4
M&G Investments	43.3
Allianz Global Investors	38.3
BlackRock Real Assets	29.1
DigitalBridge	27.3
Stonepeak Partners	27.2
MetLife Investment Management	26.9

Source: IPE Real Assets.

Annualized quarterly TSR, %

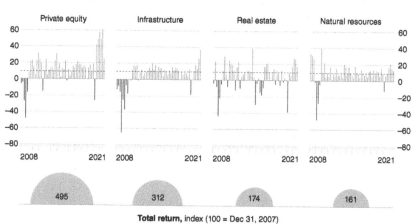

Total return, index (100 = Dec 31, 2007)

FIGURE 2.11. Annualized quarterly total shareholder return (TSR) (%).

Source: McKinsey & Company, https://www.mckinsey.com/industries/private-equity-and-principal-investors/our-insights/infrastructure-investing-will-never-be-the-same, last accessed December 14, 2022.

2.4.2 Recent Developments

Two trends have the potential to meaningfully impact infrastructure investing. The first is similar to what is happening to private equity overall, namely the strong flows of capital into the space are putting pressure on financial performance. According to McKinsey & Company, infrastructure funds raised over 50% more capital in 2021 than in 2016; IRRs in private infrastructure have declined 20–40% over the past 10 years.[26]

Second, decarbonization and the fight against climate change have the potential to significantly alter the risk-return profile of existing assets:

> In the past, individual assets sometimes moved up or down the risk/return spectrum. But with changes in energy, mobility, and digitization, more assets need to be reassessed: assets that have long dwelled squarely within an asset subcategory may need to move to a different bucket today, and there may be big shifts from super core all the way to core-plus. Dramatic reshuffling is occurring because assets that were once seen as immutably stable, such as gas pipelines, are now exposed to significant energy transition risk.[27]

On the other hand, the same need for decarbonization leads to new investment opportunities in areas like renewable energy, electric vehicle (EV) charging networks, hydrogen production and distribution, and perhaps even new nuclear generation technologies, such as molten salt reactors.

2.5 Land and Commodities

As has been the case for centuries, land offers multiple avenues for investment. In its most basic form, raw land can itself be an attractive long-term investment. For example, today's exurbs may be the suburbs of tomorrow as urban and suburban populations continue to grow, and raw land may increase in value as a potential development site in the future. When raw land is improved, it transforms into spaces for real estate development, farmland, or timberland. The drivers of economic performance for these three use cases are very different.

Raw land requires additional investment before it can be used for real estate development. The process of "finishing" land may include grading and landscaping, laying paved roads, and installing basic utility infrastructure (electricity, communications, water, sewerage). Additionally, the land should be approved for development, a process that may require permitting by a government agency, and potentially paying associated fees. Finished land is more expensive than raw land, reflecting the value of the improvements that have been made.

Farmland is a combination of the value of raw land with the income associated with livestock or crops. Investors in farmland typically lease the land to a farmer (individual or corporate) to manage the crops. Land values and the prices of commodities farmed on the land are two potential risks that, when packaged together in a single investment, may partially counterbalance each other. There are other risks associated with farmland, however, including inclement weather or natural disasters, spoilage, and disease. Depending on the jurisdiction and the nationality of the investor, buying and selling farmland may be subject to restrictions, and transaction costs (broker fees) are high. Absent these risks, farmland can be an effective diversifier during inflationary environments (increasing commodity prices) that are likely to be negative for equity investments.

Investments in timberland also represent a combination of land value and crop income; in this specific case the crop is timber for paper and lumber production. Since forests require hands-on management, investors typically contract with a specialist company (a timber investment management company, or TIMO) to manage the forest through to harvest. Whereas many agricultural commodities are at risk of spoilage, timber in contrast is more durable, providing investors more flexibility to adjust the timing of harvest to prevailing market conditions. Forests take decades to reach maturity, however, meaning that timberland investments will be very long term and expose owners to risks such as fire, flood, drought, and insect damage.

In addition to farmland (or timberland) used to produce livestock or crops, land may also be valuable for commodity extraction such as mining rights or oil and gas production. The materials that are either extracted from or grown on the land are referred to as commodities.

Although not every commodity is easily investable, a determined commodities investor has access to a wide range of assets (Table 2.12).

TABLE 2.12. Sub-categories of commodities

Sub-category	Examples
Energy	Crude oil, natural gas, refined products (e.g., aviation fuel, gasoline)
Industrial metals	Aluminum, coper, iron, lead, nickel, tin, zinc
Precious metals	Gold, palladium, platinum, silver
Livestock	Cattle, hogs, poultry, sheep
Grains	Corn, rice, soy, wheat
Softs (cash crops)	Cocoa, coffee, cotton, sugar

Usage and therefore the determinants of prices differ widely across commodities. Energy-related commodities are linked closely to measures of economic activity; they may also be temporarily affected by severe weather events such as hurricanes in the southeastern United States, or geopolitical events like the conflict in Ukraine in 2022. Industrial metals are similarly tied to economic growth, especially construction, infrastructure investment, and in the case of copper, electrification of many activities and processes in response to climate change. Precious metals like gold are considered by some to be an inflation hedge, while palladium, platinum, and silver are in demand for industrial applications, such as the manufacturer of catalytic converters. Climate also impacts grains and softs, which as agricultural products are susceptible to weather conditions, such as drought or frost in growing regions, as well as storage and transportation risks. Livestock prices may also be affected by climate risks (e.g., fluctuations in feedstock prices (grains) and substitutes such as fish or soy). Investors who look at the commodities markets as a single asset class therefore risk missing the rich diversification opportunities available.

In the commodities markets there are two principal ways to invest. *Direct* investing involves taking physical possession of the commodity, with the corresponding challenges related to finding buyers, transportation, and storage. Physical commodity investing therefore requires specialized know-how extending well beyond speculating on the future price of the commodity. *Indirect* investments, on the other hand, are made using futures contracts traded on exchanges like the Chicago Mercantile Exchange (CME), Intercontinental Exchange (ICE), BM&F BOVESPA, or the London Metals Exchange (LME); futures are the most common instrument used by professional commodities investors. Dating back to the 1970s, futures contracts represent an agreement or obligation to exchange an asset for a specific price at a specific time in the future. In all but the most unusual circumstances,[28] investors trade futures without assuming the risk of physical delivery. Futures contracts have an expiry date at which point the parties agree to deliver and receive the physical asset, but in practice investors avoid taking physical deliver either by closing the contract before expiry or "rolling" the exposure to another contract with an expiration date further in the future. Today individual investors can use ETFs to indirectly speculate on the prices of a wide range of commodities, from livestock to palladium, although the ETF structure confers an element of equity market beta that is otherwise absent from many commodity investments.

There are several different categories of participants in commodity markets. For companies producing or consuming commodities, the futures market offers opportunities to hedge against future price movements, such as an airline that wants to reduce the risk that jet fuel prices will increase in the future. Participating alongside corporates are a wide range of managed futures funds (also called commodity trading advisors, or CTAs), commingled vehicles that trade a combination of commodity, exchange rate, and interest rate futures. To identify investment opportunities, CTAs typically apply technical analysis,[29] a quantitative process of analyzing historical price and volume data to identify patterns in how new information is incorporated into asset prices. Investors can base trading decisions entirely on technical indicators or use technical analysis to inform entry and exit timing for positions identified through fundamental analysis.

Regardless of whether positions are identified through fundamental or technical analysis, commodity investors predominantly follow one of two strategies, either trend-following or mean-reverting. Trend-following is a way for investors to capitalize on price momentum, the tendency for prices to continue moving in the same direction. One popular way to measure momentum is through a "moving average." The moving average is a time-series of averages calculated on a rolling basis. For example, to calculate a 20-day moving average (20dma) today ($t = 0$), the investor calculates the average of the previous 20 consecutive daily prices, from $t = -1$ (yesterday) to $t = -20$ (20 days ago). On the following day the calculation would drop the old day $t = -20$ and replace it with yesterday's price (the old $t = 0$).

Investors applying technical analysis often look at multiple moving averages at the same time. Occasionally readers might see mention of the "death cross" or "golden cross." These patterns are based on the 50-day and 200-day moving averages. A "death cross" forms when the 50dma falls below the 200dma—short-term momentum falling below long-term momentum may signify further price weakness. Conversely, if the 50dma crosses above the 200dma, that forms a "golden cross" that may signal continued positive price gains following the positive shorter-term momentum. Since the investor must wait until there is enough data to confirm a trend has formed, trend-following is often criticized for being too slow to identify the beginning of a trend—and similarly too late to see when a trend has stopped.

Mean-reverting is the opposite of trend-following and occurs when prices regress toward the mean. Whichever strategy is followed, CTAs typically implement their strategies through systematic (quantitative) processes rather than discretionary decision-making. Trend-following strategies are the more popular variety, and when commodity markets have a clear trend to them, CTAs often perform quite well. When markets are "trendless," the models being used by CTAs are at risk of suggesting trades that are quickly reversed, generating churn for the portfolio without any meaningful investment performance.

Even compared with other traditional alternative strategies, information on CTAs can be difficult to find without professional data subscriptions. Nevertheless, available data reveal a somewhat dated list of sizeable managed futures specialists[30] ranked by average monthly AUM, many if not all of which are likely to be new names for readers (Table 2.13).

2.5.1 Performance

After a period of strong performance in the late 1990s, investors rushed into managed futures funds. Since the Global Financial Crisis ended in 2009, however, commodities markets have spent much of the time in a relatively trendless and lower volatility environment. Since many CTAs

TABLE 2.13. Sizeable managed futures investment managers ($ billion)	
Manager	AUM (June 2018)
Winton Capital Management	28.5
Man AHL	17.5
AQR	12.7
Systematica Investments	7.8
H2O AM	5.7
Graham Capital Management	5.3
Campbell & Company	4.5
AlphaSimplex	3.3
Lynx Asset Management	3.2
Aspect Capital Limited	3.1

Source: RCM Alternatives, https://www.rcmalternatives.com/2018/07/infographic-the-top-100-managed-futures-programs/.

use trend-following strategies, it has been difficult for managed futures funds to deliver the same level of performance that had been so appealing to institutional investors several decades ago. These conditions eased in somewhat in 2019, and performance has improved accordingly (although still well below the levels of 2000–2010) (Figure 2.12).

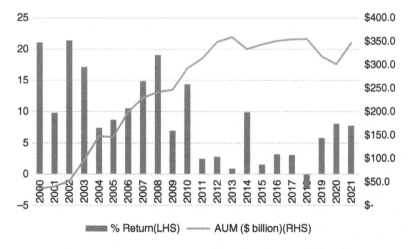

FIGURE 2.12. Managed futures AUM and % returns, 2000–2021.

Source: AUM from BarclayHedge, returns from EurekaHedge. All data as of 12/31 for each year.

When evaluating a potential investment in a commodity fund, investors must pay careful attention to the benchmark used for comparison. A global emerging markets equity fund is relatively straightforward to evaluate using a benchmark like the MSCI Emerging Markets index. For commodities, however, the benchmarks are less clear. Popular third-party indices like the Bloomberg Commodity Index, the CRB Index, or the GSCI Index have wildly different constituents and weights. As a result, two CTAs may be exposed to a different set of assets and weights than those included in any particular benchmark, adding another unwelcome layer of complication to performance evaluation.

2.5.2 Recent Developments

While the past three years have witnessed several extraordinary events in the commodity futures markets—including a negative price for oil in 2020[31] and the London Metals Exchange canceling $3.9 billion in trades and halting trading in nickel futures for a week to protect a single, large investor in March, 2022[32]—the Russian invasion of Ukraine and trade tensions between China and the United States promise to have an impact on commodity markets for months and potentially years to come. Decarbonization will also contribute to future price volatility as economies slowly shift from fossil fuels (oil, natural gas, coal) toward cleaner electricity generation that relies on rare earth minerals. Whether these factors create market conditions conducive to strong performance from managed futures funds remains to be seen.

2.6 Funds of Funds

As introduced in Chapter 1, Section 1.3, alternatives provide valuable diversification benefits for portfolios due to their lower correlation with traditional assets like stocks and bonds. However, the universe of alternatives is so broad that investing in a single hedge fund or private equity fund creates additional risk that the investor may be too exposed to a single alternative strategy. Practitioners therefore are incentivized to select a diverse mix of managers across multiple alternative investment strategies; however, developing the capabilities required to manage a portfolio of alternative investments may be out of reach for individuals and smaller institutional investors.

As described in Section 2.3, funds of funds offer a potential solution to this problem. As the name suggests, these products provide exposure to multiple alternative funds for investors lacking the resources to build their own diversified portfolio of alternatives. Funds of funds typically specialize in a particular alternative asset class (e.g., funds of hedge funds or private equity funds of funds). Applying their expertise in a specific asset class, FOFs perform manager sourcing and due diligence, portfolio construction, and ongoing monitoring on behalf of their investors. As a result, FOFs may build valuable relationships with the underlying managers, in some cases opening access to highly regarded managers that might otherwise be closed to new investments. Funds of funds may also be able to leverage their scale and relationships to negotiate better terms than individual investors would be able to obtain on their own. The benefits offered by FOFs come at a price, however, in the form of an extra layer of fees. On top of the fees charged by the underlying funds (e.g., "2 and 20"), FOFs add their own "1 and 10." Unless the funds of funds are able to negotiate fee discounts with the underlying managers, 3 and 30 may be an expensive price to pay for outsourcing an alternative investment program.

2.7 Summary

Chapter 2 has focused on five "traditional" alternative asset classes of great interest to professional and qualified individual investors: venture capital, private equity, hedge funds, infrastructure, and commodities, and introduced the funds of funds structure popular with many institutional investors. Aside from real estate, the subject of Chapter 3, these are arguably the largest and best-established alternative asset classes in the world.

The contrast between investing in private companies—whether startups like VC or leveraged buyouts in a form of PE—and public securities, such as stocks and commodity futures, is representative of the wide range of alternative strategies. Simply put, there are many different ways to invest in alternative assets that go well beyond traditional "buy-and-hold" investing in stocks and bonds. These strategies are more complex and less closely regulated, however, so with opportunity comes risk as well. Investors of all types and sizes must respect these risks and conduct proper due diligence so that, to the extent possible, they maximize the potential for positive performance and risk management through portfolio diversification.

Notes

1. Some readers may not be familiar with this term from the game of baseball; a home run is when a player hits the ball so far on the fly that it leaves the playing field while remaining in fair territory. The equivalent in cricket is called a "six."
2. See the discussion of IRR and performance measurement in Chapter 1, Section 1.2.4.
3. Readers looking for additional detail may wish to read *Venture Deals: Be Smarter Than Your Lawyer and Venture Capitalist* (4th ed.) by Brad Feld and Jason Mendelson (New York: Wiley, 2019).
4. Usually, multiple VCs work together with one firm playing "lead"; in exchange for a larger investment, the lead firm has greater influence on deal terms and often gets a seat on the board.
5. The extent to which the distribution of returns is stretched out (high dispersion) or narrowly clustered (low dispersion).
6. The degree to which an earlier event appears to influence a future event.
7. For example, if a manager has successfully invested a fund ("Fund 1") such that it ranks in the top quartile, then performance would be said to be *persistent* if the performance of the next fund ("Fund 2") also ranked in the top quartile. This concept appears to refute the common disclaimer that "past performance does not guarantee future results."
8. https://news.crunchbase.com/venture/softbank-vision-fund-strategy-turnaround-under-the-hood/.
9. https://news.crunchbase.com/venture/tiger-global-management-strategy-investing-2021/.
10. Infamous for his role in the Drexel Burnham Lambert junk bond scandal, Milken was barred from the securities industry for life in 1989. See https://en.wikipedia.org/wiki/Michael_Milken for more information.
11. For more information on DCF analysis, see Tim Koller, Marc Goedhart, and David Wessels, *Valuation: Measuring and Managing the Value of Companies*, 7th ed. (New York: McKinsey & Company Inc./Wiley, 2020).

12. This dynamic of negative near-term IRRs evolving to (hopefully) longer-term positive IRRs also applies to venture capital, especially when investing in early-stage companies.

13. Other trends include increased attention paid to sustainability factors in PE investments and secondary funds which provide liquidity to LPs by buying out investments in PE funds before they are completely wound down and distributed.

14. Without claiming anything more than interesting correlation, it is worth noting that 2022 has been a very difficult year across all asset classes, including public and private equity.

15. Chartered Financial Analyst (CFA) is a highly regarded professional designation for investors.

16. The CFA Institute classification is not the only way to categorize hedge fund strategies. Another approach divides the universe into *directional* strategies that are more willing to assume higher levels of market risk; *absolute return* strategies that focus primarily on delivering positive performance, regardless of market conditions by minimizing risk; *event risk* strategies which correspond to the event-driven category in the CFA Institute classification; and *diversified* strategies. This risk-centric partitioning of the hedge fund universe may be more useful for investors subject to tight risk constraints.

17. Roger Lowenstein, *When Genius Failed* (New York: Random House, 2011).

18. One famous example of such a trade was when George Soros and his Quantum Fund "broke the Bank of England" in 1992; see https://fortunly.com/articles/george-soros-and-the-bank-of-england/#gref.

19. Gross capital is the sum of the absolute value of longs and shorts, whereas net capital is longs minus shorts.

20. Factors are persistent drivers of returns such as size, value, and momentum. To learn more about factors, see A.L. Berkin and L.E. Swedroe, *Your Complete Guide to Factor-Based Investing: The Way Smart Money Invests Today* (Buckingham: BAM Alliance Press, 2016).

21. The use of technical indicators is a common part of many commodity futures trading strategies (see Section 2.5); https://www.investopedia.com/terms/t/technicalanalysis.asp.

22. In the United States, for example, investors are required to file a beneficial owner report (Schedule 13D) with the SEC within 10 days after accumulating an ownership stake of 5% or more in a public company.

23. See https://reenergizexom.com/the-case-for-change.

24. For example, https://www.moneylife.in/article/hedge-funds-lose-the-edge-beaten-by-the-us-market-index-again-and-again/31060.html does not once mention leverage or net market exposure, even when comparing SAC Capital's 12% return to the 18% return of the S&P 500.
25. An excellent source for additional material on infrastructure investing can be found in Noël Amenc, Frédéric Blanc Brude, Abhishek Gupta, and Tim Whittaker, "An Infrastructure Investment Primer: From Valuation to Allocation and Manager Selection," *Journal of Portfolio Management*, August 2022, jpm.2022.1.412; DOI: 10.3905/jpm.2022.1.412.
26. https://www.mckinsey.com/industries/private-equity-and-principal-investors/our-insights/infrastructure-investing-will-never-be-the-same.
27. Ibid.
28. See, for example, https://www.nytimes.com/2020/04/20/business/oil-prices.html.
29. Like the CFA, devotees of technical analysis (TA) can pursue a Chartered Market Technician (CMT) designation; see https://cmtassociation.org/chartered-market-technician/.
30. Specifically this list ranks *programs*—roughly equivalent to a "strategy" as has been used in this text—rather than firms, and only includes managed futures assets; firms like AQR will likely report higher AUM when the whole firm is considered.
31. As mentioned above, see https://www.nytimes.com/2020/04/20/business/oil-prices.html.
32. https://www.livemint.com/market/commodities/lme-halts-nickel-trading-again-on-technical-issue-as-price-plunges-11647421418882.html.

Real Estate

3.1 The Global Real Estate Market

Real estate cannot be lost or stolen, nor can it be carried away. Purchased with common sense, paid for in full, and managed with reasonable care, it is about the safest investment in the world.
—Franklin Delano Roosevelt,
32nd President of the United States

This quote continues to ring true today as real estate remains one of the largest, albeit complex, investment class. Even as the world moved from an asset-heavy manufacturing and industrial economy into one led by innovation, the millionaires who grew their wealth through the knowledge and services economy inadvertently allocated a significant part of their investment portfolio to real estate. Real estate provides a good store of wealth for investors who are prudent and are willing to actively manage the properties.

Savills Research placed a US$326.5 trillion valuation (2020) on the world's real estate assets, which included retail malls, office buildings, industrial buildings, hotels, residences, and agricultural land (Figure 3.1). This estimate is approximately four times the size of global GDP and exceeds the combined value of all global equities and securitized debt instruments. However, only one-third of the world's

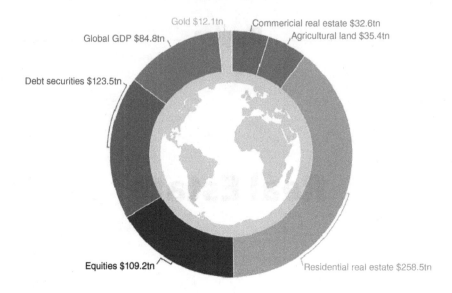

Source: Savills Research

FIGURE 3.1. 2020 global real estate universe in comparison.
Source: Savills, https://www.savills.com/insight-and-opinion/savills-news/319145/value-of-global-real-estate-rises-5--to-$326.5-trillion, accessed June 22, 2022.

real estate assets are investible; the remaining two-thirds are not publicly available for sale, such as crown properties and assets owned and occupied by governments.

3.2 Structure of This Chapter

To provide learners with a good overview of real estate as an asset class, the characteristics of selected real estate segments will be introduced. The knowledge of what drives the demand and supply of each real estate segment will lay the foundation for learners to understand the three methods of real estate valuation: (1) the income approach; (2) the cost approach; and (3) the sales comparison approach. Following that, the methods of investing in real estate through the use of public debt, private debt, public equity, and private equity will be described. These are also known as the real estate capital markets matrix or the four quadrants of capital. This chapter will conclude with an update on the recent trends in real estate investments, including the disruptions caused by new technologies and the Covid-19 pandemic. Readers who wish to delve further into real estate investments may refer to the Appendix: Real Estate Investments.

The new investment platforms and business models enabled by blockchain technology leading to the tokenization and fractionalization of real estate, as well as investments into land and properties in "the metaverse," are discussed in Chapter 4 on Modern Alternatives.

3.3 Characteristics of Real Estate

Investors considering this investment class would need to understand several of its characteristics that are different from the mainstream investments. Some of the characteristics are inherent in the bulky and physical nature of real estate assets.

First, real estate assets are immovable and no two properties are exactly alike. This is a key characteristic: properties are non-fungible and are heterogeneous. Differences arise from location, floor levels, interior decor, material used, age, and so on. As a consequence of this characteristic, the valuation of properties becomes challenging as there are many parameters that have to be taken into account: land area, location, built-up area, construction quality, occupancy, tenant mix, accessibility, and so on.

The bulky and physical nature also means that investors need to set aside a higher quantum of capital for investing in real estate. On the other hand, the fact that real estate assets are immovable means that there are many lenders willing to provide loans to investors for the long term. The availability of loans reduces the amount of capital that investors need to provide for each investment in real estate.

Given the many parameters to be considered for each property, and because some of the parameters, such as rents, expenses, and occupancy rates, vary, it is challenging for investors to assess property investment opportunities based on good quality and comprehensive data. The process of acquisition, especially performing due diligence on the asset and its related financial accounts, may take several months and, even then, the information may not be complete.

Unsurprisingly, property valuation is not an exact science and investors have to be comfortable with making their investment decisions without, for example, full knowledge of what the other buildings on the street are worth or whether an adjacent building may turn into a construction site in two years' time.

The bulky nature, the long-term cash flow available from rents, and the high cost of acquisitions and divestments result in physical real estate assets being held by investors for years, and in the case of pension, endowment, or insurance funds, for decades. Therefore, a single property may only change ownership once in 10 years, and this is why real estate is also characterized as an illiquid investment asset.

Unlike investments in gold, foreign exchange, or stocks, investors with direct ownership of properties have to provide active management oversight in order to generate good returns for themselves. There are relationships with tenants to manage; rents to collect; expenses to be paid to suppliers, facility managers, and contractors; periodic upgrading and renovation work; and, finally, there are government departments (such as the property tax department and the municipal office) to answer to. Properties that are actively managed by their owners will suffer less from the other characteristic called obsolescence, which, due to age, wear and tear, or changing trends, makes properties less desirable to tenants and users. Without active management, physical deterioration sets in and the financial value of the property will depreciate.

Investors who want to allocate capital to the real estate market, but who do not have the capabilities or resources to invest directly in, and subsequently manage, physical properties could invest in real estate via alternative methods. These passive investors could participate in the real estate market through private fund structures, invest in property development companies and real estate investment trusts that are listed on stock exchanges, or invest in real estate mortgages, and so forth.

3.4 Classifying Real Estate Segments

Real estate exists to support users' activities. Every type of real estate has its basic utility value. For example, agriculture real estate, when cultivated and managed well, will yield crops, food, and other raw materials for consumers. An office space serves the needs of knowledge workers.

A modern factory is filled with highly skilled workers, machinery, and robots to manufacture consumer and industrial products. A port and a logistics facility channel the flow of goods moving from the place of origin en route to various destinations. The list goes on.

Different types of real estate exist for different users, depending on their needs and activities. As there is a limit to the supply of land, particularly in preferred locations, real estate is a resource that has to be shared and managed equitably by all the stakeholders in the community. In most parts of the world, governments and policy-makers have taken over the role of allocating land use and the master planning of land resources to ensure that stakeholders' needs will be met.

In addition to allocating land for shelter and economic use, the authorities tasked with planning have to provide land for institutional and religious use, for example, police stations, hospitals, places of worship, and so on, and for utilities and infrastructure, such as roads, rail networks, waterworks, power plants, and ports.

As a result, land planning guidelines and controls are needed to ensure that the competing and tangential needs of different stakeholders and users can be balanced. It is easy to see why the quiet enjoyment of residential users should not be disturbed by the economic activities of an automotive repair facility nearby. But not all real estate segments and the user activities within the properties can be so clearly delineated. For example, is a home baker someone who is using his place of residence for production activities? Such activities should normally be undertaken in industrial properties.

While there are dozens of different segments within the real estate world, in the financial markets, a handful of these segments feature prominently. Investible real estate assets are usually split into two sub-asset classes: residential and commercial (or non-residential).

The residential category, especially for the market in the United States, is further subdivided into the segments of single-family homes and multi-family homes. In other markets, single-family homes could be called landed houses, terraced houses, detached houses, or bungalows while multi-family homes could be known as flats, apartments, and condominiums.

A residential property is primarily used for dwelling purposes. It is a private space where the occupiers enjoy their time and engage in their personal or family activities. The trend of working from home, supported by a plethora of technology improvements, software, and gadgets, has recently blurred the definition somewhat, due to the Covid-19 pandemic.

This is the real estate category that we are most familiar with. But while we spend most of our lives in residential properties, investing in them requires investors to lose their preconceived notions, biases, and emotional baggage that may tag along with the sense of familiarity of residential properties. Once it comes to investing in residential properties as a financial commitment with the objectives of enjoying a regular cash flow and making profits, it is advisable to follow due process: getting a written opinion from a real estate appraiser, checking the legal title, obtaining an engineering report, and so on.

The commercial category is more varied and consists of four main segments: Office, Industrial, Retail, and Hospitality. Secondary segments include data centers, student housing, retirement homes, and hospitals.

An office is a place of work, where business activities take place. Commercial entities are the main occupiers of office spaces, and they operate businesses for profits. An industrial property is one where production and related activities, such as storage, packing, logistics, and distribution, take place. The industrial segment consists of sub-segments such as factories, warehouses, data centers, and in some countries such as Singapore, Malaysia, and China, workers' dormitories.

The retail segment refers to properties where consumers purchase goods and services from businesses. The purchase transactions could include the immediate consumption of the goods and services, such as in restaurants and hair salons. The hospitality segment has properties such as hotels and serviced apartments where the principal use is for short-term accommodation with flexible lease periods of between a day and less than 6 months.

3.4.1 Analyzing the Segments

Building upon the foundational knowledge of what uses each of the real estate segments cater to and what types of activities take place in them, readers can begin to consider the utility value of each of the segments. It is important to understand the drivers of supply and demand for each segment so that, when presented with an investment opportunity, the investor will be able to form an opinion about the potential returns that the investment might bring.

It is easier to estimate the current availability and near-term supply of new floor space in all the real estate segments than it is to estimate demand. Data on real estate in most developed cities in the world are provided by government bodies or municipal offices. And for cities which have good quality investment grade properties, more data would be available through reports published by investment analysts and real estate consultants. The complication about supply arises when floor space is converted from one real estate segment into another. For example, given the "work-from-home" trend pushing up office vacancies, the owner of an office tower could repurpose the building entirely into a hotel, shifting the supply of floor space from the office segment to the hospitality segment.

Estimating current demand and forecasting demand are more challenging. But a good forward estimate is necessary for feasibility studies and for making investment and divestment decisions. Each segment has its own unique set of drivers of demand, and when market data show that the potential demand for a particular segment may be strong and sustained over the next 5 to 10 years, such positive data about demand will drive investment decisions to create new and additional supply in that segment. New supply could come from new buildings on land sites which were vacant, or it could come from repurposed buildings. The former might take two to four years of construction and development, while the latter option might see a new supply of floor space ready to welcome tenants in a year or two.

Demand estimates should not be generalized across all real estate segments. For example, a few consecutive years of strong economic growth does not mean that demand for all segments such as residential, office, retail, factory, hospitality, and so on are on the uptrend. We need to consider the context and understand the specific reasons that have contributed to the growth. If GDP growth was driven by increased labor productivity and higher value products, demand for office and factory space would increase if private enterprises were more profitable. But that is only true if these companies needed to increase the headcount of their office workers or factory workers. A city's shift to higher value production could arise from investments in automation which resulted in higher revenues generated by fewer workers.

So, counterintuitively, the higher GDP growth would actually lead to lower demand for residential, office, and factory space.

Forecasting demand for each real estate segment requires analysts to consider a combination of indicators. These could be macroeconomic indicators, such as population growth, consumer price inflation, wage growth, GDP growth, or real estate industry indicators, such as occupancy rates, rents and prices, transaction volumes, construction costs, and so on. The indicators mentioned are used in analyzing the residential segment's demand for rent and demand for home purchase. In addition, analysts might also consider other parameters, such as the unemployment rate, marriages, and household formation, interest rates for home loans, and the data on immigration versus emigration. All these indicators are useful for determining housing demand for both the single family home and the multi-family home segments.

For the office segment, in addition to macroeconomic indicators, key datasets to take heed of are employment and jobs growth, formation and cessation of new companies, and industry reports on business expectations. Analysts and investors also need to be cognizant of emerging work trends that encourage office users to take up flexible office leases or co-working spaces.

Analyzing demand for the retail segment requires us to consider a wider range of indicators. These may be related to consumption, purchasing power, household income, and tourism spend. For analysis specific to a retail mall asset, investors could additionally consider the mall's visitor traffic and footfall, or the connectivity of the mall via various transportation modes.

The hospitality segment is more varied as hotels and service apartments cater to a wide range of short-term accommodation needs: domestic and foreign business travelers, vacationers, local consumers of food and beverage services and hotel facilities, attendees of conferences and events, and so on. Given that most hospitality assets are designed to maximize the revenue from room rentals, the demand forecast should be focused on the growth of the travel market, both domestic and international. Indicators include the number of flights to the nearest airport, passenger seat capacity and utilization, number of commuters visiting the city via land transport (e.g., trains, buses, and cars) and, in some cities, via sea transport (e.g., ferries and cruise ships).

The most complex real estate segment is the industrial segment, with activities ranging from scientific and engineering research, testing and maintenance, manufacturing and production, storage, packaging, logistics and supply chain management, and so on. Forecasting demand for industrial space is very challenging. Indicators that provide some forward-looking guidance that could be considered are the Purchasing Managers' Index, surveys of direct investments in industrial activities, surveys of planned capital expenditure of industrial corporations, and so on.

Smaller segments of the real estate market, such as townships, hospitals, workers' dormitories, and so on, should be analyzed, based on their specific context, against the unique set of conditions and environment where the assets are based. As it is not possible, nor feasible, to obtain comprehensive data on a real estate investment opportunity, investors and analysts should maintain a balance between the amount of energy dedicated to analysis and making decisions to invest or to divest. If an investment case leaves lingering doubts, there is always a possibility of negotiating for a lower investment value (i.e., lower purchase price) in order to make up for the risks.

3.5 Real Estate Valuation

The worth of a real estate asset today depends on its future cash flow. This is the key reason why analysts need to understand the supply and demand factors that will affect the investment under consideration: to estimate the future rentals and expenses associated with the asset so as to derive a fair purchase price. While analyzing a specific property investment opportunity, investors may also rely on the opinions of local real estate appraisers.

The investment value of a property differs for different investors. As a property could be managed in many ways, its value depends on the investment objectives and capabilities of each investor. A passive investor could hold the property to enjoy the cash flow while an active investor could manage the tenants and suppliers to improve profits, spruce up the property to modernize it and attract higher-paying tenants, and even do a complete tear-down and rebuild. Both active and passive investors could also begin their evaluation with different investment horizons and consider different opportunity costs available to them.

Aggressive investors with higher risk appetites may take on more leverage to enhance their returns, which means that they might be willing to offer a higher price for a property than an investor with a moderate or low-risk appetite.

Real estate appraisers are called on to provide valuation reports for a wide range of purposes:

1. to provide a market value or book value to meet audit requirements;
2. to estimate the property's current "value in use" for an owner-occupier;
3. to provide an insurable value to determine what is the maximum loss or replacement cost;
4. to provide a taxable or depreciation value, etc.

Depending on the purpose of the valuation, an appraiser will apply relevant external market benchmarks, with adjustments to the assumptions, to derive the estimated property value. External benchmarks could include the risk-free rate, the inflation rate, rental growth, the escalation of maintenance and repair costs, the capital expenses that will be incurred in future to meet statutory requirements, and so on.

Three methods are most commonly used for property valuation:

1. The income approach
2. The cost approach
3. The sales comparison approach

3.5.1 The Income Approach

Under the income approach, the total operating cash flow of the property is considered by summing all the operating revenues of the asset (i.e., rents, parking charges, vending machine revenue, etc.) and subtracting all the operating expenses (i.e., utilities, maintenance, waste management, security, property tax, etc.). The result of this equation is the net operating income (NOI) of the asset. The NOI is usually calculated based on 12 months of revenues and expenses. Dividing the annual NOI by the property value will give us the capitalization rate, or cap rate, as it is usually known in the industry. The cap rate reflects the returns provided by the property and it is expressed as an annual return in percentage terms.

As an example, an office building has an annual operating revenue of $100,000 and operating expenses of $20,000. The owner purchased it recently at $1.6 million. The NOI is $80,000 per annum and the cap rate is 5.0% per annum.

The concept of using the NOI, the cap rate, and the asset value is very important in real estate investments. Once we have information for two of the three data points, we can calculate the third. Their relationship can be represented in Figure 3.2.

This quick method of estimating returns should be supplemented by more thorough and detailed analysis for the total returns of the project. Several items such as the acquisition costs, setup costs related to the investment structure, and non-operating expenses, such as interest costs, depreciation, and income tax have been excluded.

As such, some investors prefer to determine a project's value based on the building's useful life by adding up all the future cash flow streams and discounting them back to Present Value (PV). Using the Discounted Cash Flow (DCF) of the project to calculate the expected returns and the value of the project is acceptable.

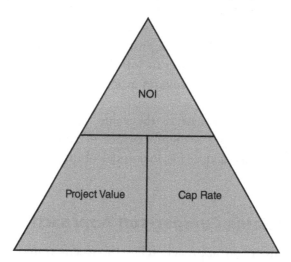

FIGURE 3.2. Pyramid relationship of net operating income, cap rate, and project value.

However, the calculations are lengthy and the assumptions about rents and operating costs 10 years or 15 years away become more and more fuzzy. Furthermore, as most properties are expected to last longer than the investment holding period, the analyst has to make an assumption about the terminal value of the project at the point of intended divestment, say, in year 15. The many assumptions that go into the DCF model may not add to improving the quality of the feasibility studies.

As the NOI and the cap rate are used so frequently in the industry, it is fundamental to understanding the daily exchanges between investors and landlords as well as the multitudes of industry reports by financial analysts and real estate consultants. Readers are advised to read Section A.4.3.1 in the Appendix to gain a deeper understanding.

3.5.2 The Cost Approach

The cost approach appraises a project's value by adding up the cost of land and construction, based on the premise that an investor should not invest any more than it would cost to buy vacant land and then construct the same building. While it seems to be a relatively straight-forward approach, it is complicated by the adjustments to the value required in this approach.

Adjustments are required because adding the current cost of land and current costs of construction would result in a brand-new building, but the target asset could be a property that was already completed 15 years ago. Some depreciation in value would have to be accounted for, so that the final value provides a better reflection of the current state of the property.

In the final adjustment to the value, appraisers will take into consideration four types of depreciation: (1) physical deterioration; (2) functional obsolescence; (3) locational obsolescence; and (4) economic obsolescence.

3.5.3 The Sales Comparison Approach

The sales comparison approach relies on recent transaction data to provide an estimate of the property's value. Given that a market with active buyers and sellers will result in frequent transactions, investors and appraisers may estimate the market worth of a target property by comparing the data of similar properties in the same location that were transacted recently.

Since no two buildings are alike in all aspects, the data comparison could be improved upon by considering attributes such as the age of the properties transacted, land size, the built-up area, the physical condition, proximity to transport nodes such as bus stops and train stations, and so on. When selecting transaction data, recent transactions will carry more weight as they would be more relevant than older transactions, due to changes in interest rates, employment, economic outlook, and so forth.

3.5.4 Other Approaches

Readers may see other variations to the three approaches mentioned in the valuation literature or used in valuation reports. Some of the variations arise from the need to modify the three basic approaches because the assets being appraised may not have regular cash flow or income and expenses that are easily forecastable. For example, the value of a multiplex cinema, a bowling alley, or a multi-story parking garage may be ascertained using the cost approach, but it is challenging to apply the income or sales comparison approach. Using the cost approach to appraise the value of a car park, which is relatively inexpensive to construct, would likely result in the parking garage being priced too low for the profits that it could generate.

Each approach has its own shortfalls. The income approach depends heavily on the long-term discount rate or an assumed cap rate and so it is not suitable for properties that have little or no income, such as a piece of land or an institutional building like a museum or a community center. The sales comparison approach depends on having market data that are sufficiently recent and rich, and thus, to appraise the value of a suburban shopping mall, where the nearest comparable asset could be 20 kilometers away, we would need to use the income approach and the cost approach.

3.6 Due Diligence

Prior to making an investment commitment and paying the seller for the property, investors need to undertake due diligence on the property. The due diligence process is a detailed examination of the claims that were made by the seller, to confirm that the property is indeed able to generate the income and profits that were presented.

In the real estate industry, the due diligence checklists include these broad categories:

- the seller's background and the management of the property;
- the historical financial performance of the property;
- the physical condition of the property, including an engineering site inspection;
- legal matters, including all the rental agreements;
- the suppliers' contracts;
- statutory matters;
- taxes.

Investors undertaking a thorough audit will reduce their risks as they could satisfy their stakeholders that they have addressed as many doubts as they possibly could. Any significant issues that could surface during this deep audit of the property could cause the transaction to be called off.

It cannot be overstated how important a detailed and thorough due diligence process is. Investors need to give the due diligence process sufficient resources, time, and attention. Investors should not take shortcuts in the process, even if competitors are rushing to purchase. Failure to scrutinize real estate portfolios and weak due diligence standards played a part in the Global Financial Crisis, which resulted in the bankruptcy and demise of famous financial institutions such as Bear Sterns and Lehman Brothers. Recently, lapses in due diligence of crypto market players have resulted in several billions of combined losses for a few of the biggest global investment fund managers. Readers may refer to Section 1.2.5 for further discussion of this topic.

3.7 The Four Quadrants of Real Estate Investment

Having covered the fundamentals—key segments of real estate, drivers of supply and demand for each segment, property valuation and the due diligence process—we can now consider the range of investment products available in the real estate universe.

Real estate investments may be categorized into four main types. The framework for the four quadrants of real estate investment is succinctly illustrated in Figure 3.3 by Timbercreek Asset Management, a multi-billion-dollar real estate fund manager.

This framework provides four investment objectives along the axes: yield, growth, stability, and liquidity. Investors who seek stable yields should focus on debt while investors who like to see their capital grow should focus on investing in equity. Investors who prefer stability should select private investments while investors who value liquidity should go for public investments (i.e., listed stocks). In combination, it means that investors who prefer stable, low-volatility investments that pay a steady income should select private real estate debt. However, at the other end of the spectrum, investors with higher risk appetites and who prefer stronger returns with better liquidity (i.e., investments can be converted to cash or cash equivalent within days) should opt for public real estate equity.

The four quadrants approach takes the perspective of institutional investors allocating capital from a large multi-asset investment

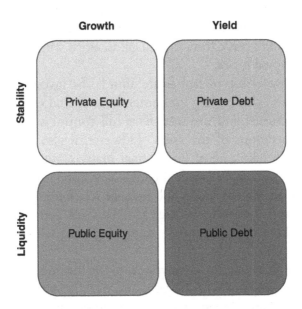

FIGURE 3.3. The four quadrants of real estate investment.

Source: Timbercreek Asset Management, https://www.investmentexecutive.com /in-depth_/partner-reports/4-quadrant-approach-to-real-estate-investing/, accessed July 26, 2022.

portfolio to real estate. The funds allocated for real estate investments could be apportioned to several, or all, of the four quadrants.

In a limited way, this framework may also be viewed from the perspective of a fundraiser. For fundraisers, such as property developers and real estate fund managers, the four quadrants provide a framework for considering how their projects could be financed. For example, a property developer which is listed on the stock exchange trying to acquire a significant property could consider paying for the acquisition with a mix of public equity (by issuing more shares), private equity (though a joint venture with a property fund), public debt (by issuing public bonds), and private debt (via a loan from a bank).

This section primarily focuses on the four quadrants approach from the perspective of an investor. Each of the four quadrants will be briefly described here. Readers should refer to Section A.6 in the Appendix for more details.

3.7.1 Private Equity

Private equity investments entail large capital investments in direct real estate ownership. These investments are illiquid due to the fact that they are not publicly traded, but they do offer the potential of stable returns and a full upside from capital gains, albeit with full exposure to the risks of capital losses.

Direct ownership of real estate affords the investors better confidentiality (i.e., challenging for competitors to find out details about investment returns) and investors have full control over the management and operations of the assets. However, it also means that the investor has to take care of operational matters, such as contracting with a property manager or a facility manager, appointing leasing managers to rent out vacant spaces and manage relationships with tenants, as well as a myriad of activities such as filing taxes, getting the property insured, working with contractors to repair damage or upgrade equipment, and so on.

The simplest way for an investor, or an investment company, is to purchase a property with its land and building titles. However, in the majority of cases, investors will choose to set up a new company to acquire a property. This has the advantages of a clean set of financial accounts, segregating investment properties and their bank accounts, and also improves tax efficiency to enhance the total returns. Large investment assets of above US$10 million are usually owned via a company that is specially set up (i.e., a Special Purpose Vehicle [SPV]), to acquire the property titles.

Investors who do not have the resources to manage properties and deal with operational issues, but who would still prefer to allocate capital privately, can choose to invest in real estate via a Private Equity Real Estate (PERE) fund. Such fund managers set up and manage SPVs that acquire and hold properties, usually for the long term, say, five years or longer.

Investors who choose to go down this route would have to take an additional step in the due diligence process: review and audit the fund manager's track record, reputation, governance, and procedures for managing the assets and the cash flow of the assets. Therefore, in addition to reviewing the property investment opportunities, investors need to be confident that the PERE fund manager can perform to standard and deliver the expected returns as projected by the manager.

3.7.2 Public Equity

Investing in real estate through the public markets may be considered a much simpler route. Real Estate Operating Companies (REOCs) and Real Estate Investment Trusts (REITs) are listed on stock exchanges, and they are required to provide regular (at least half-yearly) disclosures of their financial statements and business performance. As listed companies, they have to comply with rules imposed by securities exchanges, and this provides a layer of protection to investors.

Investors who want a very wide exposure across the listed real estate space could also invest in Exchange Traded Funds (ETFs) which are focused on REOCs and REITs.

Even though the public equity route is simple to access and the acquisition fees for shares of REOCs and units of REITs are very low, the volume of information in the public markets may be overwhelming for new investors. The starting point for an investor could be a decision about whether a steady dividend income or capital growth is preferred.

REITs are income-producing instruments that are bound to pay out most of their profits as dividends. With more than 90% of profits paid out to unit holders, there is little in terms of retained earnings, and REITs are unable to acquire properties regularly to expand their portfolio. Some investors with lower risk appetite and more conservative requirements, such as retirees who like regular payouts, insurance funds, and pension funds, prefer to invest in REITs for the stability and cash flow.

REOCs, also known as property developers in many parts of the world, are in the business of buying land to build new properties as well as buying and trading properties. As they are not compelled to pay out dividends, they have the flexibility of managing their cash reserves for major acquisitions or for the construction and development of large projects that are worth hundreds of millions of dollars. The strength of these companies and the profits they generate will increase the company's valuation, and therefore the stock prices will increase. Investors who prefer capital growth rather than steady income will allocate more funds to REOCs.

Investors could take another approach by first making a decision on which real estate segments they prefer. For example, an investor might like the story about e-commerce growth and the demand for logistics services. That narrows down the stock selection process quickly, and the investor could focus on REITs and REOCs that have property portfolios that are heavily weighted in the warehousing and logistics industry.

As with all investments, due diligence is required. In this case, stock selection of REOCs and REITs would require investors to analyze the financial reports of these companies and look at their revenues and profit margins, valuation multiples, balance sheet and gearing ratios, strength of their annual cash flow, market capitalization, and daily trading volume, and finally consider the quality of the management team and their shareholdings.

3.7.3 Private Debt

Individuals and private companies incur private debt in a variety of ways, including bank mortgages, student loans, mezzanine loans, subordinated loans, promissory notes, and debentures. The term "private" means that money is lent by lenders to a borrower directly or via an investment vehicle and the fact that this debt is not publicly traded.

Private debt can be transformed into public debt by pooling multiple loans, securitizing them, and listing them on an exchange.

Private real estate debt refers to loans backed by real estate (i.e., loans collateralized by real estate). Banks underwrite the majority of these loans for purposes such as commercial loans secured against an office building or home loans backed by residential properties. Non-bank lenders such as housing associations, credit unions, cooperatives, and other financial services companies and mutual funds may also provide private real estate debt. In some countries, real estate agencies may offer bridging loans to homebuyers who are in the process of buying a new home while selling their current one.

The single most important thing to note about investing in debt is whether the borrower is able to repay the debt and the interest payments. The fact that the borrower has pledged a property to secure the loan is a secondary issue because almost all investors of real estate debt do not wish to see the scenario of a borrower's default playing out. This is because when borrowers default, the process of seizing the assets for divestment in order to recover the debt and interest payments owed is onerous and may take years.

Investors must be familiar with the fundamentals of real estate debt in order to invest in private debt. The two main metrics for assessing the debt incurred on a property are the loan-to-value (LTV) ratio and the interest coverage ratio (ICR). Lenders generally use the LTV ratio and ICR to create loan size restrictions so as to limit the lenders' risks.

The LTV ratio of a property refers to the total amount of debt borrowed against the property, divided by the property's appraised value. LTVs under 80% are often preferred by banks acting as senior lenders. This means that the bank can seize the property and sell it for 80% of its earlier appraised worth and still be able to reclaim the entire loan when the borrower defaults. Taking a lender's perspective, debt investors may interpret an 80% LTV ratio as a 20% "safety margin," meaning that asset prices must fall by 20% before the debt investment incurs a loss. This metric is analogous to the "debt-to-equity ratio" of an operating company, and it shows the proportion of capital that is invested in the asset by the borrower versus the loan taken out against the asset. The LTV ratio is applicable to a variety of properties, from vacant land sites to completed buildings.

The ICR may be calculated using the NOI of a property divided by the anticipated interest payment for the year. Since the ICR only applies to properties that have income, its application is somewhat more constrained. For an owner-occupied building, the ICR may be calculated using the cash flow and EBIT (earnings before interest and taxes) of the owner's business. The ICR's counterpart is known as the debt service coverage ratio (DSCR). The DSCR includes both principal and interest payments, whereas the ICR excludes any payment of the principal sum. The majority of loans contracts would include a covenant stating an ICR of greater than 1.5.

Of the four quadrants, opportunities to invest in private debt are probably the most limited. The bulk of private real estate debt is lent by banks and financial institutions who then sell off the risks by securitizing the private debt portfolios for investment by public debt investors.

3.7.4 Public Debt

As the term implies, public debt refers to publicly traded entities that own sizable pools of loans that are secured against real estate. Borrowers make monthly interest and principal payments to these loan pools. Profits are made through interest income, and investors of these publicly traded companies receive dividend payments. As a result, these investments offer investors relatively predictable returns and are usually less volatile than publicly traded equities. Investors may also benefit from capital gains on the price of the listed debt instrument when investor demand rises, especially during periods when interest rates drop.

The main public debt instruments available to investors are mortgage-backed securities, traded as mortgage REITs, and debt-focused exchange-traded funds. Corporate bonds and medium-term notes issued by real estate companies and securitized against properties could be considered if these were traded on a public exchange.

Public debt instruments may provide better and more frequent financial disclosures than private debt. However, the basic principles of assessing risks apply: what are the average or median LTVs in the loan pool, what is the ICR (where applicable)? In addition, since there is an investment manager amassing the loan portfolios, investors need to understand the investment manager's capabilities, governance, and processes.

The size of the loan pool and the combined and anonymized data on borrowers' credit quality and securitized assets make it challenging for investors to obtain a confident assessment of the risks. As these loan portfolios change over time due to old loans being retired and new loans being added, investors must remain watchful and perform routine reviews of the managers of these listed instruments. Needless to say, due diligence is required on the loan portfolio and on the management quality and track record of the investment manager.

3.8 Future Trends in Real Estate

Having understood how to deploy the capital to invest, we need to turn our gaze to the future and consider the trends that will affect the real estate industry. Investors need to be aware of new growth segments to invest in, new tools and platforms that could disrupt real estate, and which market segments to avoid as they may become obsolete.

The post-Covid-19 world is turning out to be more turbulent than anyone expected. Many countries and organizations have been affected economically by high inflation, high interest rates, and volatile exchange rates. In the real estate world, extreme measures restricting activities and movements during the pandemic have created major changes to several property segments. Some of these changes are systemic and permanent: e-commerce and food delivery have reduced the demand for retail space, "work-from-anywhere" arrangements have reduced the demand for office space. Other changes, such as the dip in demand for hotels and resorts and air travel, are temporary and are likely to recover when restrictions are fully lifted around the world.

On the other hand, the industrial property segment saw a surge in demand due to the Covid-19 lockdowns. Within the industrial segment, warehouses, logistics facilities, distribution centers, and data centers were the prime beneficiaries of consumers stuck at home who ordered food, daily necessities, and other goods online. This led to a big jump in online orders for consumer goods, cooked food, and courier services, which resulted in the increased demand for warehouses and logistics facilities. Mobile and internet applications were increasingly used, and as more people stayed home, gym classes and movies were streamed to home use. Schools delivered lessons online and business meetings and seminars also shifted online. Demand for data services and communications surged, along with the demand for data centers.

3.8.1 The Data Center Segment

Cloud computing, data analysis, data mining, and blockchain technologies all require large amounts of data transmission and storage, thereby making data centers an increasingly popular real estate investment. Data centers are facilities used to house IT systems, application servers, telecommunications equipment, and storage systems. The data center facilities include cooling systems, backup power supply, redundant data communications connections, environmental controls, and a lot of security systems.

Demand for data centers is driven by new software applications, mobile applications, data mining, as well as gathering, analyzing, and generating new data from data sets. The insatiable desire for bandwidth, faster upload/download transmissions and communications for more videos, pictures, and instantaneous transactions has helped to push up demand for data centers.

Additionally, increased concerns about security also nudged demand higher as more individuals and organizations back up and duplicate data for disaster recovery and redundancy purposes. The storage and backup of information take up a very small fraction of data center capacity. The load on data centers comes from data flow: running applications, processing data, uploading and downloading of files and media, and executing payment transactions.

Interestingly, unlike more traditional real estate asset segments, the primary value of a data center is not its land or the building, but the value of the technology and equipment installed inside the building. In the past, tenants would rent space on the racks that their servers occupied, but a more efficient model has since been adopted in which data centers primarily charge their clients based on the electricity consumption. Some data center owners provide and charge clients for additional engineering and maintenance services on top of the "base rents" of a minimum commitment for power consumption.

Thus, the capacity and value of a data center are measured not by its floor area, nor by the volume of data storage, nor the value of hardware installed, but by its data processing capabilities measured by electrical power used. The biggest data centers in the world today require electrical power in excess of a hundred megawatts, sufficient to power a small town.

Investors may easily access data center investments through the public equity quadrant as many of the biggest data center assets are owned by listed REITs. However, investors need to look deeper into the business models of each REIT, as it is arguable whether data centers can be treated as real estate. First, the nature of the services offered by data center owners and operators brings in revenue streams which are different from the usual definition of steady rents paid for occupying physical space over a period of time. Second, given the high cost of IT and communications equipment, the land cost and building cost constitute only a small fraction of the total cost of a data center, unlike an office or a residential block where the land and building costs make up the bulk of the investment value. High-tech equipment and the constant need to upgrade mean that the equipment in a data center could attract significant depreciation and rapid obsolescence. Alternatively, investors might view the investment potential of a data center in the way one considers infrastructure, such as power plants, toll roads, and telecommunications, where the revenue streams are based on throughput and flow of the utility provided.

3.8.2 Key Technology Trends That Impact Real Estate

Several trends in technology development deserve close attention by real estate investors. Major cities competing on the world stage need to constantly upgrade to stay ahead of the curve. This forces city planners and policy-makers to improve the urban landscape and physical infrastructure. In the next two decades, key gateway cities around the world could look like giant construction sites in various stages of renovation and extensive regeneration (i.e., demolitions and construction).

The technology trends to keep an eye on include:

1. **Autonomous vehicles (AVs)** (i.e., cars, buses, and trucks) are on road trials in hundreds of cities around the world. Several cities in China and the USA have already enacted legislation allowing driverless taxis to operate commercial services. As passengers can call on these vehicles through mobile apps, the adoption of AVs and car-sharing services is expected to reduce personal car ownership. The widespread adoption of AVs will reduce the demand for parking lots and alter the design of pick-up and drop-off points as well as loading and unloading bays in buildings. Some in-building parking garages may be renovated to serve that purpose, but most of the car parking lots (especially those in condominiums) are likely to become dead space. In most countries, excess car parking lots may be repurposed for other uses, while in others, land use regulations and building design guidelines may have to be amended before parking lots can be adapted for new uses. Cities such as New York and Hong Kong, where parking lots have transacted at high prices, may see parking lots decline in value.

2. **Drones for transporting goods and humans** are in various stages of experiments and trials in many parts of the world. For example, an urban air-mobility company from Germany, Volocopter, announced that they will operate an air-taxi service in Singapore by the end of 2023. From a real estate and urban planning perspective, how many take-off/landing ports will be needed? Will building owners invest in fitting out the air-taxi ports? Will the buildings in the Central Business District need to install navigation beacons to guide the drones? What safety features and accident prevention measures may have to be installed in the buildings? If open spaces were configured with take-off/landing ports, what other modes of transport would passengers use to get to their final destinations?

3. **Remote teaching and online learning** have been growing ever so slowly in the last 50 years. The BBC started to air the UK Open University courses through television and radio in 1971. But the demand for in-class learning did not decrease because

learning in class provides learners with a richer experience. However, the advent of high-speed internet and rich multimedia content pushed more learning content online, and in the past 10 years, MOOCs (Massive Open Online Courses) have taken off in a big way. Due to the lockdowns of Covid-19, even more lessons were conducted online, and the introduction of 5G wireless technology will bring even richer content from schools to learners. These technological advances may result in a reduction in the need for lecture halls in schools and universities. In New York and London, where land prices are high, education institutions can reduce the physical space they occupy and cut down on rents by delivering more content online.

The three examples above are but a small set from more than a dozen technology-led disruptions to real estate. Investors need to be mindful about other advances in PropTech, which includes technology related to property maintenance, construction, 3D printing of buildings, FinTech, and blockchain.

Adopting new technologies will render some types of real estate assets irrelevant. For example, we recently witnessed the impact of e-commerce causing an increase in the number of ghost malls. As people around the world "migrate" their lives more and more onto the clouds, less real estate will be required in the physical world. The idiom "building castles in the air" takes on a new meaning in this age of the metaverse.

New investment platforms and business models enabled by blockchain technology, including the tokenization or fractionalization of real estate, as well as property investments in the "metaverse," will be discussed in Chapter 4, Modern Alternatives.

Chapter 4

Modern Alternatives

As global wealth increased and interest rates remained low through 2021, investors looked beyond stocks and bonds for new ways to preserve and build wealth, even beyond the "traditional alternatives" of venture capital, private equity, hedge funds, and real estate. This chapter is an overview of some of the "modern alternative" asset classes that the authors find most interesting and promising for individual or institutional investors, or both. With so many options and new ones arriving all the time, this is not intended to be an exhaustive list but rather a subset of investment opportunities to open the reader's eyes to the many exciting possibilities in the world of alternative investments.

4.1 Private Credit and Alternative Finance

One of the most basic corporate needs is money to finance its activities, especially investments such as hiring more employees, expanding hard assets such as plants and equipment, or developing new soft assets through research and development. Large companies are often able to directly tap into the credit markets by issuing bonds or borrowing from banks. After the Global Financial Crisis, however, many banks further reduced their lending activity to small and medium enterprises (SMEs), forcing these smaller firms to seek other venues for financing, including hedge funds and other non-traditional lenders (see Figure 4.1).

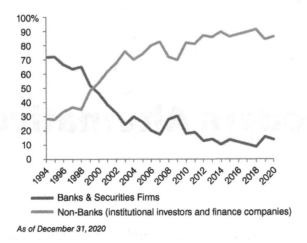

As of December 31, 2020

FIGURE 4.1. Primary market loan participation.

Source: Oaktree Capital Management, https://www.oaktreecapital.com/insights/insight-commentary/education/direct-lending, last accessed December 15, 2022.

The investment strategies described below—direct lending, marketplace lending, venture debt, trade finance, aircraft finance, and litigation finance—are sometimes referred to as "private credit" or "alternative finance"[1] and represent ways for investors to capture returns through lending activities and financing activities that traditionally belonged to the banks.

4.1.1 Direct Lending

As the banks retreated from lending to SMEs, other investors perceived an opportunity to fill the gap with dedicated lending facilities targeting this market segment. So-called direct lending funds provide loans to middle-market companies. Typically, these are senior secured loans (lower risk) with 5–7-year maturities, held by the lending institution until maturity instead of syndicated to other institutions, and target high single- to low double-digit returns.

Direct lending is a subset of private credit strategies, which also includes mezzanine and distressed debt. Depending on what an investor is looking for, the strategies within private credit can offer an attractive mix of diversification, risk management, and returns (i.e., strategies such as direct lending that prioritize capital preservation), and distressed lending that prioritizes return generation (Figure 4.2).

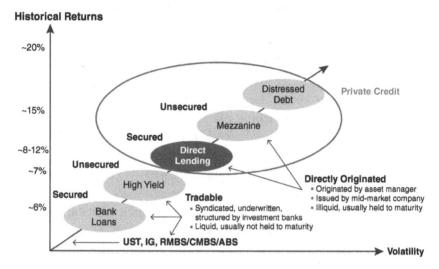

FIGURE 4.2. Direct lending in the context of credit strategies.
Source: Marquette Associates, https://biws-support.s3.amazonaws.com/Direct-Lending/Fixed-Income-Direct-Lending-Marquette.pdf, last accessed December 15, 2022.

Similar to private equity funds, direct lending funds also raise money from institutional LPs and charge a combination of management and incentive fees (carried interest). These funds often source their deals from private equity firms (GPs) that regularly need financing for their portfolio companies. The thousands of GPs and hundreds of thousands of middle-market companies around the world create a rich opportunity set for direct lending funds. Funds with the GP/LP structure are usually available to accredited investors only, and that applies to most direct lending funds as well. For readers with an opportunity to invest in this asset class, however, it may be worthwhile spending some time digging deeper into the specific strategies employed, any leverage used, and sector/geographic concentration to understand the risks involved. Although direct lending is one of the lowest risk private credit strategies, by no means should that suggest that there aren't any risks involved.

4.1.2 Marketplace Lending

The marketplace lending model is a specialized form of direct lending where borrowers and lenders find each other through an online platform. Two characteristics shared by many platforms are that the companies and average loan sizes are even smaller than in other forms of direct lending, so lenders are more likely to need different tools for credit scoring than banks would traditionally use. As a result, the set of potential loans available on marketplace lending platforms skews toward smaller and riskier loans.

Two different terms are commonly associated with non-bank financing through an electronic platform. The first, "crowdfunding," dates back to at least the eighteenth-century Irish Loan Fund[2] and involves raising money in small amounts from a large group of people. Modern crowdfunding has four main categories: (1) reward-based; (2) donation-based; (3) debt-based; and (4) equity-based crowdfunding. In the case of reward crowdfunding, platforms like Kickstarter (www.kickstarter.com) help match individuals and small businesses with investors, called "backers." In return for their financial support, backers receive a reward (usually a product of some sort) instead of financial returns—hence the term "reward crowdfunding."

A famous example of reward crowdfunding is the case of Oculus. In 2012, backers helped the firm raise $2.5 million for its initial virtual reality headset. They successfully built and shipped their product and soon thereafter were acquired by Facebook for $2 billion. While you might expect that to have resulted in a nice return on investment for the backers of Oculus, the backers had only pre-purchased a VR headset and received nothing from the sale. For this reason, reward crowdfunding, while popular, is not appropriate for those seeking financial returns.

In contrast to reward-based crowdfunding, donation-based crowdfunding allows individuals to more widely solicit donations toward a cause, project, or event than would be possible otherwise. One example, GoFundMe (www.gofundme.com) states on its website that it has helped raise $17 billion since 2010 through over 200 million donations. As this strategy falls under the category of philanthropy, it is not covered here in further detail.

The other two types of crowdfunding are equity-based and debt-based (lending). In 2012, the United States passed the Jumpstart Our Business Act, or JOBS Act, which created a way for companies in the United States to issue and sell securities via crowdfunding, something that was previously prohibited. Since then, platforms like AngelList, Microventures, and Wefunder in the United States—and many others around the world—have become important channels for small and growing companies to connect with potential equity investors. The investment process here follows any other equity investment, with the challenge that the companies are usually very small and may have limited financial, operational, or other information available. Platforms can be very different, for example, in terms of minimum investments, whether or not they serve non-accredited individuals, and the characteristics of the investments offered—investors should carefully compare different platforms before participating.

"Marketplace lending" itself is what market participants currently call the fourth type of crowdfunding, debt crowdfunding, though confusingly the term tends to be applied to platforms offering both equity and debt financing. Like equity crowdfunding, marketplace lending also refers to an online platform that facilitates the relationship between the borrower and lender.[3] Regulators require platforms to conduct typical banking functions, including identity verification, anti-fraud and anti-money laundering checks, credit checks, processing payments, and debt collection. These practices and protections give confidence to potential investors who are also interested in the relatively high interest rates charged to SMEs that might otherwise have a difficult time accessing funding from banks. Despite the relatively high cost of financing, SMEs are attracted to platforms because they are a viable alternative to banks, especially in countries with less well-developed banking sectors.

Marketplace lending platforms were developed for individuals to evaluate projects or investments one at a time. This works well for small numbers of smaller investments, whereas institutional investors usually operate on a larger scale. To address this issue, institutional investors have developed a creative workaround. Rather than evaluating individual loans, institutional investors make a deal with the platform operator. The investor sets predefined criteria for the loans they want to finance, perhaps using criteria like industry, location, size, credit rating, term, and interest rate. When a new loan is added to the platform, the platform screens that loan against the criteria set by the investor. If the loan meets the investor's criteria, the investor automatically makes the loan before it appears on the platform, up to an agreed-upon aggregate lending amount. In this way, institutional investors don't have to spend time reviewing each loan and secure pre-emptive access to some of the most attractive loans on the platform. The platform benefits because the amount of capital committed to their platform helps them attract more borrowers and lenders.

Institutional investors are particularly interested in these investments because they have historically provided attractive risk-adjusted returns, with one index of US marketplace lending outperforming other asset classes during five separate episodes of volatility from 2011 to 2018[4] as shown in Table 4.1.

TABLE 4.1. Risk-adjusted returns vs. traditional asset classes during market turmoil periods 2010–2018 (%)

		Orchard US consumer marketplace lending index	Fixed income	Equities	REITs
1	Double Dip: May—Oct '11	2.23	3.52	−15.30	−18.44
2	Taper Tantrum: May—Sept '13	2.65	−3.67	3.03	−14.43
3	Grexit Fears: Feb—Jul '15	3.03	−2.15	4.36	−13.57
4	U.S. Election: Aug—Dec '16	0.85	−3.28	1.97	−13.52
5	Feb '18 Dip	0.45	−0.95	−3.69	−7.94

This sounds attractive but keep in mind that investors in different locations may have had a very different experience with marketplace lending platforms. For example, China experienced a lot of fraudulent activity in this sector before 2016 when the regulators stepped in. As a result, where there had been over 6,000 such platforms in 2015, by 2019, there were fewer than 300 remaining.

Individuals are unlikely to have access to the kind of relationships that institutional investors enjoy with marketplace lending platforms.

Instead, individuals can get direct exposure to SME lending returns by signing up as lenders on these platforms (subject to minimum investment levels and other onboarding requirements). As with equity crowdfunding, no two platforms are exactly the same and investors should evaluate the available options before deciding whether or not to participate.

4.1.3 Venture Debt

Traditional bank loans require the borrower to provide collateral for the loan in the form of assets, cash flows, or profits, but young growth companies in sectors like technology and life sciences often lack these forms of collateral. Venture debt is designed for young, high-growth companies that have pre-existing venture capital funding. Loan terms are based on the startup's growth prospects and perceived ability to raise new capital as a means to pay off the debt.

Venture debt enables companies to fund expansion or cover unexpected operational issues without additional dilution from another round of equity financing, and at a lower cost of capital. Loans are typically closed shortly after a fresh round of equity. The size of the equity round and the borrower's burn rate are key determinants of the size of the loan. A rule of thumb is that the principal amount of the loan may be equal to 30% of the most recent equity round.

Like venture capital investing, private funds are the preferred way to invest in venture debt. Lenders benefit from close ties to the venture community due to the relationship nature of the business, and fund managers are concentrated in venture-rich ecosystems like Silicon Valley, New York City, Israel, and even Southeast Asia (Singapore).

4.1.4 Other Credit

Of the many specialized forms of credit available to investors, this section highlights two large, well-established markets, trade finance and aviation finance, that have yet to achieve their full potential as allocations in institutional portfolios.

4.1.4.1 Trade Finance

Global trade relies on a vast network of banks and other intermediaries that facilitate transactions between buyers and sellers. Enabled by a combination of different short-term structures provided by banks, such as letters and lines of credit, importers and exporters send and receive payments when shipments are made and goods are received, mitigating the risk of non-shipment or non-payment. According to recent figures, trade finance could represent a large and appealing market, given its combination of short duration and low default rates—if products are built to accommodate traditional capital markets investors.[5]

While at the time of this writing trade finance remains largely the purview of banks and specialist firms, early efforts to transfer risk to the capital markets are gaining momentum. In one example, the bank will syndicate (sell) a portion of its trade finance portfolio, raising capital that the bank needs to protect its regulatory capital ratios. This model has the advantage that investors are able to leverage banks' existing role as the originators of trade finance business. For companies that are unable to access traditional bank trade finance channels (e.g., some SMEs in emerging economies), a new set of trade finance funds is replicating the origination and administration activities of the banks. These funds are potentially exposed to higher counterparty or execution risk, for which they compensate through higher fees and higher returns to investors. As more business models arise and technology continues to reduce the frictional costs associated with trade finance, investors may discover more opportunities to allocate to this differentiated form of credit.

4.1.4.2 Aviation Finance

The airline industry is extremely capital-intensive and, as such, presents an interesting opportunity for financing solutions. Airlines have two options when planning how best to finance their fleet: they can own their own planes or lease aircraft if they prefer to reduce their balance sheet, maintaining flexibility for future fleet growth, or when they are dissatisfied with the price of buying direct from the manufacturer. Leases typically take one of two forms, either a finance-only structure or an operating lease where the lessor is responsible for operating the aircraft as well.

The global airline industry largely survived the Covid-related challenges of 2020–2021, including the leasing companies. As the global travel market continues to rebound, improvements in passenger and cargo traffic support have renewed interest in aviation finance. In addition, two structural factors suggest that the market for aviation finance will continue to grow. First, as part of the overall trend toward sustainable investing, additional investment is required to replace older planes as part of low-carbon transition plans for the industry. Second, the incessant growth in dry powder (uninvested capital) in the private equity industry has led to the launch of new aviation finance funds. While this influx of capital may ultimately lead to downward pressure on returns, new fund launches translate into new opportunities for institutional investment in this asset class.[6]

4.1.5 Litigation Finance

Lawsuits and arbitrations can be expensive for claimants, requiring financial commitments well before reaching an uncertain verdict or settlement—even more so if the case is appealed. Although the practice has its roots in the 1800s, modern litigation finance has evolved to where there are multiple opportunities to invest in this asset class.

The most straightforward lawsuits involve two parties, either individuals or companies. More complex lawsuits are also possible; over 30 countries around the world allow individual claimants to jointly bring a lawsuit by forming what's referred to a "class." Class action lawsuits require a lot of work but often result in very large settlements, especially in cases involving consumer protection, environmental disasters, and securities fraud.[7]

In some cases, the claimant(s) may lack the financial resources required to pursue the lawsuit to its conclusion. Some countries permit lawyers to accept cases on a conditional or contingency basis, where they only receive payment if their client wins the case. Under such arrangements the payment is often tied to the amount awarded to the claimant, which in some countries—especially the United States—can be quite large. This fee arrangement merely transfers the financing burden from the claimant to the law firm, rather than eliminating it, but if the potential award is large enough, the law firm may be incentivized to take the financial risk.

Because some lawsuits (and especially class action lawsuits) are expensive to pursue, litigation finance funds provide capital required to prosecute the case in return for a percentage of the lawyer's share of the award or settlement. These investors possess specialized expertise to evaluate the legal merits and potential financial outcomes of a case before providing funding.

There are several third-party funds that (institutional) investors can allocate to, and since returns are driven by lawsuit activity, financial performance should exhibit low correlation to traditional market indices. For individual investors, Burford Capital is a litigation finance specialist whose stock trades in the UK (LSE: BUR) and the United States (NYSE: BUR).

4.2 Insurance-Related Finance

Most readers are likely to be familiar with several forms of insurance for individuals, including health insurance, life insurance, and perhaps renters or property insurance. Businesses require insurance as well, and their needs may be rather more complex than individuals. This chapter describes two investment products linked to underlying insurance markets: one for insurance sold to companies and one for individuals.

4.2.1 Catastrophe Bonds and ILS

To understand the first insurance-related alternative asset class—catastrophe bonds—it helps to begin with a very oversimplified view of how the insurance market works.[8]

Company A ("the Policyholder") is exposed to a set of risks, such as fire, flood, theft, and injuries to its employees. To mitigate some of that risk, it purchases an insurance policy from Insurance Company X ("the InsureCo"). In essence, it trades the risk of unknown losses for the certainty of a premium payment for the insurance policy.

Now consider the InsureCo. It too is exposed to a set of risks, and though these include the same risks as Company A, the difference is that the InsureCo is also exposed to events that might affect large numbers of its policyholders at the same time. If Company A's building burns down, that is bad for Company A but only represents one policy for the InsureCo. Insurance premiums reflect the probability of potential losses for each individual policy and assume that the odds of a single fire causing damage to buildings of many policyholders at the same time are relatively low.[9] When large wildfires occur as experienced in Australia in 2019 or in California in 2017–2021, however, lots of policyholders could be affected at the same time, causing large losses for the InsureCo. To protect against this extreme event, the InsureCo buys its own insurance using something called "reinsurance"—insurance for insurance companies.

Just like Company A transferred its risk to the InsureCo, now the InsureCo transferred some of its own risk to a reinsurance company. But of great interest to investors, the InsureCo has other options. If it feels like the cost of reinsurance is too high for the risk being transferred, the InsureCo can use several different structures (collectively called "insurance-linked securities" or ILS) to transfer that risk to the capital markets. This section is focused on a structure called a "catastrophe bond" since it is the largest and most widely investable instrument in this asset class.[10]

Catastrophe bonds are similar to traditional bonds with a few important exceptions. First, proceeds from the bond sale are placed in a special purpose vehicle[11] (SPV) instead of going directly to the accounts of the issuer. In aggregate, the insurance industry is wellcapitalized, but it is not impossible for an insurance or reinsurance company to go bankrupt. If that were to happen, the bondholders would lose their principal, so to avoid that risk the catastrophe bond proceeds are held in very conservative investments within an SPV.

The second difference concerns interest payments and the return of principal. Unlike traditional corporate bonds, catastrophe bond payments are contingent upon covered events that occur during the duration of the bond (just like an insurance policy). If there are no qualifying events during the duration of the bond, investors should receive all interest payments along with their principal. If a covered event does occur, however, then investors may lose some or all of their interest payments and principal.

Each catastrophe bond contains language describing under which specific circumstances a catastrophe will result in a loss of payments or principal. One component is related to the region and type of peril, for example, Japanese typhoons; if this is the "covered peril," then losses due to fires in California will not affect the bondholders. Another important component of a catastrophe bond is referred to as the "trigger." The trigger describes the specific catastrophic conditions under which bondholders will reimburse the issuer. There are three major types of triggers:

- **Indemnity:** The issuer's own specific losses are used to calculate payouts. This can take months or years to determine.
- **Industry loss:** Rather than look at what happened specifically to the issuer, an industry loss trigger uses aggregate damages across the industry.
- **Parametric:** This trigger is based on a specified parameter of the peril, for example, the magnitude of an earthquake, or the wind speed or storm surge for a hurricane.

The choice of trigger introduces "basis risk," or the potential for a difference between the issuer's actual losses and what is received from the catastrophe bond. Imagine that the InsureCo loses $150 million in a large US hurricane. If the InsureCo had sold a $100 million catastrophe bond for US hurricane risk, the bond trigger helps determine the payout. A parametric trigger might be based on the category of the storm; if the trigger is set for Category 3 or above, and the hurricane was only a Category 2, the InsureCo receives nothing from the bond. If, however, the catastrophe bond used an indemnity trigger based on actual losses, then the InsureCo should receive something like $100 million from the bond, potentially wiping out the bondholders.

The market for catastrophe bonds has reached over $40 billion in outstanding notional value, and investors can allocate to asset managers who specialize in these strategies. These asset managers rely on a combination of analysis of credit risk and interest rates, and very specialized expertise required to assess the projected maximum loss due to the insurance conditions, such as covered perils, geography, and underlying insurance exposures. Dedicated catastrophe bond investors may have meteorologists, vulcanologists, and insurance actuaries on their staff in addition to traditional financial investors.

Investors are interested in catastrophe bonds for two primary reasons. First, financial returns are uncorrelated with traditional markets because performance is driven by natural phenomena like the weather. Second, the returns have been very attractive. According to industry data provider Artemis (https://www.artemis.bm), returns for a benchmark of ILS managers were exceptionally stable until 2018, with only two negative months in the preceding 10 years. Beginning in the fall of 2018, however, a series of catastrophes in the United States caused large losses on some bonds. Since then, catastrophe bonds have been hit with a long stream of natural disasters. Investors must consider whether this is a string of bad luck or if perhaps climate change is behind what will be a less attractive new normal for the asset class.

Direct investing in catastrophe bonds, or indeed any form of ILS, is probably best left to the experts; some institutional investors have built up the requisite expertise to do so, but many more access this asset class through specialist managers. In some jurisdictions, individual investors may be able to get exposure to catastrophe bonds through unit trusts or mutual funds marketed through private banks.

4.2.2 Life Settlement

Of the two insurance-linked asset classes in this section, catastrophe bonds are based on insurance for companies (insurance companies, actually). The second asset class, life settlement funds, is based on an individual insurance product: life insurance. An individual ("the insured") buys a life insurance policy on his or her own life, pays a premium every year, and then when the insured dies the designated beneficiary receives the death benefit. Those are the important terms: insured, premium, beneficiary, and death benefit.

Although the practice dates back over 100 years, the life settlement market grew quickly in the 1980s during the AIDS epidemic. Investors sought terminally ill AIDS patients with life insurance policies and gave the patient cash to pay for expensive medical treatment in return for being named the owner and beneficiary of his life insurance policy. The investor paid the premium on the policy until the insured died (which was expected to happen quite soon at the time), and then collected the death benefit. As medical treatment began to extend the lives of AIDS patients, investors were less interested because the returns were better when you knew that the policyholder was going to die soon.

From these rather morbid and perhaps ethically questionable beginnings, life settlement funds have evolved into something a bit more mainstream. Under the current model, investors look for elderly policyholders rather than terminally ill AIDS patients. They use actuarial techniques to determine how much to pay for a policy—the same statistics that insurance companies use to determine what premium to charge. And they build portfolios to help manage three important types of risk.

The first risk is "basis risk" again, only this time it represents the risk that the insurance company will raise the premiums unexpectedly, negatively impacting the value of the policy. The second is longevity risk. If the insured lives longer than expected, the policy is less attractive for investors because they pay more premiums before receiving the death benefit. Finally, the third is liquidity risk. The secondary trading market for insurance policies isn't very liquid, and investors must pay premiums to keep a policy in-force. If LPs in a life settlement fund withdraw their money when the GP is liquidity-constrained, the GP may find it difficult to make premium payments and might have to let a policy lapse for non-payment of premiums.

The market for life settlement funds is an example of a niche asset class with attractive returns that appears to have a low correlation to traditional markets. Several institutional investors have made small (less than $50 million) allocations to life settlement funds,[12] and some funds are accessible to accredited individual investors. Especially if the product expands to countries with large life insurance markets like Japan, this could be an interesting asset class to watch.

4.3 Impact Investing

In the past decade, and especially in the past few years, much has been written about sustainable investing. According to the Global Sustainable Investing Alliance (GSIA), "[s]ustainable investment is an investment approach that considers environmental, social and governance (ESG) factors in portfolio selection and management."[13] Sustainability-focused investors may follow one or more strategies to achieve this goal, relying on ESG-related information provided by companies through what is called corporate social responsibility (CSR) (e.g., greenhouse gas emissions and employee diversity statistics). The market is large and growing, by recent estimates accounting for over $35 trillion and 35.9% of global assets under management.[14]

Investments in stocks and bonds as well as traditional alternative asset classes may incorporate sustainability-related information to different degrees, but only one very specific strategy is so different that it merits mention as an alternative asset class: impact investing.

Impact investments are "made with the intention to generate positive, measurable social and environmental impact alongside a financial return."[15] Investing for impact has been around since at least the 1960s and is a prominent feature of development finance institutions (DFIs), such as International Finance Corporation (IFC, www.ifc.org). The term "impact investing," however, is thought to date to a 2010 research report by JPMorgan and the Rockefeller Foundation.

Impact investing follows similar key steps common to venture capital and other forms of private markets investing (see Chapter 2, Section 2.1): (1) screening for investments, (2) structuring the terms of the investment, (3) providing ongoing support for portfolio companies, and (4) exiting the investment.

Screening in the impact context considers many of the same risk factors as traditional investments, including evaluating the founders or management, and checking prior experience or past performance of the enterprise. The difference is that impact investors also screen for impact, including the nature of the impact (e.g., reducing water usage in drought-prone areas), how the impact is measured (e.g., surveys, sensors), and the quantum of impact generated in relation to the financial investment and returns.

Impact deal structuring also has a few different components, starting with the financial terms of the investment. From the onset, the organization and impact investors must agree what type of instrument will be used (e.g., loans, bonds,[16] equity) and whether the investment will be made at a market or below-market ("concessionary") rate. Impact investors often prioritize impact over financial returns by investing at concessionary rates, one of the main ways that impact investing differs from traditional investing.

Another important part of deal structuring is to agree on impact metrics, targets, and measurement. Proper impact measurement is very deliberate, benefits from experience, and requires commitment from all parties to the investment. Specialist organizations like the Global Impact Investor Network (www.thegiin.org) have worked for years to collect and standardize different impact metrics that can be customized for a specific investment, but the process is still manual and requires significant experience to do well. For example, in a YouTube video, the director of a large impact investor shared that it took them a year to develop and agree to the impact metrics for one of their investments. This focus on measurable—and attributable—impact is arguably the defining feature of impact investing.

It bears emphasizing that choosing impact metrics involves a considerable amount of judgment in part because the act of measurement is itself less precise than the ideal. For example, when considering projects targeting positive environmental impact, it can be very challenging to measure the impact even when there are generally accepted metrics that can be used. Emissions reduction may sound straightforward—just measure the change in greenhouse gas emissions—but every step in the chain has some degree of uncertainty (where did the electricity come from? How were goods shipped for sale?). Furthermore, impact measurement may face tradeoffs between different objectives. If animal husbandry is a significant source of emissions, how should investors evaluate the impact of providing microloans to smallholder farmers in emerging markets in order to support raising livestock? Impact measurement stands to benefit from the broader industry effort to identify and measure risks and opportunities from ESG and sustainability issues, but until then investors must apply a healthy amount of judgment.

After the investment is made, impact investors provide hands-on help to investees or portfolio companies like traditional venture capitalists, helping them grow their impact and to refine impact metrics and measurement. Depending on the deal terms, the investors may arrange periodic site visits for impact measurement, often requiring a trip to underserved communities in hard-to-reach places.

Finally, at some point, impact investors will exit their positions, either naturally when loans expire or bonds reach maturity, or through a sale in the case of investments with an equity component. Traditional VC investments are more likely to exit through an industry sale or IPO, a more unusual (although not impossible) scenario for impact investments, especially those made on a concessionary basis.

One of the common critiques of impact investing has to do with concessionary investments (i.e., that there must be a tradeoff between "doing well" and "doing good"). In other words, sustainable or impact investments should be expected to deliver worse financial performance than non-impact investments. We can visualize this using two graphs. On the left, skeptics would say that any movement along the x-axis, meaning incrementally positive impact, would require a negative change in expected returns on the y-axis (Figure 4.3).

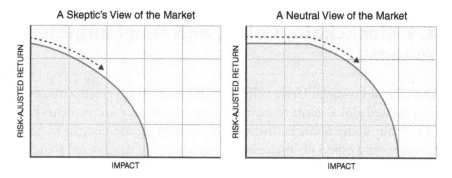

FIGURE 4.3. Competing views on the tradeoff between social and financial returns.

Since impact investments are typically private markets transactions, a rigorous evaluation of impact investing performance is subject to the same issues as private equity funds (see Chapter 2, Section 2.2), but with the added complication of monitoring the tradeoff between financial return and impact return. The data on impact funds are limited, but analyses suggest financial returns from impact investments are similar to market-rate private investments, especially for fixed income, but impact investors are willing to accept ~4% lower IRR than market rate private equity funds.[17] When it comes to measuring the *impact* performance of impact investing, however, research is further behind due to a lack of data, but the situation is improving: in 2020, faculty from three of the world's top business schools formed the Impact Finance Research Consortium (https://impactfinanceresearchconsortium.org) to collect data on impact investing for academic research.

Investors interested in impact funds face similar constraints to traditional venture or private equity investing (i.e., most impact funds are private and for accredited investors only), with few if any options for retail participation. More recently, some equity mutual funds have begun to include the term "impact" in their name; some do an admirable job of engaging with public companies on ways to measure impact from their operations. Few investments in public equities, however, will satisfy the most rigorous definition of impact investing referenced above since public companies are less likely to *intentionally* generate *measurable* impact, and if the fund doesn't own the shares then someone else will.

4.4 Blockchain, Coins, and Non-Fungible Tokens

The Global Financial Crisis (GFC) in 2008–2009 triggered a massive, coordinated global effort to stave off deep recessions. Governments had to bail out many financial institutions, deepening the distrust in governments and especially financial institutions. This distrust led some to imagine alternative ways to store, transfer, and invest money outside the traditional financial system. One such alternative, called bitcoin, was launched in the middle of the GFC.

From the launch of bitcoin in 2008, the global market for cryptocurrencies has twice exploded in popularity, first in 2017–2018 and then more recently during the Covid-19 pandemic (and especially the first half of 2021). There are many resources available for readers interested in a deep exploration of the history of "crypto," its technologies and protocols, and investment opportunities. This section is focused on crypto as an alternative asset class. It begins with an overview of the building blocks of blockchains, coins, and tokens—including so-called "non-fungible tokens" (NFTs)—before summarizing some of the strategies used by investors in this space.

4.4.1 Blockchains and Coins

In the traditional financial system, government institutions like the Depository Trust & Clearing Corporation (DTCC) in the United States manage what is essentially a list of every share of publicly traded stock, who owns it and in which account, and other important information. Around the time of the Global Financial Crisis, some people distrusted the traditional financial system so much that they wanted to create an alternative that didn't require trust in a centralized authority and that would be less susceptible to monetary policy decisions (especially devaluing currencies). On October 31, 2008, under the pseudonym "Satoshi Nakamoto," a White Paper was published describing an invention called "bitcoin" which runs on a "blockchain." Blockchain technology addresses the trust issue because while anyone can see the transaction-level data in blocks on the blockchain, the parties are anonymous. And because bitcoin has a fixed, lifetime supply, there can never be the equivalent of central banks printing money.

In contrast to the existing system of centralized record-keeping, a blockchain uses distributed ledger technology where participants in the network (called "nodes") each maintain a local copy of the equivalent list of ownership, using software to maintain and validate the ledger. When a transaction takes place between two parties, that transaction is broadcast to all the nodes. The nodes validate the details of the transaction and eventually combine the transactions into a new block in the chain. Validation requires work, and bitcoin uses a technique called "proof-of work" that requires node operators to solve cryptography problems, for which the successful operator is compensated with one bitcoin—this process is called mining.

Bitcoin is the original and largest cryptocurrency in the world, but today there are many other blockchains, coins, and tokens designed to serve different purposes. The second biggest blockchain is called Ethereum, built specifically as a platform for "smart contracts." With a smart contract, computer code replaces the usual set of paperwork that accompanies a transaction. For example, the terms of a loan can be written into an Ethereum-based smart contract, and then all the cash flows from that loan could flow between lender and borrower without any human intervention.

Coins like bitcoin are native to their own blockchain and function almost like cash in that ecosystem. Readers may also have heard of the term "altcoin," which includes variants on bitcoin that use different techniques with technical improvements like faster transaction times or reduced energy consumption. Another interesting twist is the "stablecoin," which is meant to hold a stable value relative to a fiat currency like the US dollar. Some stablecoins are backed by fiat and pegged to 1 US dollar, a cash-equivalent asset that is not as volatile as other crypto assets.[18] As of November 7, 2022, across all categories there are over 20,000 coins and tokens with an aggregate market capitalization of over $1 trillion. The screenshot in Figure 4.4 shows the 10 largest cryptocurrencies along with their relevant price and volume information:

#	Name	Price	1h %	24h %	7d %	Market Cap	Volume(24h)	Circulating Supply	Last 7 Days
1	Bitcoin BTC	$20,892.64	0.03%	1.34%	1.99%	$400,904,018,420	$40,226,384,716 1,926,569 BTC	19,200,562 BTC	
2	Ethereum ETH	$1,584.84	0.44%	1.97%	0.14%	$193,875,344,652	$12,795,534,800 8,076,625 ETH	122,373,883 ETH	
3	Tether USDT	$1.00	0.00%	0.01%	0.02%	$69,370,287,811	$56,933,913,843 56,926,038,950 USDT	69,360,692,564 USDT	
4	BNB BNB	$337.61	0.50%	3.55%	9.51%	$53,990,259,706	$1,332,559,742 3,948,458 BNB	159,976,513 BNB	
5	USD Coin USDC	$1	0.00%	0.01%	0.01%	$42,712,812,073	$2,742,769,297 2,742,844,387 USDC	42,713,981,439 USDC	
6	XRP XRP	$0.4671	1.40%	4.38%	2.54%	$23,471,890,730	$1,123,361,907 2,403,318,822 XRP	50,215,300,844 XRP	
7	Binance USD BUSD	$1.00	0.01%	0.02%	0.03%	$22,545,535,943	$7,060,027,418 7,059,602,322 BUSD	22,544,178,442 BUSD	
8	Dogecoin DOGE	$0.1174	0.86%	5.15%	0.86%	$15,550,891,120	$1,364,595,630 11,641,901,064 DOGE	132,670,784,300 DOGE	
9	Cardano ADA Buy	$0.4071	0.44%	3.43%	1.66%	$13,964,511,527	$497,146,660 1,222,664,925 ADA	34,343,814,874 ADA	
10	Solana SOL Buy	$32.24	0.71%	9.92%	2.56%	$11,580,519,478	$1,774,448,789 55,120,383 SOL	359,728,679 SOL	

FIGURE 4.4. Top 10 cryptocurrencies by market cap (November 2022). *Source:* www.coinmarketcap.com, retrieved November 7, 2022.

Part of the broader adoption of digital assets involves efforts to replicate the instruments and functionality of traditional financial markets ("TradFi"). Ambitious projects use smart contracts to replicate traditional financial market functionality in the crypto space. Collectively, this is referred to as decentralized finance, or "DeFi." Recent DeFi projects fall into five major categories:

1. lending and borrowing;
2. derivatives;
3. decentralized exchanges or DEXs;
4. synthetic assets;
5. prediction markets.

Lending and borrowing on platforms work like traditional banking where borrowers post coins as collateral and lenders charge an interest rate paid in coins. Derivatives also look a lot like finance in the real world. Many platforms allow traders to buy and sell derivative contracts based on the value of an underlying asset, index, or interest rate. Other DeFi projects are similarly designed to replicate TradFi functionality, but on the blockchain.

4.4.2 Non-Fungible Tokens (NFTs)

With the advent of blockchain technology, the concept of fractional ownership has moved well beyond the older applications of property timeshares and shared jet ownership. Previously, investors would buy the right to use a vacation property for several weeks a year, or a certain number of flight hours in a private jet. There was a limited resale market, at least for vacation properties, but returns were typically weak.

The next level of this is called "tokenization," meaning the process of issuing tokens to represent ownership of real-world assets. Unlike coins which are native to a specific blockchain, tokens are created on top of existing blockchains and fall into two broad subcategories. One kind of token[19] of interest to investors represents an asset like a building. By trading in tokens (or fractions of tokens), investors can own part of the building at a much lower price than buying the building outright. Section 4.5 discusses tokenization of real estate in more detail.

Another type of token is referred to as a "non-fungible token" or NFT. These tokens are digital assets that exist on a blockchain and can be bought and sold just like any other crypto asset. Whereas one bitcoin has the same value as another,[20] just like each $100 bill is worth $100, "non-fungible" means that each NFT is one-of-a-kind. The most common kind of NFT is digital artwork, and for a while in 2020–2021 the market for NFTs was booming. As an example, consider the 2017 project called EtherRocks.[21] Each rock has the same shape and areas available for shading, but the actual color used for each shaded region can be different (Figure 4.5). Only 100 such images exist, and while anyone can copy the image and keep it on a phone or computer, the NFT confers ownership of the original computer image.

Other art projects exist like CryptoPunks (https://www.larvalabs .com/cryptopunks), Bored Ape Yacht Club (https://boredapeyachtclub .com), or CryptoKitties (https://www.cryptokitties.co). These and thousands of other projects are traded on secondary markets like OpenSea

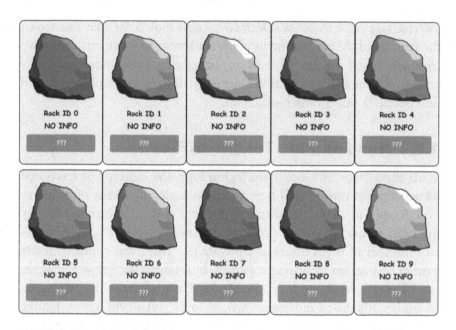

FIGURE 4.5. EtherRocks.
Source: http://www.etherrock.com/.

or one of several competing marketplaces. What all these projects have in common is that the images exist as non-fungible tokens with ownership rights stored on a blockchain. Because the image is available online and can be copied, like an image of the Mona Lisa, skeptics say that NFTs are nothing more than "tokenized bragging rights." If that's the case, it has greater appeal to insiders within the crypto community who know how to tell who[22] paid millions of dollars for a digital image of a rock.[23]

Along with the rest of crypto prices, the market for NFTs also crashed in 2022. Prices for some projects dropped 90% or more, and trading volumes all but dried up. That said, crypto advocates and many venture capital investors believe it has the potential to deliver "Web 3.0" where money and power accrue more directly to content creators rather than platforms like Meta (Facebook) and TikTok. If compelling use cases for blockchain and smart contract technology are found, it is reasonable to assume there will be better times ahead for crypto investors—especially if stronger regulatory oversight is put in place.

4.4.3 Investment Strategies

One of the first things that any investor will notice about cryptocurrencies is that prices are extremely volatile.[24] In the case of bitcoin, from the "genesis block" on January 3, 2009 until December 2017, the price of bitcoin traded from $0.08 to as high as $19,834. In hindsight, this period appears to have been a short-term bubble characterized by a lot of hype, new projects, and coins—many of which turned out to be fraudulent—and many new individual investors who were chasing returns. Between 2018 and 2020, the froth left the market; in December 2018, the price of bitcoin fell all the way to $3,300 before making new all-time highs above $40,000 on January 8, 2021. One reason for the recovery was that progress in more technical areas such as custody and administration allowed institutional investors to participate in the market. In 2021, companies like Microstrategy (NASDAQ:MSTR) and Tesla (NASDAQ:TSLA) added bitcoin to their corporate treasuries, and El Salvador declared bitcoin to be legal tender. To many, these events suggested that digital assets were poised to go mainstream, and on November 10, 2021 it reached its all-time high of $68,742.

From an investment standpoint, trading digital assets is relatively easy and increasingly common, especially among younger investors. Before the big price declines of late 2021 to 2022, on any given day as many as 15–20 assets had a market cap over $10 billion and traded more than $1 billion every 24 hours; the top 100 assets were investable in at least small institutional size. Many coins and tokens are correlated to each other, but there is still plenty of asset-specific price movement, similar to what is observed in equity markets. As a result, most equity strategies have a corresponding strategy in the world of crypto assets—ranging from fundamental analysis to searching for arbitrage opportunities due to price differences across multiple trading venues—just using different data.

Another way in which investing in crypto resembles traditional finance is a popular strategy called "yield farming." As the term "yield" suggests, the strategy involves lending or "staking" (like depositing) tokens for use by a protocol like Aave or Compound. In return for locking up the tokens for a predetermined period of time, investors receive interest payments in the protocol's token. So if someone staked 1,000 of Compound's COMP token, and the yield was 10%, the investor would receive 100 COMP at the end of the period. This seemed like a great idea for much of 2020–2021 as the market went up, but two risks negatively affected investors in 2022. First, because of the extreme volatility in crypto, investors may have been unable to sell their tokens during the market crash because their tokens were locked up. Second, since the yield was paid in tokens like COMP, the value of the tokens staked as well as the tokens earned as yield both dropped significantly, greatly reducing the effective yield of the investment.

For those who prefer to let others make the investment decisions, there are hundreds of digital asset funds pursuing a wide range of strategies. Since digital assets lack traditional financial statements, fundamental crypto investors use a new set of "on-chain" metrics such as "total value locked," user adoption, and transaction rates. For example, using third-party tools investors can track the number of new owners of a token, the size of transactions, and even if the parties to a transaction are making or losing money at the current price.

Investors use other strategies from traditional finance as well. Technical analysis is used widely in commodities markets and is said to work reasonably well in crypto markets. There are index strategies, venture strategies, and with the advent of third-party crypto funds, even fund-of-funds strategies. One digital asset manager website describes a multi-strategy approach with bitcoin acting as market beta, fundamental and quantitative trading strategies, plus more opportunistic and venture strategies. As of 2022, there are even funds specializing in investment opportunities in NFTs.

To justify an allocation to crypto, one popular analysis compares the performance of a traditional 60/40 portfolio[25] to a portfolio that allocates 1% or 2% to bitcoin. In Figure 4.6, from a paper published in October 2020, an allocation of only 2% adds 228bps of annualized performance, improves one common measure of risk-adjusted returns (Sharpe ratio) by 25%, and the maximum drawdown is essentially unchanged. Note, however that the volatility of bitcoin is much, much higher than stocks or bonds: bitcoin was trading around $300 in January 2015, but even after the major price declines of 2018 and 2022 the price is still over 60x higher (roughly $20,000) as of this writing. Naturally a small allocation to bitcoin will look attractive when the price has gone up so much over time.

Summary Portfolio Metrics (January 2015 through September 2020)

Stocks/Bonds/Bitcoin	60%/40%/0%	59.5%/39.5%/1%	59%/39%/2%	58.5%/38.5%/3%
Annualized Returns	6.83%	7.98%	9.11%	10.24%
Change vs. 0% BTC (bps)	N/A	114	228	341
Annualized Volatility	11.67%	12.04%	12.54%	13.16%
Change vs. 0% BTC (bps)	N/A	37	87	149
Sharpe Ratio	0.59	0.66	0.73	0.78
Change vs. 0% BTC	N/A	14%	25%	34%
Max Drawdown	-14.23%	-14.22%	-14.21%	-14.20%
Change vs. 0% BTC (bps)	N/A	-1	-2	-3

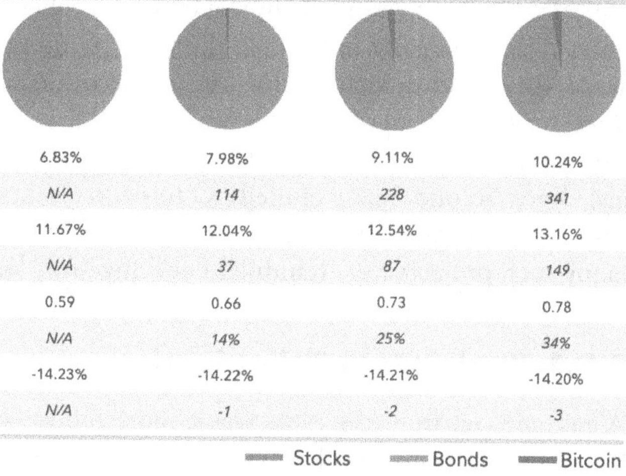

Stocks   Bonds   Bitcoin

FIGURE 4.6. Effect of adding bitcoin to investment portfolios.
Source: FMR LLC 2020, https://www.fidelitydigitalassets.com/sites/default/files/documents/bitcoin-alternative-investment.pdf, last accessed December 15, 2022.

Looking ahead to 2023 and beyond, although crypto enthusiasts may be licking their wounds today, it may be premature to rule out increased adoption and higher asset prices. Investors should be wary of a repeat of the hype cycle that accompanied the frenzied activity during Covid-19 while keeping an eye out for improved regulatory supervision and compelling use cases for blockchain-related investments.

4.5 Real Estate Tokenization and the Metaverse

The story of tokenized real estate has its roots in equity crowdfunding as a number of real estate investment platforms entered the market after the GFC. Subsequently, regulators imposed tighter controls and platforms started to feel the pinch of rising expenses to comply with these regulations. Many of the early crowdfunding platforms went out of business.

In the midst of weakening prospects for the real estate crowdfunding platforms, blockchain technology was being applied to the issuance of digital tokens that represented ownership in real estate investments. Between 2015 and 2018, a wave of initial coin offerings (ICOs) raised billions of dollars to fund new businesses, new business models, and projects—including real estate investments. Those real estate ICOs typically offered investments in real estate via tokens representing contractual rights to gains or losses in the value of the securitized real estate asset. This trend quickly fizzled out as execution of such plans faced three major challenges. First, it was, and still is, difficult to convert large sums of cryptocurrency into fiat money to be paid to the sellers of real estate. Second, many of the ICO initiators lacked sufficient knowledge of structuring real estate investments. Finally, and unfortunately, many such projects were fraudulent and investors lost all their money.

4.5.1 Real Estate Tokenization

What emerged from the ashes was a more robust solution. For example, one of Asia's first blockchain-based real estate investment platforms, FundPlaces, was launched in July 2017. FundPlaces was originally established as a real estate crowdfunding platform in Singapore in 2015, mainly offering Australian real estate debt to its investors. The company then incorporated blockchain technology for the issuance of digital tokens, called Tiles, to represent contractual rights to real estate ownership.[26]

These tokens were created on a private blockchain platform unrelated to the public cryptocurrencies such as bitcoin and Ethereum. Each property asset or debt was represented by a separate series of tokens, non-fungible with tokens associated with other assets. These tokens represented the same rights as traditional shares of the investment would possess. From the financial markets and regulators' points of view, these tokens were considered "securities" and the blockchain platforms that the tokens traded on had to be licensed as "recognized market operators" or "digital asset exchanges."

Investors funded their accounts with fiat money and purchased the tokens on an exchange, and sellers of the tokens received fiat money in return. An advantage of the tokens trading in fiat instead of cryptocurrency was that the value of the tokens followed the value of assets that were securitized. Similarly, the tokens were not subject to the high volatility of cryptocurrency prices and additional transaction fees associated with blockchains like Ethereum.

Hacks at various crypto exchanges led regulators around the world from late 2017 to impose and tighten regulations on platforms like FundPlaces in Singapore or Fundrise and Yieldstreet in the United

States. So, despite the promise of applying blockchain technology to real estate investing, FundPlaces fell victim to declining investor confidence in blockchain platforms and wound down in 2019.

4.5.2 Growth Prospects

The upturn in crypto prices and rising familiarity with DeFi as a venue for investing from mid-2019 led to a revival of interest in tokenization of real estate. At the same time, increasing clarity of regulations around the issuance of asset-backed tokens and the operation of token exchanges helped to reassure investors about the legitimacy and foundations of tokenization. As of 2022, real estate tokenization had become firmly entrenched in the investment world. The Swiss Digital Asset Market Report 2022 revealed that there were 60 security tokens offered in Switzerland in 2021, nearly double the number offered in the previous five years. The security tokens offered included non–real estate token offerings such as tokenized stocks and bonds.

Recent publications contend that the market for tokenized real estate is poised for growth. A 2020 report by OECD[27] stated that asset tokenisation has emerged as one of the most popular use-cases of distributed ledger technology as shown in Figure 4.7. With assets such as real estate being tokenized, there will be potential impacts on financial market participants, practises, market infrastructure and regulators.

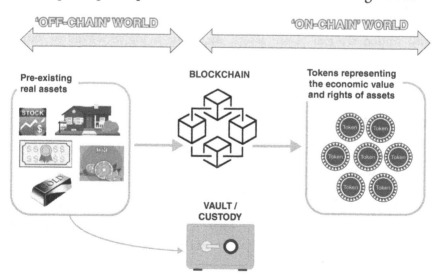

FIGURE 4.7. Tokenisation of real assets that exist off the chain.

Source: "The Tokenisation of Assets and Potential Implications for Financial Markets" by OECD.

In late 2022, the Boston Consulting Group and Singapore-based asset exchange ADDX estimated that the tokenization of illiquid assets could grow to US$16 trillion globally by the year 2030.

Separately, a research article in the *Journal of Property Investment & Finance* concluded that:

> Real estate tokenization is a nascent market but platforms like BrickX, KASA, ADDX, and Minterest have successfully launched real estate tokens in Australia, South Korea, and Singapore respectively. Tokenization may prove to be a viable funding source for the relatively poorly capitalized financial markets in the APAC region.[28]

In Thailand, a well-known developer of real estate (Sansiri, BKK:SIRI) launched the SiriHub Token, the first regulated, real estate–backed, token offering based on the Tezos blockchain. The 2021 offering consisted of one office building, Siri Campus, valued at THB2.4 billion, as the underlying security. In Korea, the Financial Services Commission created a financial regulatory sandbox for Fin-Tech companies and other start-ups to trial their business models. A real estate tokenization platform and exchange called Kasa has been offering asset-backed securities, named DABS, since November 2020. Kasa's real estate tokens are backed by commercial real estate assets in South Korea. Through June 2022, Kasa's platform had tokenized and traded six real estate assets, including a logistics facility worth US$9 million which saw the tokens fully subscribed within 24 hours of offering.

4.5.3 Challenges

The potential for tokenization to disrupt traditional real estate investments is widely acknowledged, but a few key challenges must be overcome in order to achieve more widespread adoption.

From a business operations perspective, improvements in the underlying blockchain technology have reduced implementation costs, but management teams must have the right combination of business and technology know-how to take advantage of these improvements. From a regulatory perspective, most regulators have declared that asset-backed tokens are equivalent to traditional securities. Having clear rules is helpful for platform operators, but the cost of satisfying the same compliance requirements as traditional finance companies is very high. Market participants, policy-makers, and investors benefit from increased trust in market practices, but applying current securities frameworks reduces tokenization to a small improvement in efficiency.

Tokenization platforms might be able to improve efficiency and drive costs down if they could standardize investment documents and investment structures. Standardization will improve familiarity, build trust, and simplify the decision-making process for investors who still have to navigate through hundreds of pages of documents for every investment. Government-led initiatives and private sector innovations may create new paths to improve on the contracting process, registration of property interests, and systems of governance. The Monetary Authority of Singapore's Project Guardian initiative is an example of a Public-Private-Partnership to develop and pilot use cases for asset tokenization in order to improve transaction efficiencies and reduce intermediation costs.

Realizing the advantages of DeFi—allowing investors and businesses to conduct financial transactions on a peer-to-peer basis—may require a more bespoke regulatory solution. Tokenization of real estate assets holds great promise to make real estate transactions faster and lower costs by reducing friction and ensuring that only middlemen who add value to the transaction process are rewarded. Just as real estate transactions may occur directly between buyer and seller or through a broker without direct regulatory oversight, the full potential of the blockchain technology can only be realized by treating real estate tokens as real estate and not as a security.

4.5.4 The Metaverse

Beyond tokenizing the properties in our physical world, blockchain platforms and the movement toward decentralization have expanded into the internet and what is called a "metaverse." The term "metaverse" was coined by science fiction author Neal Stephenson in the 1992 novel *Snow Crash,* describing a world in which humans, through their avatars, interacted with systems-generated characters in a simulated world.

Due to the infancy and complexity of the metaverse there is no single definition that succinctly describes the space that it represents. Dictionary.com provides the following definitions for "metaverse":

1. (in science fiction) a shared, realistic, and immersive computer simulation of the real world or other possible worlds, in which people participate as digital avatars.

2. a theoretical or emergent networked online space with digitally persistent environments that people inhabit, as avatars, for synchronous interactions and experiences, accessing the shared virtual space through virtual reality, augmented reality, game consoles, mobile devices, or conventional computers.[29]

The finance and business world has an alternative definition. From Investopedia:

The metaverse is a digital reality that combines aspects of social media, online gaming, augmented reality (AR), virtual reality (VR), and cryptocurrencies to allow users to interact virtually. Augmented reality overlays visual elements, sound, and other sensory input onto real-world settings to enhance the user experience. In contrast, virtual reality is entirely virtual and enhances fictional realities.[30]

Many large corporations have started to develop their metaverse strategies. Luxury goods brands such as Balenciaga, Gucci, and Louis Vuitton have experimented with marketing physical products as virtual products in the metaverse, together with their exclusive designs sold as non-fungible tokens (NFTs). While these luxury brands led the fashion industry as innovators in the metaverse, a metaverse developer Everyrealm purchased a virtual plot of land in Decentraland to build a shopping mall. A subsidiary of Tokens.com called Metaverse Group has purchased virtual real estate in Decentraland's Fashion

District equivalent to 450,000 square feet in the physical world. There they hosted Decentraland's first virtual fashion week in March 2022. Dubbed the Metaverse Fashion Week 2022, the three-day event saw participation from more than 60 fashion brands.

Virtual real estate has already seen millions of transactions with real buyers and sellers spending fiat money on metaverse properties. Speculative investors are betting that virtual properties will turn out to be highly valuable. Today they can choose from virtual worlds such as Decentraland, The Sandbox, Roblox, Somnium Space, Earth2, and Next Earth. Interestingly, Earth2 and Next Earth are digital twins of the real Earth we occupy and allow users to invest in and develop virtual plots of land that are mapped onto our planet.

To purchase land in the metaverse, investors pay with cryptocurrency for an NFT representing "ownership" of the land. The land may be held, sold to other investors, or investors could choose to develop properties, create games, put up an advertisement signboard, or host events on the land. Selecting land in the metaverse involves some of the same steps as in the real world, including selecting the specific plot of land, considering the plots surrounding it and looking at the transaction records to learn about the price history and the identities of the previous owners. Unlike the real world, where being close to a school or a transport hub may indicate high pedestrian traffic, the metaverse may not operate the same way. Therefore, buying the land plot adjacent to a "tall" virtual building may not offer much in the way of price appreciation.

When considering an investment in metaverse real estate, investors should be cautious and closely monitor how the virtual worlds are evolving. An October 2022 Coindesk report[31] revealed that activity on metaverse platforms is at best lukewarm. While Decentraland reports an average of 8,000 users a day, the number includes everyone hanging out on the platform, not only transacting. An active user is defined as when a user's wallet transacts with the smart contracts in the metaverse. Based on that definition, on the typical day examined in the report, Decentraland had only 38 active users and The Sandbox had 522. It seems that the metaverse platforms are not crowded with users or investors.

As use cases for digital real estate in the metaverse are still evolving, the value of any land plots, buildings, and properties or digital assets is merely speculative at this moment. There are no valuation methods to guide investors on the entry price or to estimate the potential investment returns. Most virtual land, especially those outside of gaming environments, does not pay any recurring income.

To complicate matters further, property developers in the real world have begun selling homes with NFTs included. A brand-new luxurious mansion near London was put up for sale by a developer with a price tag of £29 million. The price includes the land and house, as well as an NFT that contains the copyrighted blueprint and a digital twin of the property. Savvy home buyers should think carefully about this new asset, including:

- What is the value of the land and house in the real world versus the value of the NFT?
- Does having an NFT of the house add to the future resale value of the property?
- What would the value of the digital real estate (NFT) be if I wanted to continue living in the physical real estate (splitting up the physical and virtual assets)?

A few more items investors should include on a due diligence check list:

1. **Counterparty risks, including cyber security risks:** A platform may not fulfill its part of the agreement or default on its obligations. Malicious actors may identify vulnerabilities in the smart contracts and hack into the transactions. Identity theft and financial breaches are frequently reported.

2. **Limitless supply:** Consider that there is no limit on the number of metaverse platforms or the number of land plots for sale. Where supply is abundant and demand is limited, virtual real estate will have little value.

3. **Longevity of counterparties:** As was the case during the Internet Bubble, we do not know which platforms will emerge as Amazon and Google and which platforms will go the way of Buy.com and Netscape.

4. **Withdrawal into fiat money:** A primary concern for investors is how cryptocurrency in the metaverse can be converted to fiat

and withdrawn into a traditional bank account. Converting fiat into crypto is easier than the reverse as most regulators are justifiably concerned about money laundering.

Decentraland only launched in 2020. It has been less than two years since The Sandbox metaverse launched and a year since Facebook changed its name to Meta. Given the nascent stage of development, investors should tread cautiously and go into the metaverse only with money they are willing to lose.

4.6 Collectibles

Items become more collectible when they have artistic, personal, or historical significance. A quick look at the departments in Sotheby's, one of the leading global auction houses, shows the incredible range of very specific interests that collectors may have (Figure 4.8).

Why invest in collectible assets, aside from appreciation for some of the wonderful creations of mankind's imagination and ingenuity? Reasons may include the potential price appreciation, low correlation (maybe) with traditional financial assets, and perhaps appraisal-arbitrage for tax savings. And of course, ego.

4.6.1 Traditional Collectibles: Art, Jewelry, Antiques, Stamps, and Coins

Wealthy individuals and institutions have been collecting fine and rare objects for hundreds of years. Among the oldest collectible items are fine art, jewelry and diamonds, furniture (antiques), and stamps and coins. According to the specialist firm Knight Frank, these are also some of the most relevant collectible assets for high net worth individuals.

The number of billionaires in the world has more than quadrupled since 1995, and the number of millionaires has grown even faster. With so much wealth concentrated in the hands of so few, and a fixed or shrinking number of traditional collectible assets to go around, prices have risen as well. Knight Frank conducts annual surveys of price performance for different collectible assets, ranging from the traditional (fine art, jewelry, antiques, etc.) to "modern" collectibles

FIGURE 4.8. Collectible departments in Sotheby's.

Source: Sotheby's, https://www.sothebys.com/en/about/departments, retrieved February 02, 2023.

0-9
19th Century European Paintings
20th Century Design

A
Aboriginal Art
African & Oceanic Art
African Modern & Contemporary Art
American Art
American Furniture, Decorative Art & Folk Art
Ancient Sculpture and Works of Art
Automobiles | RM Sotheby's

B
Books & Manuscripts
British Paintings 1550-1850
British Watercolours & Drawings 1550-1850

C
Canadian Art
Celebrated Collections
Chinese Paintings – Classical
Chinese Paintings – Modern
Chinese Works of Art
Clocks & Barometers
Coins and Medals
Contemporary Arab, Iranian & Turkish Art
Contemporary Art
Czech Art

D
Diamonds
Dutch & Belgian Paintings

E
English Furniture
European Ceramics & Glass
European Sculpture & Works of Art

F
French & Continental Furniture

G
German, Austrian & Central European Paintings
Greek Art

H
Handbags and Accessories

I
Impressionist & Modern Art
Indian & South Asian Modern & Contemporary Art
Indian, Himalayan & Southeast Asian Art
Irish Art
Islamic Art
Israeli & International Art
Italian Paintings

J
Japanese Art
Jewelry
Judaica

L
Latin American Art

M
Modern Art | Asia
Modern & Contemporary Southeast Asian Art
Modern British & Irish Art
Musical Instruments

N
NFT

O
Objects of Vertu
Old Master Drawings
Old Master Paintings
Orientalist Paintings

P
Photographs
Pre-Columbian Art
Prints

R
Rugs & Carpets
Russian Art

S
Scandinavian Paintings
Scottish Art
Silver
Sneakers, Sports Memorabilia & Modern Collectibles
Sotheby's Concierge Auctions
Space Exploration
Spanish Paintings
Stamps
Swiss Art

T
Toys

U
Unique Collections

V
Victorian, Pre-Raphaelite & British Impressionist Art

W
Watches
Whisky & Spirits
Wine

like whisky and fine wine.[32] Over the 10-year period ending in 2020, the leading performer was rare whisky, with an increase of 478% over the previous decade, and in fact none of the best performers over that period came from the traditional collectible assets. Stamps, for example, which had been included in earlier surveys, were removed from the report altogether in the 2021 edition. Since much has already been written about investing in fine art, jewelry, antiques, and stamps and coins, the remainder of this section will focus instead on the "modern" collectibles that have attracted considerable attention and assets in recent years.

4.6.2 Modern Collectibles: Cars, Wine, Whisky, Watches, Streetwear, and More[33]

The first four assets covered in this section—collectible cars, fine wine, whisky, and watches—all appear in the Knight Frank report. The fifth, streetwear, is a nod to younger readers who may be as interested as many of their peers in sneakers, "BAPE drops," and the like. It is an exciting category with interesting technology businesses supporting the growth.

4.6.2.1 Collectible Cars

There are an estimated 13–14 million collectible cars globally; in 2019, their global market value was estimated to be between US$20–22.5 billion. Annual turnover, predominantly tracked through auction house sales, exceeded US$1 billion in 2018. The market comprises different segments based on the age of the vehicle and manufacturer. Ferrari is the clear market leader, and the record for the most expensive single vehicle ever sold belongs to the Ferrari 250 GTO (US$38.1 million in 2016 for a 1962 version built for racing legend Sir Stirling Moss). A report by the global consultancy Knight Frank suggested that cars had the greatest cumulative price appreciation among collectible asset classes over the trailing 5–10-year periods through 2017.

The direct purchase of collectible cars starts for most investors with one of the many car auctions held around the world. Some auctions, such as the Pebble Beach Concours d'Elegance run by car specialist Gooding & Co., feature the finest examples of cars across major categories, and million-dollar cars are relatively commonplace at these events. Other auctions, such as those run by American specialist Barrett-Jackson, are more focused on sub-categories like American "muscle cars" from the 1950s to the 1970s. Auction houses typically charge 10% commission to the seller (less for more expensive cars) and as much as 11% to the buyer. After the successful purchase of a car, the owner must arrange for its transportation, storage, and maintenance and pay any applicable duties or taxes, which could be very expensive.

According to one expert, pure financial investment only makes economic sense for cars worth over US$300,000. As of this writing, there are only a handful of third-party-managed funds offering investors an opportunity to profit from investments in classic cars.[34]

4.6.2.2 Fine Wine

The global market for wine is large, with roughly 270 million hectoliters of wine produced annually and over US$300 billion in sales. A small fraction of this market, perhaps US$5 billion in annual sales, is considered "fine wine"; the market for collectible wine is smaller still. The main drivers of whether a wine will ultimately be considered of interest for collectors include scarcity (number of bottles/cases produced); age, since wine is a perishable and consumable item; perceived quality (producer, vineyard, vintage, and professional reviews); and provenance (ex-château bottles and professional storage are preferred). In the wine business, the producer and vineyard are the equivalent of make and model for cars, and certain combinations are far more expensive and collectible than others. For example, there are a number of producers of red burgundy (pinot noir) from the famous Grand Cru vineyard "Richebourg," but all else being equal, a bottle from Domaine de la Romanée-Conti (DRC) could cost more than 10 times the price of a bottle from another producer in the same vineyard.

Vintage is also extremely important as growing conditions affect the quality of the wine from year to year. The price of wine from the same producer and vineyard might double in a great vintage. In terms of regional variation, Burgundy, Bordeaux, and Champagne account for well over half of auction proceeds, while collectible wines from other parts of Europe (e.g., Italy, Spain, Germany) and the rest of the world (e.g., the United States, Australia, Chile) have strong followings as well.

London International Vintners Exchange (Liv-ex) has emerged as a reference for fine wine trading, providing real-time and historic data and 35,000 price updates daily based on more than US$35 million worth of bids and offers submitted every day by its more than 400 global members. The Liv-ex index that tracks the most "investable" wines in the market has delivered very strong performance since 1988, rising an average +11.94% on a 10-year CAGR. Over shorter time horizons, meaningful drawdowns resulted in three-year CAGR as low as -11.57%.

The most common means of acquiring wine for investment are direct from the winery, through a retailer, or at auction. Direct sales are especially important for limited-production wineries in the United States, and it is not uncommon to wait several years for a spot to open on the mailing list offering an opportunity to purchase a coveted bottle or two. In contrast, auctions are the most important venue for buying older or rare bottles. Sotheby's and Christie's are the global leaders (Sotheby's 27 auctions in 2019 accounted for nearly US$120 million across over 17,000 lots) but there are smaller, regional auction houses active in the wine market as well. Looking at the industry on a regional basis, Asia (led by Hong Kong, Taiwan, and China) accounts for two-thirds of fine wine auction sales, surpassing the traditional markets of the United States and the UK. The global nature of the wine business means that investors must carefully consider currency, storage, and transportation when making direct investments.

There are a small number of third-party funds dedicated to investing in fine wine. One firm, Cult Wines, manages bespoke portfolios, acting as both broker and storage facility as required. A firm called WSF SICAV manages separate funds for investments in vineyards (Vineyard & Terroir Fund) and bottles (Wine Source Fund). Third-party funds generally have relatively short track records, which make it difficult to assess performance.

4.6.2.3 Whisky

Scotch single-malt whisky, American bourbon, and Japanese whisky make up the lion's share of this collectible market. Investing is similar in nature to the wine market, with ratings providers, multi-level distribution, and an active secondary market through brokers and auctions. Collectible bottlings are typically limited production or older bottlings no longer available in the market. Reports indicated that the UK whisky auction market alone accounted for over US$71 million in turnover in 2019 from the sale of nearly 144,000 bottles at an average selling price of over US$500 per bottle.

According to the 2019 Knight Frank Wealth Report, whisky was the best performing collectible asset in the preceding decade, rising +582%. Individual bottlings, however, could see their prices go up by multiples of that figure. Hanyu Ichiro's Full Card Series is a set of 54 limited-release bottles from a defunct Japanese distillery. An extremely rare complete set of all 54 bottles were recently sold at auction for US$943,000, nearly US$17,500 per bottle. Also, in 2019, a single bottle of 1926 Macallan cask 263 was sold at auction for a staggering US$1,811,000. An example of the importance of scarcity, only 40 bottles have ever been confirmed by the distiller to have come from that historic cask.

Direct purchase of rare and collectible whiskies, like fine wine, is possible through auction markets and specialized brokerage houses. For those wishing to leave investment decisions to a third-party manager, several funds have been launched with different structures, from private investment vehicles to a fund listed on the Nordic Growth Market.

4.6.2.4 Watches

The size of the overall watch market is in excess of US$28 billion per year, of which the top brand watches (Patek Philippe, Breguet, Rolex, Vacheron Constantin, and Audemars Piguet) are estimated to account for more than US$5.5 billion. An "investment grade watch" is often (but not always) a high value, limited supply timepiece. Key variables affecting the valuation are age (vintage vs. contemporary), type (with or without complications,[35] type of movement[36]), metal (gold, platinum, stainless steel, diamonds), brand, and production quantity. The last does not necessarily mean that only limited edition models are valuable, but simply that values are higher when there is limited supply of (or at least an indefinite waiting list for) a particular model.

Retail prices for most investment grade watches start at around US$10,000, similar to the range of price points available in wine and whisky. However, entry-level but still collectible watches can be purchased for a tenth of that price. Watch magazines and blogs (e.g., aBlogtoWatch) review and give exposure to both iconic and lesser-known watch brands.

According to Knight Frank, watches returned +73% over 10 years through 2017. While this performance trailed many other luxury assets, the consistently positive returns on a 12-month basis indicates that watches have delivered more stable returns relative to other collectibles.

The market for collectible watches is heavily concentrated among specialized dealers, auction houses, and brokers. At the very high end of the market (unique pieces that might cost upwards of US$1 million), liquidity could be a concern since the number of potential buyers was relatively limited. To address this concern, some firms offer loans using luxury watches as collateral.

Collectible watches can be purchased direct from the manufacturer or specialized retailer, but truly rare pieces are very difficult to buy without connections. Expertise is required, especially since most transactions are completed without opening the caseback (thereby avoiding the risk of environmental contaminants entering the watch)[37] to verify the condition and contents of the timepiece. Most readers will relate to the idea of buying a car without being able to inspect the engine and understand the degree of trust involved with an expensive watch purchase. As a result of a thriving market for investment grade vintage watches, authentic models often pass through unauthorized or "unskilled" sources; in the process, some of the authentic or original components might have been removed or replaced with generic parts. It could also happen that brand authentic parts, though not original to the piece or the time period, will have been used to put a watch back together, considerably reducing the value of the piece. Changes to the watch movement are impossible for anyone less than an expert to spot.

Several private third-party watch funds[38] are available for those investors who would rather leave the investment decisions up to a professional.

4.6.2.5 Streetwear and Sneakers

Streetwear refers to "a style of casual clothing which became global in the 1990s. It grew from California surfskate culture, and eventually New York hip hop fashion, to encompass elements of sportswear, punk and Japanese street fashion."[39] This relatively new category within the fashion world includes products from clothing-oriented brands such as Supreme and Off-White™ as well as major footwear companies such as Nike and Adidas. The segment's early products were predominantly T-shirts and other lower-cost apparel, but it has since expanded to encompass a wide range of clothing, lifestyle products, home furnishings, and other items. Reflecting the diverse origins of the streetwear segment, brands such as Supreme periodically release co-branded items developed in collaboration with other, often luxury brands, such as Louis Vuitton. The limited-edition merchandise developed through these "collabs," as they are called, often resells at a significant premium to the original purchase price. Many brands release limited quantities of product (referred to as "drops"), and due to the scarcity of the items, the only opportunity for most consumers to buy them is through specialized resale marketplaces such as StockX and Goat. According to the market-leading reseller StockX, the global secondary sneaker market is worth US$6 billion per year.

Due to the relative newness of this category, an index that accurately reflects the performance of sneakers or streetwear overall has yet to be developed. The value of individual items can rise dramatically depending on the firm and the product. Most streetwear and sneakers are valued at under US$500, but certain very rare items can cost much more. As an example, in 2016, Nike released 89 pairs of sneakers based on the self-lacing model featured in the *Back to the Future* movies and raised US$6.9M for charity; these shoes seldom appear in the resale market and can cost up to US$50,000 a pair.

Buying direct from the manufacturer is very challenging due to the "drop" model introduced by Supreme in the mid-1990s. By aggressively constraining supply for these limited collections or lines, firms such as Supreme, Off-White™, and others created such outsized demand that it has spawned a new industry of "bots"[40] that are designed to improve the chances of a successful online purchase during a drop. Given the difficulty of purchasing items from the retailer, reselling has emerged as the most important channel, dominated by a limited number of global platforms, regional players (e.g., Novelship in Asia), and local resellers (e.g., Poizon in China). Given the global issues surrounding counterfeit apparel, establishing the authenticity and condition of the item is critically important. Resellers provide authentication services to ensure that items were "dead stock" (authentic, new, unused) or used and have had their condition graded. Sneakers, in particular, are subject to physical degradation over time due to the degeneration of glue or the discoloration of certain materials.

As of mid-2020, the first investment funds dedicated to streetwear were entering the market. Until these funds reach scale and develop a track record, investors are more likely to gain exposure to this market through private equity investments in leading streetwear producers, marketplaces, or other members of the ecosystem.

4.6.2.6 Other Collectibles

Sports memorabilia is especially important in the US market. More valuable items are often signed by the player or have a documented connection to an important event, such as a jersey worn during a championship match. Also associated with sports are trading cards featuring the image of sports players; these have been printed by tobacco and bubble gum companies for over a century. Over time and depending on the success of the player, cards can be quite valuable as demonstrated by a recent auction sale of a single, 110-year-old baseball card for over $6 million.

More recently collectors have begun investing in the things they collected as kids. Comic books date back to the 1930s, video games to the 1980s, and Pokémon cards were introduced in 1996. Examples of rare items in top condition across these and other categories are fetching higher and higher prices at auction.

In the United States, specialized platforms like Rally (www.rallyrd.com), Collectable (www.collectable.com), and others enable peer-to-peer sales and even fractional ownership across many categories of collectible items. Aside from the rarest, highest value items, however, individual asset prices are relatively low; the relative lack of experienced third-party managers means institutional investors may find it difficult to allocate sufficient capital to these newer collectibles.

4.7 Other Opportunities

Any book on alternative investments will struggle to build an exhaustive list of all the assets that can fit into this category. This final section on modern alternatives covers two with potentially attractive characteristics for very different reasons, and then provides a list of other alternative investments that may be of interest to the reader.

4.7.1 Patents, Royalties, and IP

Intellectual property (IP) is an intangible asset that can be owned and recorded as an asset on balance sheets, hinting at the different investment opportunities in this asset class. Included in this category are patents, copyrights, and trademarks. For example, patents represent the exclusive right to an invention and are typically held by companies, individuals, or universities where the invention was made. These may be worthless or extremely valuable depending on the nature of the invention. Owners of intellectual property may license or otherwise permit the use of the IP by a third party, for which the third party pays a fee called a "royalty." In the past, investors gained exposure to IP by purchasing shares in the business that owned and monetized the IP; pharmaceutical companies are an example of this type of investment. Recently, however, it has become possible to unbundle the IP from the firm or creator, allowing investors the opportunity to directly invest in this economically meaningful revenue stream. Examples include patents, brands, and media ranging from art, music, and film.

In the corporate world, patents often involve technologies developed through research and development (R&D) that are subsequently used to design and manufacture goods or to provide services. In the pharmaceutical industry, prescriptions for drugs protected by patents generate billions of dollars of revenue every year. Drugs that have been widely adopted by the medical community deliver a consistent revenue stream that can be monetized like an annuity, allowing the IP owner to recycle capital into new R&D or other projects. Note that newer drugs or those for less prevalent medical conditions may be more difficult to value. The age of the patent is also important since patent protection is a finite, wasting asset—up to 20 years in the United States. When drugs go "off-patent," the competition from generic versions inevitably cannibalizes some of the value that previously had accrued exclusively to the patent holder.

Companies often buy and sell patents between themselves, but most patent-related transactions involve licensing, where one company pays the patent holder for the right to use the patent. These types of patents are less likely to be available for purchase by financial investors, but marketplaces like Techquity (www.techquity.com) do offer some patents for purchase by investors. If an investor would prefer to use a third-party manager instead, private investment funds are a common structure for institutional investors, and publicly traded Royalty Pharma (NASDAQ: RPRX) offers exposure to royalties from patented drugs in a listed equity format.

In part because of the public nature and star power of the music industry, readers may be familiar with the concept of music royalties. There are two broad categories of copyrights associated with a song, one for the composition (the publishing side) and another called the master for the recording itself. Royalties may be owed to the songwriter, the recording artist, the publisher, or the record label, depending on how and where the music is being used.[41] For example, different royalties are paid if the original song is played on the radio vs. over a streaming service, or if another artist covers the song, or if the song is used in a commercial or movie. Investors, therefore, may choose to invest in one or more of these royalty streams using different techniques. One of the early artists to monetize his music catalogue was the British rock musician David Bowie, who securitized his royalty income through a bond offering in 1997. When recording artists were unable to go on tour in 2020–2021 due to the Covid-19 pandemic, some very popular artists chose to sell some portion of their copyrights and royalties to investors in deals that in some cases reached over $100 million.

Similar to pharmaceutical royalties, private funds are popular investment vehicles for institutional investors seeking exposure to music royalties. Individuals wanting to directly invest in royalties from music, movies, or trademarks might use a platform like Royalty Exchange (www.royaltyexchange.com), which operates a marketplace similar to Techquity described above. Alternatively, one of the most active investors in music royalties is Hipgnosis Song Fund; its stock is publicly listed in the UK (LSE: SONG).

4.7.2 Income-Sharing Agreements

Income-sharing agreements or ISAs are a relatively new form of student loan gaining traction in the United States, where the cost of university education is extremely high. Instead of traditional federal student loans which apply the same fixed rates to all borrowers regardless of field of study or institution, with an ISA the student commits to paying a defined percentage of future income instead. Students are obligated to make payments for a fixed period of time, only if the salary exceeds a certain threshold, and only up to a maximum amount.

This arrangement addresses issues facing students from lower-income families and those who choose to pursue lower-paying jobs after graduation. For example, two students borrowing the same amount in federal student loans at the same time will have the same payment schedule—even if they are an economics major from an Ivy League school going to Wall Street after graduation and an English major from a small, local college choosing to become an elementary school teacher. The ISA structure acknowledges and adapts to the different earning potential of the two students. Furthermore, if the borrower is out of work, not only does she not have to make payments while she is unemployed, but the lender helps the graduate find a new job because the lender's incentives are aligned with the borrower. Under the federal student loan system, borrowers are obligated to make payments irrespective of employment status or financial condition.

While the ISA market is still in its early stages of development, the potential is extremely large—the market for federal student loans is over $1.5 trillion. As of this writing, there appear to be a few third-party funds acting as ISA lenders which accept private investments from accredited individuals and institutions.

4.7.3 The Rest

Any attempt to build an exhaustive list of alternative investments is bound to be incomplete, as investors around the world exhibit relentless creativity in their search for financial returns. This chapter has focused on a combination of traditional alternatives as well as those with greater adoption or potential. Left off this list are many investment opportunities that may be of interest to the reader, including the following:

- Billboards
- Domain names (ODYS, dan.com, sedo, afternic)
- Newsletters
- Racehorses
- Social media accounts (see Fameswap and Trustiu)

- Specialized real estate: islands, tax liens
- Websites (Flippa, Empireflippers)

The authors encourage readers to read a lot and keep an open mind to identify the emerging alternative investments of the future.

Notes

1. Private credit is the broader term used to describe nonbank lending and includes various forms of private debt as well as structured products like asset-backed securities (ABS), collateralized loan obligations (CLOs), and mortgage-backed securities (MBS). Structured products are described in the Appendix, Section A.6.6.1 on securitization. See https://www .cambridgeassociates.com/insight/private-credit-strategies-introduction/ for an introduction to the private credit market.
2. A helpful history of crowdfunding is available at https://smallbrooks .com/history-of-crowdfunding/.
3. This business model was originally called "peer-to-peer lending" (or P2P), assuming that individual lenders would provide financing to individual SMEs. While that still happens, today much of the capital invested through marketplace lending platforms is from institutional investors. As a result, the industry has moved away from "peer-to-peer lending," preferring terms like "marketplace lending" and "alternative finance."
4. *An Introduction to Alternative Lending* (Morgan Stanley, July 2018).
5. Impediments to institutional investment include high transaction cost relative to expected returns due to a lack of standardized forms and processing. See https://alpha-week.com/trade-finance-comes-age-asset-class for more information.
6. https://www.whitecase.com/publications/insight/facing-headwinds/ overall-investment-outlook-global-aviation-finance.
7. https://www.gjel.com/blog/largest-class-action-settlements.html for a representative list of large settlements.
8. See https://corporatefinanceinstitute.com/resources/wealth-management/ property-and-casualty-insurers/ for an introduction to property/casualty insurance.
9. Or at least have some relatively predictable probability.
10. See https://content.naic.org/cipr-topics/insurance-linked-securities for more information.

11. SPVs are further explained at https://corporatefinanceinstitute.com/resources/management/special-purpose-vehicle-spv/.
12. For example, https://www.artemis.bm/news/city-of-zurich-pension-to-double-insurance-linked-securities-allocation/.
13. http://www.gsi-alliance.org/wp-content/uploads/2021/08/GSIR-20201.pdf.
14. Ibid.
15. https://thegiin.org/impact-investing/need-to-know/#what-is-impact-investing.
16. One type of bond known as a Social Impact Bond often represents an outcomes-based contract between investors and funders, and rather than a fixed return, the payments are linked to successful achievement of the desired outcomes. The first such bond was issued in the UK in 2010 to fund a prison rehabilitation program. Investors committed capital to fund a rehabilitation program run by a third-party organization whose results were verified by an independent third party. When the program met its outcome goals, the government repaid the investors, in essence only paying for successful outcomes. These bonds are typically considered part of the impact investing toolkit, though these structures have the potential to be adopted more broadly to address a wide range of issues.
17. B.M. Barber, A. Morse, and A. Yasuda, "Impact Investing," *Journal of Financial Economics*, 139(1) (2021): 162–185.
18. "Algorithmic stablecoins" are not backed by fiat assets, and in the "crypto winter" of 2022 TerraUSD and its sister coin Luna crashed. https://www.weforum.org/agenda/2022/05/crypto-crash-ust-luna/.
19. The other kind of token is meant to be used in an application ("dApp") built on top of an existing blockchain. For more information on the different types of coins and tokens, see https://www.sofi.com/learn/content/understanding-the-different-types-of-cryptocurrency/.
20. Strictly speaking, this may no longer be the case: https://medium.com/geekculture/are-all-bitcoins-really-the-same-e7ac0f044251.
21. The labels "NO INFO" and "???" are there because the authors did not install the plug-in required to see current prices and trade EtherRocks at www.etherrock.com.
22. Transactions are made using a digital wallet with an ID, rather than using people's names, so ownership is based on the wallet information.
23. https://www.cnbc.com/2021/08/23/people-are-paying-millions-of-dollars-for-digital-pictures-of-rocks.html. Readers may be interested to find current prices (still over $250,000) at https://twitter.com/etherrockprice.

24. See https://coinmarketcap.com/alexandria/article/bitcoin-price-history-and-events-timeline for a useful summary of historical events and prices for bitcoin.
25. 60% stocks and 40% bonds—the original "diversified" portfolio.
26. In another real estate blockchain use case, FundPlaces also created a utility token platform for a Malaysia-based hotel owner. Each utility token represented the rights to one room night of hotel stay. This enabled the hotel to pre-sell room nights to investors who could use the hotel rooms for their own stay or trade the tokens for higher prices when the tourism market was hot.
27. https://www.oecd.org/finance/The-Tokenisation-of-Assets-and-Potential-Implications-for-Financial-Markets.pdf.
28. Chow, Y.L. and Tan, K.K. (2022), "Real Estate Insights Is tokenization of real estate ready for lift off in APAC?", Journal of Property Investment & Finance, Vol. 40 No. 3, pp. 284–290. https://doi.org/10.1108/JPIF-10-2021-0087.
29. www.dictionary.com/browse/metaverse.
30. www.investopedia.com/metaverse-definition-5206578.
31. https://www.coindesk.com/web3/2022/10/07/its-lonely-in-the-metaverse-decentralands-38-daily-active-users-in-a-13b-ecosystem/.
32. https://content.knightfrank.com/research/83/documents/en/the-wealth-report-2021-7865.pdf.
33. Much of this section is taken from the management case "Merlion Investments: Investing in Collectible Assets," co-written by one of the authors in 2020 (https://hbsp.harvard.edu/product/ISB220-PDF-ENG).
34. For example, https://www.hetica.capital/en/klassik-fund.
35. Complications refer to features that go beyond just telling the time, e.g., date display, power reserve indicator, moon phase indicator, etc.
36. There are three types of watch movements, also referred to as "caliber": (1) quartz movements are powered by a battery, and the second hand moves in individual ticks; (2) mechanical movements require manual winding, and the second hand moves smoothly without ticks; and (3) automatic movements are powered by kinetic energy from the wearer's wrist.
37. The caseback is the back of the watch, which covers and protects the movement or battery compartment and the rest of the interior of the watch. If the caseback is removed and contaminants are permitted to enter the watch, this could compromise the accuracy of the movement, for example.

38. See https://luxurybazaar.com/wp/precious-time-luxury-watch-hedge-fund for more information on one such fund.

39. Wikipedia, "Streetwear." Retrieved from https://en.wikipedia.org/wiki/Streetwear.

40. "Bots" are automated scripts that speed up the checkout process on a website. By entering purchase information in advance, bots are able to complete a transaction in a fraction of a second. The most popular items on websites may be nearly impossible to purchase without a bot.

41. See https://blog.groover.co/en/tips/all-you-need-to-know-about-royalties/ for a more detailed discussion of this topic.

Chapter 5

Building Portfolios

After considering the wide range of traditional and modern alternatives, investors with a long-term orientation may be better prepared to create portfolios that benefit from the diversification offered by these asset classes (see Chapter 1, Section 1.3). This chapter describes several approaches to portfolio construction, starting with the easiest and most common options before moving to more sophisticated techniques favored by institutional investors.

5.1 The Portfolio Management Process

Especially for institutional investors, portfolio management is a deliberate process that leads to an appropriate combination of assets and weights: a portfolio. The starting point is baseline information about the investor in the form of objectives and constraints, from which an investment strategy may be derived. With the addition of market data such as returns and volatility by asset class and asset, this information is used to generate an asset allocation plan that can be translated into a portfolio of assets and weights. These steps are described below; noteworthy by omission are important process elements that take place after the portfolio has been decided, including trading and implementation, performance measurement and monitoring, and rebalancing as required. Since asset prices change over time, the important point for individuals is to remember the process part of "portfolio management process." By monitoring performance on a regular basis, investors improve their ability to keep their portfolio fresh and ready to deliver the best possible results.

5.1.1 Objectives and Constraints

The portfolio management process starts by understanding the objectives and constraints specific to the investor. Objectives often refer to a level of investment performance (e.g., 8% return), the amount of assets available for distribution to fund spending (e.g., contributions from an endowment to the operating budget of a university or saving enough money to pay for a child's college education), or any other combination of investment outcomes typically denoted in terms of return or risk. Constraints represent the boundaries which define what the investor is able or permitted to do and may be internally created or imposed externally. Table 5.1 shows some important issues to consider.

TABLE 5.1. Issues to be considered when setting portfolio constraints

Issues	Consideration	Comments
Risk	How will risk be defined and measured? What is the investor's attitude toward risk? What limitations on risk taking must be accounted for? What is the specific risk objective?	Differences in how investors approach risk have profound impact on portfolio construction. While usually a quantitative measure such as volatility (variance), individual investors may be more comfortable with a qualitative risk measure.
Return	How will return be defined and measured? What is the specific return requirement to satisfy future obligations, e.g., funding for pension payments or retirement savings? Absolute vs. relative returns?	The most common measure used is total return including price appreciation and other investment income such as dividends. Investors must decide whether to adjust returns to account for inflation and/or taxes. Often there is tension between return objectives and risk, hence the common optimization approach described in Section 5.3
Constraints	Time horizon for investments? What are the known liquidity requirements? Are there significant regulatory, legal, or tax concerns?	Different types of investors may face vastly different constraints due to preference, financial obligations, or regulation.

5.1.2 Investment Policy Statement

Once the objectives and constraints are known, the investor is prepared to write its investment policy statement (IPS), a policy document for all investment decisions consistent with its guiding principles. Beginning with a statement about the identity of the investor and any advisors, their roles and responsibilities, the IPS includes important information about the overall investment objective, return and risk constraints, and anticipated liquidity needs. For example, family trusts may specify in advance any assumptions about annual distributions to family members to support their spending needs. Additional sections may address issues such as reporting requirements (e.g., annual reports to stakeholders), risk management processes, the impact of tax considerations, and permitted/restricted investments.

5.1.3 Investment Strategy

At a more detailed level than contained in the investment policy statement, the statement of investment strategy explains succinctly how the manager will approach the analysis and selection of investments. An important element to address is the degree to which the investor believes in active management, a passive index-based approach, or some combination of the two. To the extent possible investors should state the criteria (e.g., minimum fund ratings by a third-party provider) they will use to select investments to add to the portfolio as well as how they will decide when to exit an investment. The process by which target allocations are to be developed should be described here, as should the process for portfolio rebalancing.

5.1.4 Strategic Asset Allocation

The final stage of the portfolio planning process is termed strategic asset allocation. In this step the investor prepares its target portfolio, taking into account the objectives and constraints described earlier. A critical input is a comprehensive inventory of existing investments; preparing this inventory may be challenging for institutions and wealthy individuals. Armed with historical return and risk data by asset class (and potentially at the individual security level), as well as relevant assumptions about future market conditions or returns, the investor will be able to construct a portfolio of assets and weights that best satisfy its needs and preferences. Implementing the target portfolio may require time to close any gaps between its existing investments and the target allocations. Once completed, ongoing monitoring and subsequent rebalancing ensure the investor remains compliant with its investment policy statement.

5.2 Traditional Portfolios

Strategic asset allocation encompasses both the current and target portfolios for the investor, both of which are a list of assets and the amount of money (currently or to be) invested in each asset. To build portfolios for different objectives, investors vary the set of assets in the portfolio and the portfolio weights (i.e., the percentage of the portfolio allocated to the asset in question). Described below, the simplest and most common approaches to portfolio construction—equal weighting and "60/40"—can be followed with the help of a spreadsheet or a calculator.

5.2.1 Equal Weighting

In an equal weighted portfolio, each asset receives the same amount of capital. Over time the portfolio will drift away from the equal weighting. To compensate for this drift, investors periodically adjust the portfolio weights back to equal weight in a process called "rebalancing." Sometimes an investor may believe it has reason to place different amounts of capital in different assets. When an investor is consistently able to improve upon the performance of an equal weighted portfolio by adjusting the weights, professional investors refer to this as "position sizing skill." It is challenging to consistently add value through position sizing decisions, even for professionals, hence the popularity of equal weighting and rebalancing.

5.2.2 "60/40" Portfolio

By focusing exclusively on the portfolio weights, the equal weighted approach fails to account for one of the important ways in which assets differ from each other: risk. A high-flying social media stock is likely to be more volatile, or risky, than a supermarket stock, so why should an investor equal weight positions in those two stocks? One simple way to reduce the risk of a portfolio is to include a mix of stocks and bonds; the riskier stocks are somewhat counterbalanced by the less risky allocation to bonds.[1] Over time, conventional wisdom has gravitated toward a mix of 60% stocks and 40% bonds, hence the "60/40 portfolio." Most of the risk of the portfolio is attributable to the allocation to stocks, and the allocation to bonds typically reduces risk during market downturns—2022 was a notable exception, as bonds had their worst performance since the 1970s at the same time as stocks struggled.

Investors often use the 60/40 allocation as a starting point and then adjust the percentage of riskier equity assets based on the investor's objectives and risk tolerance. Institutional investors such as pension funds have fixed liabilities and tend to follow a more conservative allocation than university endowments; pension funds accordingly may follow the 40% weight to bonds more closely than other investors. Individual investors can also use the 60/40 portfolio as a starting point, with deviations based on age—lower allocations to bonds early in life, increasing through retirement—and personal preference.

5.3 Mean-Variance Optimization

The foundational approach to building portfolios to satisfy investor goals was developed in the 1950s by economist Harry Markowitz. The intuition behind what is referred to as mean-variance optimization is the concept of an "efficient" portfolio: for a given set of potential assets and a desired level of return, an efficient portfolio meets the return objective with the least amount of risk. That is, for an efficient portfolio it is impossible to re-weight the assets to achieve the same return with lower risk. On the other hand, efficient portfolios can also represent the best possible return for a desired level of risk. The set of all possible efficient portfolios that can be built from a given sample of assets is referred to as the "efficient frontier." According to Markowitz, therefore, investors should always select a portfolio on the efficient frontier.

Markowitz saw that the two potential formulations of investor goals—either maximize return subject to a given level of risk or minimize risk subject to a given level of return—could be expressed as a mathematical optimization problem. He called this "mean-variance optimization" because the core elements are return and risk. In non-mathematical terms this might be described as follows:

Applicable conditions Action

(1) Objective function Maximize the expected return of the portfolio

(2) Subject to Set portfolio variance (risk) equal to the investor's target l level

(3) With constraints a) The sum of the weights for all assets must equal 1

b) Weights must be greater than or equal to zero

Statement (1) is what the investor is trying to maximize, namely returns. However, the investor has a level of risk tolerance captured in (2), so optimal portfolios represent the highest return given the investor's risk tolerance. The constraint in (3a) means that the investor can invest up to 100% of its assets, but no more than that (i.e., no leverage). Assuming the investor is unable to short, (3b) specifies that the weights must be non-negative. While these are the primary components of mean-variance optimization, investors are free to add additional constraints, for example, a maximum allocation to any individual asset of 5% to avoid unwanted concentration risk. Furthermore, while the classic formulation is to maximize return subject to a level of risk, investors may prefer to solve for a portfolio that minimizes risk subject to a desired return.

In order to perform mean-variance optimization, investors require certain data for (1) and (2): historical return data[2] for each of the assets, and the covariance[3] between each of the assets. With the data in place, investors may solve this set of equations using a spreadsheet[4] for smaller datasets, or specialized portfolio optimization software for institutional applications. Notwithstanding the theoretical and practical importance of this technique—for which Markowitz won a Nobel Prize in Economics in 1990—investors must respect important limitations to mean-variance optimization. Fundamentally the output is only as good as the inputs, and this technique is less accurate when the underlying returns are non-normally distributed, especially with negative tail events.

Investors may be able to address this problem by adding further constraints to the optimization, for example, a maximum level of skew[5] for the portfolio. The technique is also susceptible to creating portfolios with weights skewed toward the assets with the most extreme return or risk data, and investors should exercise caution when assuming that past performance will be a good predictor of future results. Similar caveats apply to estimates for the covariance matrix since it assumes that covariance is stable over time.

5.4 Adding Alternative Investments

Relative to the stocks and bonds typically included in equal weighted or 60/40 portfolios, alternative assets offer the potential to contribute improved returns, reduced risk, or both. With respect to returns, some alternative investments are set up to deliver strong absolute returns through use of leverage and other techniques, while other alternative investments are designed to deliver bond-like returns with minimal correlation to traditional assets. As described in Chapter 1, Section 1.3, these characteristics of alternative investments can provide valuable diversification benefits when included in portfolios. Compared with traditional investments, the lack of daily, transparent returns for most alternative assets makes it difficult to apply portfolio optimization techniques to a portfolio with large allocations to alternatives.

Investors should take care as well to ensure that potential allocations to alternatives do not cause unintended concentration in sources of risk or return. For example, strategies such as merger arbitrage are prone to event risk; as described in Chapter 2, Section 2.3, diversifying across multiple funds can be an effective way to reduce this risk. In the same way, investments in multiple long/short hedge funds could hedge away otherwise desirable sources of return if one manager is long a sector while another is short the same sector. If multiple managers are overweight cash at the same time, the investor's performance may suffer from the drag of unproductive cash holdings. These issues may be more common to hedge fund portfolios, but overconcentration in exposures to regions, sectors, or market cap bands is possible in portfolios of private equity funds, for example. Balancing risk as well as potential hedging and overconcentration is an important part of any alternative investment portfolio.

5.5 The Endowment Model

Endowments are investment funds associated with colleges and universities. In line with the long-term mission of a university and the role that endowment income plays in funding the annual operating budget, endowments are generally long-term-oriented in their investments. The "endowment model" of investing is most closely associated with the late David Swensen, former Chief Investment Officer of Yale University, as described in the 2000 book *Pioneering Portfolio Management*.[6] Coming from the perspective of a large, long-term investor, the principles of the endowment model are: (1) to underweight liquid bonds; (2) to favor illiquid investments such as private equity over liquid investments like public equities; (3) to favor alternative investments such as hedge funds and natural resources; and (4) to protect against inflation through investments in real assets.

Compared to a 60/40 portfolio or even one including alternative investments and derived from a mean-variance optimization, the endowment model is noticeably skewed toward higher-risk, illiquid investments. The success that endowments like Yale have had investing in alternatives over longer periods of time supports this point, but only because endowments are able to look past the liquidity risk in order to realize the stronger long-term performance. Accordingly, this approach may be less appropriate for smaller investors or those with more immediate liquidity needs.

5.6 Risk Budgets, Risk Parity

Rather than optimizing for returns, some institutional investors use risk to determine allocations in the portfolio by imposing risk constraints on the aggregate portfolio and/or at the asset-class level. For example, an investor may wish to have no more than 10% aggregate risk in the portfolio based on the standard deviation of historical returns. Risk may be defined as value-at-risk (VaR), systematic (market beta) risk, or other measures that most closely align with an investor's specific risk tolerance. An investor also may set the maximum amount of expected risk that can come from each asset class or subclass in a process called "risk budgeting"—like a household setting a budget between housing, transportation, food, and other expenses. The allocator "spends" the risk budget by choosing which assets to invest in and with what quantity, often through a process similar to mean-variance optimization outlined above. Some risk budgeting applications may apply one level of optimization to the risk categories and overall portfolio and then another level of optimization to determine the best allocation within each risk category. Risk parity is a special case of risk budgeting where investors seek to balance the contribution of assets to the overall risk of the portfolio. Through this process each asset class contributes the same amount of risk to the portfolio; this equal weighting leads to the use of the term risk parity.

One of the pioneers of the risk parity approach is Bridgewater, the investment management firm founded by Ray Dalio and currently one of the largest alternative investment managers in the world. Its "All Weather Strategy"[7] is an attempt to create a portfolio that would perform well across all different types of market environments. The process starts by recognizing that assets can be separated into different components and then re-aggregated in different ways to build portfolios. In a risk parity framework, assets (cash, stocks, and bonds and strategies investing in those assets) and their component parts are viewed through the lens of "return per unit of risk." The insight Bridgewater had was to assess the risk of assets according to four environmental factors: growth, inflation, and either rising or falling market expectations. Mapping assets to these environmental factors using a four-box framework allowed the firm to identify the best combination of assets for each (Figure 5.1). The All Weather portfolio applies leverage to adjust the weights of each asset so the amount of risk in each quadrant is the same. For example, since equities and nominal bonds appear together in the "Inflation/Falling" (bottom-right) quadrant in Figure 5.1, the weights will be set so that their combined risk will equal the risk from the combination of nominal bonds and inflation-linked bonds in the "Growth/Falling" (bottom-left) quadrant.

As a general rule, risk budgeting applications tend to avoid large allocations to risky assets like equities and alternatives, and overweight

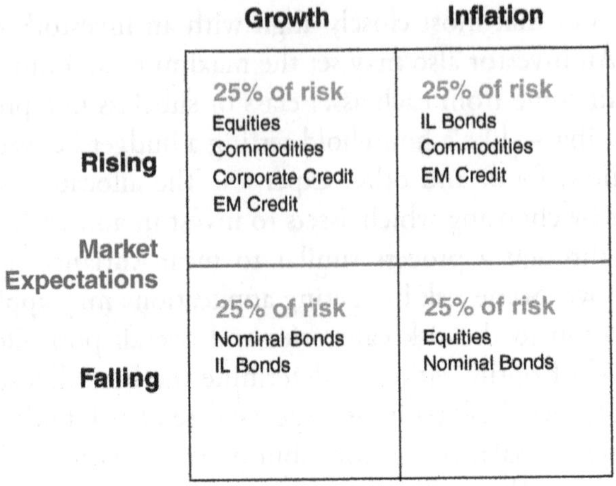

	Growth	**Inflation**
Rising	**25% of risk** Equities Commodities Corporate Credit EM Credit	**25% of risk** IL Bonds Commodities EM Credit
Falling	**25% of risk** Nominal Bonds IL Bonds	**25% of risk** Equities Nominal Bonds

Market Expectations (row axis label, between Rising and Falling)

FIGURE 5.1. Bridgewater's All Weather portfolio strategy.
Source: https://www.bridgewater.com/research-and-insights/the-all-weather-story.

less volatile assets like bonds in order to achieve the same aggregate risk as allocations to riskier assets. Especially for risk parity strategies, leverage can be applied to the resulting low-risk portfolio in order to achieve a higher overall risk level if needed to satisfy an investor's specific objectives.

5.7 Summary

Even the most sophisticated portfolios start with a deep understanding of an investor's objectives and constraints. Many institutional investors will be familiar with an investment policy statement and strategic asset allocation, but these concepts may be new for retail investors that have not had the opportunity to work with a financial advisor. When return and risk are well specified, investors are prepared to build a portfolio of assets to meet their needs. To appeal to readers of different backgrounds, this chapter takes what is inherently a deeply quantitative topic—portfolio construction—and presents it in a conceptual way to illustrate the role of return and risk, asset selection, and diversification. These are some of the critical characteristics of alternative investments, and indeed alternatives can play an important role in many investment portfolios. Viewed in the context of changing interest rates, inflation, regulation, taxes, and the performance of traditional assets, it is not hard to see why institutional investors are increasing portfolio allocations to alternative investments.

Notes

1. In the 60/40 portfolio, the 40% weight to bonds usually includes any allocation to cash as well.
2. Returns may be expressed as average (expected) returns or as returns in excess of a benchmark (excess returns).
3. Variance and covariance are mathematical terms frequently used in statistics and probability theory. Variance refers to the spread of a data set around its mean value, while a covariance refers to the measure of the directional relationship between two random variables.
4. For example, the Solver add-in for Microsoft Excel.
5. Skew and kurtosis are common statistical measures of distributions; skew is a measure of symmetry, and kurtosis measures the tails relative to a normal distribution. See any statistics textbook or https://www.itl.nist.gov/div898/handbook/eda/section3/eda35b.htm for more information.
6. D.F. Swensen, *Pioneering Portfolio Management: An Unconventional Approach to Institutional Investment* (New York: Free Press, 2000).
7. See https://www.bridgewater.com/research-and-insights/the-all-weather-story.

Appendix: Real Estate Investments

A.1 The Characteristics of Real Estate as an Asset Class

The following characteristics differentiate real estate as an asset class.

A.1.1 Non-Fungibility and Heterogeneity

Unlike investments in commodities and equities, no two properties are identical. For instance, two shares of the same class of a company's stock confer the same ownership rights to different shareholders regardless of their dates of transaction and the prices they were bought and sold for. On the other hand, each real estate asset is fundamentally unique. No two property titles are comparable as factors such as location, size, natural light, layout, floor level, and even ownership history all make it impossible to duplicate a property.

A.1.2 Difficulty in Valuing Real Estate

Being heterogeneous complicates real estate valuation. Two apartments within the same condominium block may have vastly different valuations depending on their sizes, floor levels, interior furnishing, energy efficiency, quality of material used, and renovation history, among a myriad of other factors. Furthermore, due to the high investment values and high transaction costs, most properties change owners once in every 5 to 10 years, while some investment properties are held for decades. During the holding period, the property could have been renovated and upgraded, or it could have deteriorated due to a lack of maintenance. Thus, assessing the value of real estate is far more complex than, for example, stocks and bond valuation, which are frequently transacted on the major stock and bond exchanges and investors can avail themselves of up-to-date data on the prices of these investments.

A.1.3 High Unit Value (or High Investment Value)

The physical nature of real estate (i.e., the size and the immovable land that it is built on) means properties are costly to own. Every property has a land value and a building value. Real estate assets have a higher dollar value than most other investment classes such as bonds or stocks, which may be accessible to investors with several hundreds or thousands of dollars. In contrast, the investment value of properties represents several years of an employee's salary. Even with banks providing mortgages, the capital required to enter into a property investment could be equal to a year of salary or several years of personal savings. However, this is on the cusp of change as recent technological advances allow for fractional ownership of properties via electronic contracts. These electronic contracts, built on blockchain technology, represent a new trend of real estate tokenization which reduces the investment hurdle to smaller, bite-sized investments starting from as low as a single US dollar. The subject of real estate tokenization is elaborated upon in Chapter 4.

A.1.4 High Transaction Cost and Friction

Real estate transactions often involve lawyers, real estate agents, surveyors, financiers, and other professionals to provide due diligence. For larger properties, this list may even include accountants and engineers. The necessity and fees for each professional service also vary across countries. In addition, governments impose various taxes and stamp duties on real estate transactions. Hence, the transfer of real estate from seller to buyer is both time-consuming and costly. The costs of each transaction, expressed as a percentage of the asset value, are significantly higher than trading stocks or commodities. In general, acquisition costs may add about 3–5% to the price of the property. Depending on the property type and investment holding structure, sellers may also incur hefty costs related to the asset sale. In places such as Hong Kong, Singapore, and Australia, governments have sought to cool over-heated residential property markets by imposing additional stamp duties of as high as 35% on top of the usual acquisition costs.

A.1.5 Illiquidity

As a consequence of the factors above, taken in combination, real estate assets are considered illiquid as there are relatively few available for sale at any time. Real estate investments are generally held for longer periods than other asset classes. Passive investors would hold their investments for several years before the property values have risen sufficiently to return acceptable levels of profits on their capital. Investors who are active managers may embark on asset enhancement initiatives to upgrade the properties through renovations, optimizing the tenant mix, and enhancing the services to users. The renovations and tenant improvements could take between 6 months to several years and are expected to result in improved cash flow, and therefore higher valuations, for the properties. During such periods, the properties are generally not available for sale as the owners would prefer to sell after the enhancement works are completed in order to enjoy higher profits.

A.1.6 Active Management and Operations

Unlike investments in stocks and bonds, successful real estate investments require active management to perform tasks such as paying property taxes and maintenance fees, negotiating leases, collecting rents, and managing tenant relationships, just to name a few. The property owner could appoint a tenant services agent to rent out the space and manage the tenants' needs. The owner could also appoint a Property Manager to coordinate operations at the building level, such as maintenance, security, utilities, landscaping, and cleaning. In some cases, property owners could engage the services of an Asset Manager to represent the owners' interests to supervise the Property Managers and leasing agents, pay statutory and income taxes, and liaise with government departments.

A.1.7 Obsolescence

Physical deterioration, functional obsolescence, location obsolescence, and economic obsolescence can cause properties to become less desirable, resulting in lower demand from tenants, lower rents, and leading to depreciation of the real estate's property value. Even under ideal economic and management conditions, the property may still lose value if the cost of physical deterioration outweighs other factors which increase its value. These factors reinforce the need for active asset management.

A.1.8 Equilibrium of Supply and Demand

It is difficult to match the demand and supply of real estate. On one hand, tenants are committed to leasing properties for months and years so that when supply is in excess and rents decline, most tenants are unable to take advantage of the market situation to enjoy lower rents. Relocation costs and renovation costs are relatively significant versus monthly rents and therefore most tenants are "sticky" to the properties they occupy. On another hand, when demand for space rises quickly, landlords will increase the asking rents for any vacant spaces which they own, and these landlords are likely to enjoy increased income because additional new supply would have to wait an average two to three years for planning and construction. A stable market where demand and supply of real estate are balanced could take a few years of steady economic condition, usually with slow and predictable growth, to achieve.

Having covered the unique characteristics of real estate assets, let us examine real estate based on different use-types or segments, such as residences, offices, and hotels, to learn about their similarities and differences. Understanding the demand and supply factors that drive each segment's performance is important for learners who may be involved in assessing the investment potential of real estate assets. Most of us are involved with residential property transactions, either as a tenant or as a buyer. On a personal level, it would be useful to understand where the residential market is heading so that we could economize on our rental expenses, conclude a tenancy agreement with better rent-review terms, or purchase a property with better investment returns potential.

A.2 Classifying Real Estate Segments

Real estate can be broadly classified into residential and non-residential (commercial) property. These two categories can be further divided into many segments, as illustrated in Figure A.1. Each segment has its unique drivers of demand and supply, thereby offering different risks and returns. To determine which investment segment best suits their needs, investors must understand the dynamics and characteristics of these segments.

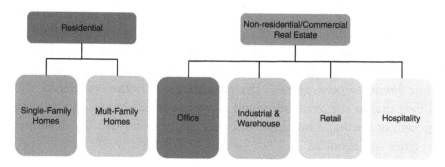

FIGURE A.1. Residential and commercial real estate sub-asset classes.

The segments in Figure A.1 are far from exhaustive, because the entire class of investible real estate includes many other property types, such as farmland, timberland, hostels, data centers, golf courses, and so on. Some investors would even classify infrastructure such as toll roads and ports, or civic and institutional properties, such as hospitals, prisons, and schools, as real estate.

A.2.1 Residential Real Estate

Residential real estate refers to properties with the primary purpose of providing dwelling. This category includes single-family homes, condominiums, townhouses, multi-family homes, public housing, and vacation homes. When combined, the value of residential properties accounts for more than three quarters of all global real estate and is the segment most widely owned by individuals and families.

The two primary segments of residential properties are single-family homes and multi-family homes. A single-family home is a standalone dwelling unit, usually with its own land title, that is occupied by a single household or an extended household. Multi-family homes are residential buildings with many apartments with single or extended households in each apartment. The owners of the apartments in the multi-family property development share the land title that the development sits on. Multi-family homes are usually referred to as condominiums, especially in Asia.

In most countries, the basic need for dwelling is met through home-ownership (see Figure A.2). For OECD countries, approximately 60–70% of dwellings are owner-occupied. These percentages tend to be highest in countries with government policies that encourage home-ownership through programs such as easy access to mortgages and first-time home-owners' grants. The percentage of home-ownership also differs due to the availability and supply of rental homes, population growth or decline, household incomes, and the affordability of homes in cities and suburbs.

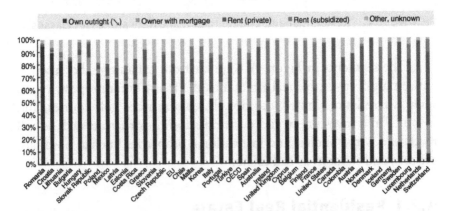

FIGURE A.2. Share of households in different tenure types, in percent, 2020 or latest year available.

Source: OECD, https://www.oecd.org/els/family/HM1-3-Housing-tenures.pdf, accessed July 6, 2022.

The propensity for home-ownership versus rental is also dependent on government policies, such as grants, tax and estate duties, and other factors, such as tenant's protection, accessibility, and costs of financing a home purchase, and so forth.

In Asia, the apartment units in a multi-family residential block are usually separately owned by individual families under strata-title ownership. This form of ownership allows each individual apartment unit in a building to be owned under a separate "strata-title" as they share the common ownership of the land title that the condominium sits on. In comparison, in the United States, it is more common for a multi-family residential development to be owned by a single investor, such as a property developer, a high-net-worth individual, or an investment company. In Europe, it is a mix of both. The UK real estate market tends to favor strata-title ownership, whereas in Germany and Switzerland, the real estate market is primarily dominated by entire multi-family blocks owned by investment companies.

A.2.2 Non-Residential/Commercial Real Estate

Non-residential real estate refers to all properties that are not designed for long-term accommodation and dwelling purposes. Note that multi-family blocks owned by investment funds for the intent of renting and rental income may be classified as commercial real estate, as the primary goal of the investment is to generate profits for the investors. The terminologies are used somewhat loosely and readers should be mindful to ask for specifics when reading market reports or when engaging in conversations about commercial real estate.

This category also includes, but is not limited to:

1. **Office property:** Investments in office properties can range from strata-title ownership of a single office unit or sections (single or multiple floors) of an office building, to ownership of the entire building and its land title. The offices could have single or multiple tenants. Tenants who need office space on a short-term basis, ranging from one day to several months, could seek co-working offices or serviced offices for rent, both of which operate within the office property segment.

2. **Industrial property:** Industrial properties can include warehouses, logistics and distribution centers, manufacturing facilities, and data centers. Depending on the activities of the tenants, the industrial building might have to be renovated to

suit the users' requirements, such as the strength of the floor loading, ceiling height, loading bays, electricity and energy supply, and waste management.

3. **Retail property:** Retail properties include shopping malls, shopping complexes, and standalone shops that are used as retail space for the purpose of selling goods and providing services to consumers. Examples of goods and services available in retail properties are fast-food outlets, hairdressing salons, stationery stores, fashion outlets, furniture shops, supermarkets, etc.

4. **Hospitality property:** Hospitality properties refer to real estate that provides short-term accommodation for dwelling purposes, ranging from hours to weeks of use, such as hotels, motels, serviced apartments, ski-lodges, and bed and breakfasts. In these properties, the tenants are usually referred to as guests. Unlike residential and other commercial real estate, the revenue stream for hospitality properties is more likely to fluctuate across the year, as room rates as well as occupancy rates vary according to seasonal demand.

A.3 Analyzing the Real Estate Segments

When analyzing the investment potential of the real estate segments, it is critical to consider factors such as demand and supply, similarities and differences across segments, and changes in market trends which could potentially impact each segment. Understanding the demand and supply drivers is fundamental to forecasting the property's revenue and profit potential. At the same time, it is necessary to consider the similarities and differences between the various segments, as competition for tenants exists within each segment and between the segments. For instance, a doctor who wishes to operate a clinic may select a retail space, an office unit, or a unit within a medical center. Having a good grasp of the drivers of demand and supply for each of the real estate segments will allow investors to determine the most suitable tenants for their property and therefore achieve the most optimal returns.

A.3.1 The Residential Segment

As daily users of residential property, this segment of real estate is the most familiar to us. However, the sense of familiarity may hamper our ability to study the financial returns and the supply and demand parameters objectively. Figure A.2 shows that in the OECD countries, a significant share of households live in rented residential properties. With the exception of the former communist countries (such as Poland, Hungary, Romania, etc., where home-ownership rates may exceed 90%), more than 30% of all residential properties are occupied by renters. These residential properties are considered investment properties as they generate rental income for the investor-landlords.

A.3.1.1 Residential Investment Properties

When analyzing the residential segment, investors have to consider whether the target residential investment property will be generating immediate rental returns, or will rentals be delayed as the property is still under construction. Investors should also be cognizant about whether the property is more suitable for the tenants' market or for the owner-occupier market.

The following is a list of factors which impacts our analysis. Do note that these factors and their relative weightings are difficult to quantify with confidence. Buyers of residential properties for own-use and enjoyment could have similar considerations as investors do, but they would also consider other parameters such as the tranquility of the neighborhood and proximity to schools for their children. For the purposes of this chapter, we will focus on residential properties as an investment, not for owner-occupation.

1. Macroeconomic variables exist, such as:
   a. **Inflation:** The effects of inflation vary by country. In general, a mildly inflationary environment would result in workers' incomes rising. Therefore, if these workers were tenants, the higher salaries would mean that that could afford to pay higher rents and landlords would benefit from higher returns. This simplistic train of thought has led to a fallacy stating that the ownership of real estate provides a

hedge against the negative effects of inflation. While it is true that rents could rise along with inflation, this is only true if the residential demand were strong and if supply did not exceed demand. On the other hand, inflation will cause material costs and labor costs related to building maintenance to increase, such that landlords may not realize as much financial profits as before. An additional point of note: for the professional real estate investor, the expected long-term inflation is often used as a reference to set the discount rate for estimating investment returns, so if the increase in rents is lower than the discount rates and operating costs of the property, the property value may not go up. The relationship between property prices and inflation is probably tenuous and learners should cautiously consider the factors that contribute to inflation before drawing conclusions about whether the ownership of real estate can hedge against the negative effects of inflation.

b. **Unemployment rate and wage growth:** During periods of strong employment, home buyers are likely to be confident about job security and are less likely to default on their home loans. The demand for homes will increase and if the new supply of residential properties cannot match the pace of demand growth, prices will increase. Similarly, a strong employment market will push up the average worker's salary and disposable incomes, resulting in higher demand for residential properties, higher rents, and higher property prices. Conversely, a weak jobs market with increasing unemployment will mean that there will be fewer tenants, existing tenants may downsize to lower-cost apartments, borrowers are more likely to default on their mortgages, and fewer people can afford to purchase their own residential properties. These will result in lower demand, lower rents, lower home prices, and lower investment returns for residential properties.

c. **Gross domestic product (GDP) growth:** Strong GDP growth is an indicator of a buoyant economy with a positive jobs market and steady income growth for workers. Higher household incomes are likely to lead to increased demand for purchases and for renting better and larger residential properties. Do note that GDP growth is a very broad economic indicator. So, if a substantial contributor to the growth came from the construction sector instead of the manufacturing or the services sectors, analysts might sound caution about the real estate markets because it could imply that a deluge of new homes could be added to the market, leading to more competition for tenants and buyers, and potentially lower home prices.

d. **Population growth:** The population growth of a city is an indicator that additional housing will be necessary, and we may expect residential property demand to increase. The converse is likely to be true. However, we need to dig deeper into the population data. Japan as a country has suffered from a declining population for a decade but her capital city, Tokyo, has continued to grow in population because of its strong employment market and ability to attract top talents to reside there. Readers should also note that the population numbers in some cities, with summer homes and winter homes that cater to the rich, are seasonal. While the resident population data may seem small, the demand for residential properties may be strong. Different generations, however, favor different styles of housing. So, while an increasing or shrinking population could signal an increase or decrease in demand for residential real estate, this change will not be uniform across all types of residential properties.

e. **Foreigners and immigrants:** An increase in the employment of foreigners will lead to additional demand for residential properties, as the foreigners arriving to take on their new jobs will need housing. Likewise, a country that has its borders open to migrants and refugees will see additional demand for housing. Again, we need to break down the data to determine the types and the numbers of additional housing units that will be needed.

f. **Interest rates and mortgage rates:** Interest rates and mortgage rates almost always move in tandem. When mortgage rates move up, the cost of property ownership financed by loans will increase, there will be less incentive to borrow and thus demand for residential property will weaken. When mortgage rates are low, the monthly mortgage payments will be smaller and the propensity for home buyers to borrow is higher, so demand for residential properties goes up. In countries with long-term fixed rate mortgages, such as the United States, demand for residential properties will increase when mortgage rates are expected to rise, because home buyers want to lock in the low mortgage rates. In countries where mortgage rates vary during the term of the loan, for example, where they are pegged to interbank rates, demand for residential properties may weaken when mortgage rates are expected to increase as investors hold back and wait for mortgage rates to trend down before investing. Looking at this subject from another angle, readers could recognize that an economic environment which has interest rates trending up could be brought on by an increased demand for money due to booming business and investment activities. In such a scenario, rentals should go up and property values are expected to increase. But in case the residential market is over-supplied and vacancies are high, a rosy economic environment with high employment rates and wage growth will not lead to higher rents. In this scenario, investors may choose to put their money in fixed deposits or invest in stocks and bonds where investment returns could be more attractive than investing in properties.

2. Real estate indicators are:

   a. **Occupancy rates:** Headline occupancy rates vary across cities and countries and they provide a broad indication of the physical occupier demand of a city or a country. In some countries, this demand for residential properties may be expressed as a vacancy rate. They are related in the equation: Vacancy Rate = 100% - Occupancy Rate. Investors need to note the historical occupancy rate and whether the occupancy rate might trend down, as new supply being added exceeds demand, or trend up when population growth and demand increase faster than supply. Furthermore, investors looking to buy a specific property would need to look beyond the headline occupancy rate to check if data are available at the precinct level and or if data are categorized by classes of residential properties. For example, when considering an investment in a middle-class multi-family apartment block in Shibuya, Tokyo, investors should look for data on the occupancy rates of a similar class of residential properties for the district of Shibuya. In neighborhoods with a high concentration of luxury homes, occupancy rates could be lower than average because those homes could be the vacation homes of wealthy investors and are likely to be vacant for most of the year. There is no benchmark for a "healthy" occupancy rate for each city or precinct. In some cities, a 90% occupancy rate could mean that demand is strong, supply is limited, and rentals are inching up, but in others, even a 95% occupancy rate could mean that tenants could strike a good bargain with landlords.

b. **Rents:** Rental income is the main source of revenue for real estate investors. When comparing rents, it is not sufficient to focus on a simple metric such as "the median rent for a two-bedroom dwelling unit is US$1500 per month in this precinct." Investors need to consider the median rent expressed as a unit rate (i.e., the monthly rent expressed in "dollars per unit area," such as dollars per square foot or dollars per square meter). This is a better indicator as the size of two-bedroom apartments or houses may range from 600 square feet to well over a thousand square feet. Focusing on the median rent of US$1500 per month would not be sufficient to make comparisons.

c. **Prices:** Every investor would like to buy at low prices and sell at higher prices. While the price at the point of acquisition and point of divestment are important considerations, most investors focus on the cash flow during the holding period (i.e., the years between acquisition and divestment). As such, the gross yield, or annual rental return, is a key consideration. This is obtained by calculating the total annual revenue and dividing by the purchase price. Comparing gross yields is one way to check on the relative performance of two or several properties. Another method is to compare prices based on the unit rate (i.e., dollars per square foot). Two similar high-rise apartment units in the same neighborhood, even with the same floor area and on the same floor level, would have different dollar per square foot prices. The price difference is usually qualified by the difference in the building quality, interior furnishings, facilities and amenities in the condominium block, and so on. Professional investors tend to be more precise with the price metric. These investors prefer using the "Net Operating Income (NOI) yield" as a measure. This is derived from the total annual revenue minus the operating costs that are required to keep the property running, such as maintenance and cleaning costs, leasing commissions, utilities, insurance, property tax, and so on. The concept of the NOI in real estate is similar to the concept of EBIT, or earnings before interest and tax, in finance and accounting. The NOI yield, expressed in percentage per annum, is derived from dividing the NOI by the purchase price of the property. This number provides a high-level indication of the annual returns that the property could give. Comparing the NOI yields of similar properties allows investors to make better investment decisions.

d. **Transaction volumes:** Transactional volumes for buy-sell and rent in a particular location could also point to high demand and popularity. It is an indication of how "liquid" the market is and whether investors will be able to find buyers when they are ready to divest their investments after a few years. A location that has zero or few transactions each year would be one where comparable property valuations are difficult to ascertain. It appeals to only a select group of buyers and therefore would be more challenging to divest. Exceptions to this rule would be the iconic properties in prestigious locations which could be much sought after, but because wealthy investors tend to hold on to such iconic properties for say, ten years or more, there are very few transactions recorded.

e. **Expectations of future rents and prices:** Investors need to consider whether rental rates have been trending up or down in recent years, and if rents trend up, investors should check if the demand for residential properties could match the supply of properties under construction in the next few years. When demand for homes is increasing at a faster pace than the supply that is under construction, the number of dwelling units available for rent and owner-occupation goes down, rents will go up. This will further push up valuations as investors are more willing to pay higher prices to earn the higher rents. The reverse is true when supply is stronger than demand, when real estate rents and prices are expected to drop.

A.3.1.2 Analyzing the Indicators of Residential Demand and Supply

It is important to understand that many of the aforementioned indicators are intertwined. For instance, an increase in the median rents of apartments is not always a cause for celebration for investors of residential properties; it is crucial to examine and identify the cause of this rent increase. Has the rent gone up due to sustained strong demand or was the increase caused by a sudden shortage of supply perhaps caused by the reconstruction of a neighborhood? If it were due to the latter, the increased rent may not persist beyond the reconstruction as the new supply could bring on more competition among landlords and cause a decline in the rents of older, less popular properties. Alert investors will monitor the demand and supply situation closely, keeping their options open to divesting before the reconstructed property is completed.

Most of the indicators are historical and backward-looking. Since many trends may not persist, past performance certainly does not guarantee future results. There are risks in extrapolating historical data for use as future estimates to guide investment decisions. For example, investors studying the trends in the residential market would note that the increase in gig-economy occupants in recent years has led to more shorter-term rental contracts being signed. This trend has also led to the rapid increase in supply of co-living spaces and share-houses. Hence, while the volume of rental contracts signed might have increased, the overall quality of the rental market may not have improved because the rental market is increasingly filled with more transient, short-term tenants (i.e., tenants staying six to nine months) as compared with long-term tenants who sign two-year contracts.

When analyzing these factors of demand and supply, investors must also research the sources, calculation methodology, and definitions used so as to ensure accuracy. For example, many national databases provide data on the number of dwelling units and the number of households. If the data show that a landed housing precinct has 2,000 houses and there are 2,500 households residing in this precinct, investors should not conclude that the occupancy rate in this precinct is high and it is worth investing in the homes here. In most population census reports, grandparents, parents, and children living under the same roof are counted as two households. In a neighborhood that is predominantly filled with landed houses, the number of households living in each house could average, say, 1.5. In this example, the 2,500 households would be occupying fewer than 1,700 houses, implying that less than 85% of the houses are occupied (i.e., more than 15% of the houses are vacant). Investors buying into the houses will face the risks of vacancy, where many months could pass without rental revenue while having to sustain expenses related to maintenance, utilities, and property taxes.

Analyzing the total number of dwelling units available versus the number of households in a geographical area provides a rough estimate of the size of the demand-supply gap. Where the number of dwelling units exceeds the number of households, there is a likelihood of a supply surplus. Conversely, if the number of households exceeds the available supply of dwelling units in that area, it is likely that demand exceeds supply. A supply surplus can add downward pressure on housing prices while a demand surplus can lead to increasing housing prices. However, before we jump to any conclusions about the demand and supply balance, we would have to consider second-order information. In the case where the number of dwelling units exceeds the number of households and occupancy rates were low, we need to find out if the dwelling units were purchased for use as holiday homes by owners from other cities. In the opposite case where the number of households exceed the number of dwelling units, we should question if there are many large residential properties which could be housing two or three households under the same roof.

The approach and thought process elaborated in the examples above may be applied to the analysis of other real estate segments. As such, the rest of the sections describing the Office, Retail, Hospitality, Industrial, and Data Center real estate segments will be more succinct.

A.3.2 The Office Segment

An office space refers to a physical location such as a room or a building, where business and professional activities are conducted. The business activities could be related to government, not-for-profit organizations, administrative and trading functions, and so on. Examples of professional activities include doctors' clinics, investment advisory and accounting services and so forth.

A.3.2.1 Indicators of Office Demand and Supply

The macroeconomic indicators given above for the residential segment are generally applicable when we consider the office segment. Rents and valuation of office properties are affected by inflation, GDP growth, and interest rates (or borrowing costs). The real estate indicators given in the residential segment above—occupancy, rents, prices, transaction volumes and expectation of future rents and prices—may also be applied, with some adjustments, when analyzing the office segment.

In addition, investors allocating funds to the office segment should take note of the following indicators:

1. **Population and employment:** While the total population of a city is an important metric to note for investing in the residential segment, the important population parameters to consider for the office segment are the size of the labor force and the strength of the employment market, and whether these are expected to strengthen or weaken. Specifically, we should examine the categories of employment in services and administrative jobs instead of categories such as manufacturing or ship building, as a massive growth of jobs in the latter categories is unlikely to result in any significant demand for office properties. A rule of thumb used by corporate real estate consultants to estimate office space needs is to allocate 100 square

feet (or about 10 square meters) of space per office worker. This estimate would represent a fully functional office including a reception area, meeting rooms, a pantry or recreation area, larger office rooms for senior management, as well as common areas for archive systems and IT and communications equipment.

2. **Competition between segments:** Competition for office tenants does not exist purely between office landlords. For example, a healthcare practitioner, a distributor of consumer products, or an architect could consider setting up their businesses in a retail space, an industrial space, or an office space, depending on their specific needs, such as rental and operating costs, accessibility and convenience for their workers, customers, and suppliers. Investors studying the office market to review the investment potential of an office asset need to keep in mind that the supply of space in the retail and industrial segments may compete for tenants in the office segment.

3. **Formation and cessation of new companies:** This is a good indicator to track when investors are looking ahead to forecast the near-future demand for office space. Coupled with other financial indicators such as the growth of direct investments, fixed asset investments, and planned capital expenditure, investors may feel more confident that demand for office space would be on the uptrend. Conversely, a reduction in the number of companies and new investments usually signifies reduced business optimism which could mean lower office demand and declining occupancy rates.

4. **Office grade classification:** Office spaces are often classified under different grades with Grade A offices having the highest specifications and being well located, and Grade C offices being the lowest. No standardized set of criteria exists for the grading of offices, as this is a subjective system used by marketers for comparing properties. In general, the parameters considered when assigning a grade to an office building include location, age of the property, speed and capacity of lifts,

security of access, quality of construction and materials used, connectivity of the building to amenities and transportation, and telecommunications infrastructure. Grade A offices are able to attract higher rents but investors need to consider the relativity of the various locations. For example, within the London office market, a new Grade A office in Canary Wharf is likely to fetch lower rents than an older Grade B office in Mayfair. Different grades of office properties appeal to different tenants with different needs and different budgets. Grade A offices tend to see the most demand and are sought after by multinational companies due to their location, high specifications, large floor plates, and prestige. Tenants' needs have changed significantly in the last few years, accelerated by the post-pandemic trends of social distancing and work-from-anywhere. Coupled with continued improvements in telecommunications and security technologies, and ESG factors, the definition of "Grade A" office will keep on upgrading.

Diving deeper, investors in the office segment must also consider the industries in which their tenants operate. Where possible, landlords should aim for a balanced tenant mix instead of being over-reliant on tenants from any one industry. For example, during the Global Financial Crisis in 2008, the banking and financial services industries responded to the same macroeconomic trends through downsizing and giving up office space. Landlords who were overexposed to tenants from the industry suffered. Figure A.3 illustrates the tenant mix of a portfolio of buildings owned by a Real Estate Investment Trust (REIT).

Investors wishing to purchase an office building can better assess the risks of tenant default and the demand for office space by analyzing historical information and reviewing market forecasts on the tenants' industries. Most trade and industry associations and national statistics bodies conduct business surveys that measure the future expectations of industry members. For instance, the United States' Institute for Supply Management's Purchasing Managers' Index (PMI) provides monthly reports on the manufacturing industry's expectations.

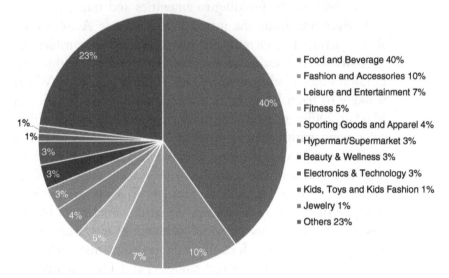

Example of a retail REIT's tenant portfolio

- Food and Beverage 40%
- Fashion and Accessories 10%
- Leisure and Entertainment 7%
- Fitness 5%
- Sporting Goods and Apparel 4%
- Hypermart/Supermarket 3%
- Beauty & Wellness 3%
- Electronics & Technology 3%
- Kids, Toys and Kids Fashion 1%
- Jewelry 1%
- Others 23%

FIGURE A.3.   Tenant mix of a retail REIT.

A.3.2.2 Office: Emerging Trends

Prior to the Covid-19 pandemic, the evolving trends in the office segment were centered around ESG (environmental, social, and governance) factors and the proliferation of co-working offices. The ESG theme led to a slew of building improvements for energy efficiency, waste management, carbon reduction, and user-centric designs for comfort and safety.

However, the pandemic appears to have permanently changed the arrangements between employers and employees. More workers are opting for work-from-home and flexible work arrangements and more companies have acceded to the employees' needs by reconfiguring their work processes. As a result, many companies have begun to downsize their office spaces, reducing the number of desks and workstations for their employees. Additionally, many businesses are reconsidering the requirements for an office space and switching to non-traditional office formats, such as co-working spaces. These two trends will cause a large-scale shift away from traditional office-metrics of providing 100 square feet of space per office worker, toward less space and more flexible spaces in the future. These trends unfolded relatively quickly and in August 2022, just two and a half years into the pandemic, Manulife US REIT announced that they are exploring "hotelization" possibilities to convert some of the office space into gyms, lounges, chill-out areas, and so forth to provide a "hotel-feel" for the office users.[1]

Given the rapid change in office demand, forward-looking landlords are already considering their options to convert office buildings into other uses, such as residential, serviced apartments, and hotels. Analysts and investors need to stay vigilant when reviewing investments in the office segment where foundations are shifting in the next few years.

A.3.3 The Retail Segment

The retail segment refers to properties that are used primarily by businesses to market and sell goods and provide services to consumers. Examples of tenants in retail real estate include fashion brands, department stores, pharmacies, supermarkets, sports goods retailers, food and beverage outlets, beauty salons, healthcare practitioners, and so forth. Properties in this segment include, but are not limited to, malls, shopping centers, standalone stores, and commercial businesses.

The traditional business model of retailers has been disrupted by the internet for more than two decades where the likes of Netflix, Amazon, and Expedia have led to the closures of video shops, bookstores, and high-street travel agencies. However, it was more recent developments in fulfillment and logistics, as well as the Covid-19 pandemic, that accelerated the shifts in consumer demand and the retail property segment.

A.3.3.1 Indicators of Retail Demand and Supply

Just like the residential and office segments, macroeconomic indicators given above may also be applied to the analysis of the retail segment. Rents and valuation of retail properties are affected by inflation, GDP growth, and interest rates (which affect consumers' disposable income as well as investors' property financing costs). The real estate indicators given in the office segment (occupancy, rents, prices, transaction volumes and expectation of future rents and prices) may also be applied, with some modifications, when analyzing the retail segment. In particular, investors who invest in malls with multiple tenants need to be mindful about the tenant mix (see Figure A.3), as a good mix of complementary tenants will generate higher consumer traffic for the mall.

The key to understanding the demand and supply for retail properties is realizing that it is dependent on consumers' demand for goods and services. Stores selling items with decreasing consumer demand will eventually be unable to continue operations and will close, leaving landlords to search for new tenants. The search for a new retail tenant can be time-consuming and costly, and vacancies in some malls may never be filled.

To minimize such risks, investors exploring investments in retail properties need to research consumer demand by geographical region, the consumer demographics that fall within the mall's catchment area, and a slew of other inter-related indicators:

1. **Consumer base and local demographics:** The size of a neighborhood's or a region's consumer base provides insights into retail demand. The total population of a country or a city rarely translates to the consumer market size that will affect a particular mall. Hence, research should be conducted to determine the mall's target demographic, followed by analyzing the earning and spending power of that target demographic.

2. **Household income:** Average household income and its related statistic average household expenses provide a helpful gauge of the total addressable market for consumer goods and services. The breakdown of such numbers by spend categories (e.g., wearing apparel and footwear, cosmetics, furniture, recreational goods, etc.) can help landlords determine the most suitable tenant mix. For instance, regions with high household incomes may favor designer fashion brands as opposed to middle-income regions that favor affordable mass market brands. However, certain necessities, such as staple food ingredients and medicines, are required in malls with little differentiation across income groups.

3. **Location and connectivity:** Retail property prices differ significantly across locations. For instance, properties in city center, suburban, and rural areas will vary drastically in price. Similarly, rents and valuations can differ between cities and

between neighborhoods in the same city. These differences arise from the variation in foot traffic and spending power of the consumers in each location. Malls and retail centers which are better connected by good transport links will do better, especially malls connected to transport hubs where commuters change modes of transport.

4. **Layout:** A retail property's layout plays an essential role in determining its success (Figure A.4). For a strip mall, the placement of food and beverage services shops, essential services shops, such as clinics and banks, the liquor store and supermarket are designed to encourage shoppers to walk past, and hopefully visit, a few more stores. As for high-rise malls, the successful ones are typically designed to be "inward-looking" with hardly any windows to the world outside the mall, so that shoppers are not distracted and are less aware of the passage of time. This is sometimes referred to as the "Gruen Effect," where shoppers feel comfortable and relaxed and wander around in the mall buying things that may not be on their shopping lists.[2] Other favorable characteristics of retail space design include sufficient circulation and rest areas, corridor width that allows for at least two groups of shoppers with shopping bags to pass each other, sheltered pick-up and drop-off points, and an atrium or a plaza for hosting seasonal or festive events.

5. **Footfall:** While a mall's foot traffic may appear to be a good indicator of demand, there is often a gap between footfall and spending at a retail property. People may enter a mall for air conditioning or heating, or as a short cut to another street (i.e., their presence adds no value to the property). Investors in the retail segment need to pay closer attention to where shoppers are actually spending their money. For instance, the mall owners could install point-of-sales systems for their tenants to monitor spending patterns and, depending on the tenant mix, survey the proportion of customers leaving the mall without shopping bags.

6. **Car park congestion:** Car park congestion as a measure of demand is subject to the same limitations as footfall. A full car park merely signifies many cars, with their passengers, going to

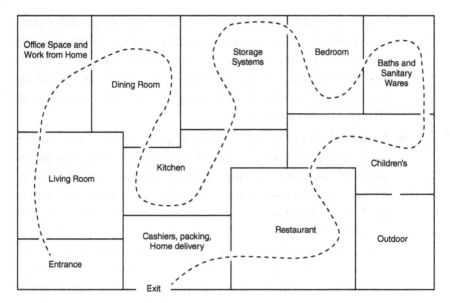

FIGURE A.4. A furniture store designed with a "fixed path" layout guiding shoppers through most of the departments in the store.

the mall. However, the presence of visitors does not guarantee spending in the stores. Some retail malls provide discounted or free parking when shoppers spend at the mall. This is a good method to judge if the parking congestion is due to the mall being a magnet for shoppers or if it is merely a convenient parking lot for visitors to transit to other destinations on foot.

7. **Tourism:** The retail sector in some cities is far more reliant on tourists than local consumers. Investors in the retail segment should analyze data pertaining to visitor arrival statistics and their trip spend. Prior to Covid-19, international gateway cities such as Singapore and Hong Kong had about four to six times the number of foreign visitors than the local population (Figure A.5). Domestic tourism may play a huge part to a city's retail scene: Kyoto City in Japan has fewer than 2 million resident population, and each year, the city welcomes more than 40 million domestic visitors! Without a doubt, the impact on consumption and the retail real estate segment is significant and investors need to take these datasets into account.

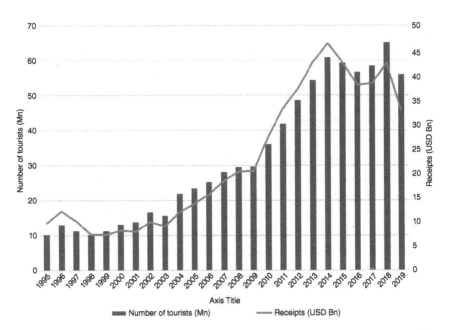

FIGURE A.5. Number of tourists and annual tourist spending in Hong Kong.
Source: https://www.unwto.org/tourism-statistics/key-tourism-statistics.

Along with the aforementioned indicators of demand and supply for retail properties, investors should be cognizant of other market factors that affect their rental returns and profits. For instance, rents for stores within the same shopping mall vary greatly depending on factors such as floor level, width of store front, and the number of shoppers likely to walk past the shop. Units on the ground level with wide frontages and great visibility for passers-by tend to have the highest demand and thus their unit rent (i.e., dollar per square foot rent) is the highest.

Retail landlords may also offer different types of leases for stores within the same mall. While some stores will be subjected to a traditional lease of, say, $5,000 per month for three years, other tenants sign a turnover lease where rents are paid to the landlord based on a percentage of the tenants' monthly revenue, usually subject to a minimum monthly rent. The turnover lease allows the landlord and tenant to share business risks as both will enjoy the upsides from higher consumer spend during festive and holiday seasons while falling back on a base rent during the slower months. A differentiating feature of retail leases is that mall owners usually include additional fees in the lease agreement, such as advertising and promotion fees, shoppers' loyalty program fees, and so on. These fees paid to the mall owner will be spent on activities to draw shoppers to the mall.

Tenants may also rent a property for reasons outside of selling goods and providing services. A welcoming and sleek-looking retail space may be used for purposes such as product positioning, advertising, and building brand recall and loyalty among followers. For instance, consumer electronics giant Apple has large, luxuriously adorned stores, yet a minimal amount of space is actually used to display products for sale. One key priority of such a store front is brand reinforcement and recognition. Sales revenues rank behind. Using a prominent retail store front for advertising and branding purposes is especially prevalent for luxury fashion brands, where revenues at some outlets barely cover rents and operating expenses. Instead of categorizing rental expenses as administrative or corporate fixed costs, premium brands consider it as a marketing expense, i.e., a direct cost rather than an indirect cost. This is because a well-presented storefront can contribute to building brand loyalty and driving sales, just as much as advertising in digital or print media.

A.3.3.2 Retail: Emerging Trends

The retail segment is evolving fast as consumers' attention span shortens and shifts. Two decades ago, there was a proliferation of fast fashion brands with affordable clothes offering new designs every fashion season, just as haute couture brands do. A decade ago, retail malls were filling up with health, wellness, and beauty (HWB) brands. All that time, the internet was gaining users and in the last 20 years we have seen the closure of thousands of retail shops such as video and music stores, toy shops, travel agencies, bookstores, shops selling film and camera equipment, and so on.

E-commerce is not an emerging trend but its continued growth and adoption are impacting retail properties in a big way. E-commerce grew rapidly at the turn of this century with the adoption of the internet, but shopping online only gained widespread acceptance as improvements in payment security, logistic fulfillment, and returns of goods established sufficient trust among consumers. Mobile e-commerce provided a boost to online sales as mobile phones and mobile apps provided consumers with access to millions of products and the convenience of payments in their hands.

The Global Financial Crisis of 2009 brought a wave of consumers online to search for lower-cost products. The lockdowns during the Covid-19 pandemic compelled another wave of e-commerce adoption, including food delivery. This growing trend of shopping online resulted in a declining need for space in physical stores. To combat the declining rents, landlords and tenants in retail have implemented omni-channel touch points, online-to-offline (O2O) integration, repurposing malls to increase the Food & Beverage or Entertainment components. But these strategies can only slow the inevitable (Figure A.6). This switch toward e-commerce has also caused an increased demand for warehouses and distribution centers, which is discussed in more detail in Section A.3.5.

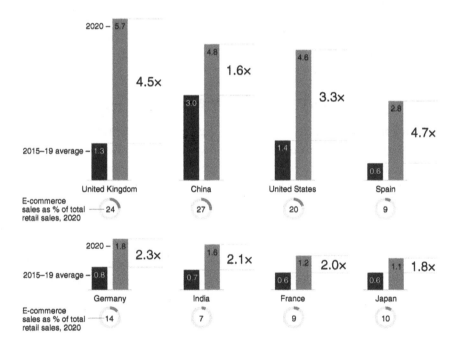

FIGURE A.6. Growth of e-commerce as a share of total retail sales in eight countries.

Source: https://www.mckinsey.com/featured-insights/coronavirus-leading-through-the-crisis/charting-the-path-to-the-next-normal/how-e-commerce-share-of-retail-soared-across-the-globe-a-look-at-eight-countries.

While e-commerce is largely hurting physical retail, luxury brands have not been as affected as mass market fashion. The experience of being pampered in the luxury fashion and jewelry stores cannot be replicated online. Consumers prefer to purchase big ticket items in person so that they can touch and feel the items before making a purchase decision. Furthermore, walking out of a luxury brand store with a big shopping bag sporting the luxury brand's logo draws the envy of other shoppers. And for some consumers, that alone is priceless.

The overall demand for space in the retail segment seems to be a shrinking one. Existing malls which have lost their relevance have either been repurposed for other uses (e.g., office or residential) or mothballed as "dead malls." While it is unlikely that we will see the new construction of large sprawling malls or multi-story shopping centers, there is still a need for retail space in the development of every new neighborhood, new industrial township, or new business park. Investors and property developers need to be a lot more measured in sizing up the retail segment when conducting their feasibility studies and new designs.

A.3.4 The Hospitality Segment

The hospitality segment refers to properties for accommodation that are leased for short occupancy periods, spanning a single night to a few months. The short-term tenants are known as guests, and because of the temporal nature of the stay, a certain level of service is included in the "tenancy agreement." These properties include hotels, motels, resorts, and serviced apartments.

Hospitality assets require much deeper understanding and a lot more consideration than most other segments of real estate. For instance, hotels and serviced apartments need to allocate a significant percentage of the built-up area to be the lobby and reception, baggage holding area, business centers, and sometimes laundromats. Furthermore, additional space has to be provided for access for housekeeping and back-of-house operations. Owners of hospitality buildings must ensure that all of these expectations are not only met but also stand out from their competitors. In this sense, hospitality assets tend to require more active management than other forms of real estate.

A.3.4.1 *Indicators of Hospitality Demand and Supply*

Tourism data are by far the most important indicator for the hospitality real estate segment. In many countries, this information is made available by business associations that track tourism data, such as hotel or serviced apartment associations and national or regional tourism authorities. In many countries, especially those in the emerging markets, tourism and visitor data can be non-existent or difficult to obtain.

In addition to knowing the numbers of visitors to a city and the seasonality of their visits (i.e., how many visitors in each weekday versus weekend or each month) investors need to understand the demographics of visitors. If visitor arrivals are dominated by foreigners, which countries are they from? What is the purpose of their visit? How frequently do they visit? How many days do they stay per trip?

Investors in the Japanese hospitality segment, for instance, would know that the country has a large domestic tourism market. Figure A.7 from the Japan External Trade Organization depicts the breakdown of travel expenditure by inbound, outbound, and domestic travel in 2019. Pre-pandemic data were selected, as travel restrictions significantly limited the ability of foreigners to enter Japan. Hotel owners can rely on these data to shape the services they offer to serve the needs of domestic tourists and foreign visitors.

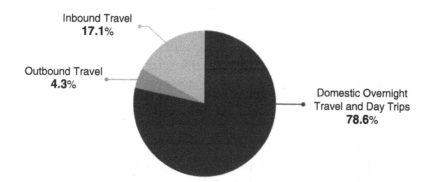

FIGURE A.7. Breakdown of travel expenditure in Japan in 2019 (overall 27.9 trillion JPY).
Source: https://www.jetro.go.jp/en/invest/attractive_sectors/tourism/overview.html, accessed June 24, 2022.

Solely analyzing the size and demographic of a region's tourism, however, does not necessarily provide hospitality investors with a holistic understanding of the market. For instance, a beach town may host a large tourist population in the summer, however, only a minority of that population will choose to stay in a hotel. Instead, the majority may opt to stay in private residences through home-sharing platforms such as Airbnb. On the flipside, domestic vacationers having staycations could be popular in a particular region and account for a significant proportion of the hospitality sector's revenue. These travelers may not cross any state or federal borders and thus are not accounted for in tourism data. Hence, the broad data on visitor arrivals do not necessarily equate to demand for hotel rooms. Analysts researching this segment need to dive deeper into the numbers.

Beyond the number of visitors, the purpose of travel and the visitor spend should be researched. Hotel investors ought to know if visitors are arriving for leisure, business, or other purposes such as healthcare, conferences, and exhibitions. The visitors' motivation for travel will influence their preferred accommodation, length of stay, and budget. This form of research provides hospitality investors with a more comprehensive insight into the market. Such data are often available to investors and hotel operators, as many local and federal governments publish statistics on the breakdown of tourism numbers by purpose of visit and type of accommodation. For instance, Figure A.8 and Table A.1 are taken from the Office of New York's State Comptroller's April 2021 report, which provides an insightful breakdown into the city's tourism industry. Again, pre-pandemic data were selected due to the impact of travel restrictions on this category's data.

Some additional useful resources investors can look into are:

1. Airport traffic into and out of the region.
2. Potential growth in numbers of flights.
3. Development in infrastructure to support land transportation, such as railways and toll roads.
4. Number of cruise and passenger ships docking in the region.
5. Presence of large-scale events in the area.

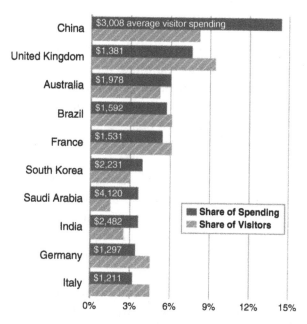

FIGURE A.8. Share of total international spending and visitors by country of origin, 2019, showing top 10 countries by spending.

Source: https://www.osc.state.ny.us/reports/osdc/tourism-industry-new-york-city, accessed June 27, 2022.

TABLE A.1. New York City's share of visitors by category, 2018–2019 (%)

Category	Share of domestic	Share of international	Share of total
Business	22	17	20
Leisure	78	83	80

Source: NYC & Company, OSC analysis, https://www.osc.state.ny.us/reports/osdc/tourism-industry-new-york-city, accessed June 27, 2022.

6. Possible growth of business visitors.

7. Real estate consultants' report, such as those from HVS, JLL, or CBRE.

8. Financial analysis reports, such as hospitality REIT reports.

A.3.5 The Industrial Segment

While the hospitality segment is full of operational intricacies, it has a relatively narrow definition as real estate for short-term and temporal accommodation needs. On the other hand, the industrial segment has a wide range of definitions and is a very complex real estate segment to analyze. The industrial segment includes properties such as factories used for the production of goods, warehouses for the storage of goods, data centers, and logistics services facilities.

Data centers and logistics facilities have seen record growth in valuations in recent years in response to the increased adoption of e-commerce. However, both data centers and logistics facilities represent more than the land and the buildings that are built; these real estate assets have high valuations which include expensive and sophisticated equipment.

The sub-segment classified as factory space includes a wide range of uses including wafer fabrication plants, food factories, car maintenance and repair facilities, petrochemical plants, aircraft maintenance facilities, garment factories, and so on. Given the wide variety of uses, the industrial segment is one of the most complex to analyze.

The physical characteristics of industrial properties also vary widely. Investors getting into the industrial segment must be knowledgeable about specifications and design considerations that would be relevant to industrial tenants' needs. For instance, some factories are built with dock levelers, which ease the process of loading and unloading goods. A factory without dock levelers will require forklifts for goods to be loaded onto a container truck, and hence are less efficient for the tenant's operations. Prospective tenants would either be unwilling to rent or would bargain for a reduced rent if dock levelers could improve their efficiency. Other important physical characteristics include the floor loading capacity, the safety and security systems installed, the electricity supply and back-up supply, and so forth.

Further complicating this segment is that the tenancy agreement is a lot more detailed and complex than those of the other segments. The terms of the lease need to conform to the technical specifications of the industrial property as well as comply with government regulations for industrial activities, including ESG (environmental, social, and governance) factors. The lease agreements also spell out the insurance cover required for the tenant to cover potential liabilities that may result from accidents.

A.3.5.1 Indicators of Industrial Demand and Supply

The indicators of demand and supply within the industrial segment are largely determined by the industrial categories that the tenants operate in (e.g., aerospace, biomedical, petrochemical, food, precision engineering, automotive, general manufacturing, etc).

Some indicators, however, influence demand and supply across the majority of industrial properties. These include overall economic growth, energy costs, commodities and raw material costs, interest rates, and so on. The location of an industrial property, just as in the other segments, is an extremely important consideration for an industrial tenant since proximity to suppliers and customers and the ease of transportation of goods will influence the tenant's bottom line.

The heterogeneous drivers of demand and supply across the industrial segment can greatly complicate the analysis of these indicators. So, while there is an abundance of information available on the industrial segment (see examples in Figures A.9 and A.10) and data on manufacturing and logistics businesses are regularly published by economists and financial analysts, piecing the information together can be difficult. One valuable data source is the regular reporting of financial results provided by industrial REITs. These provide the relevant research on the performance of their different assets. In fact, keeping track of industrial REITs' performance is a good practice, as these reports often provide insights into rentals and price trends as well as possible future headwinds or opportunities.

Another useful set of data is the price and rental index for industrial properties, which are published by relevant government bodies or tracked by real estate consultants, such as Jones Lang LaSalle, Savills, and Cushman & Wakefield. These data show the past rental and price trends, which may be used as indicators for price levels in the next 6–12 months.

In addition to these backward-looking indicators, the PMI and business expectations survey, as discussed in Section A.3.2, provide investors with forward-looking indicators of demand and supply.

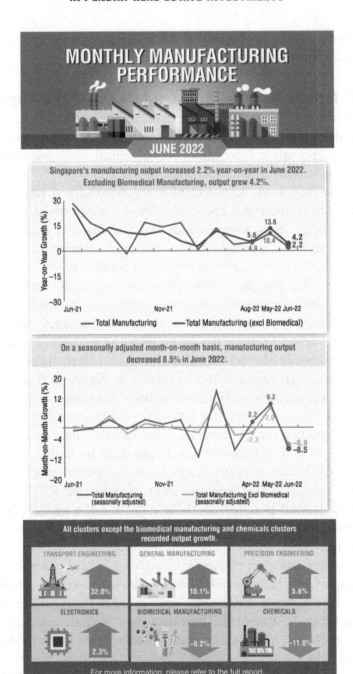

FIGURE A.9. Manufacturing output report for Singapore (June 2022).

Source: https://www.edb.gov.sg/en/about-edb/media-releases-publications/
monthly-manufacturing-performance.html, accessed July 26, 2022.

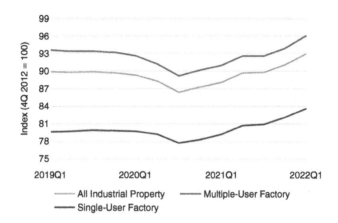

FIGURE A.10. Price index of industrial space in Singapore.
Source: https://stats.jtc.gov.sg/content/static/price-sub-page.html, accessed July 26, 2022.

These forward-looking indicators, however, are obtained through surveys, and are therefore dependent on respondents' outlook on their business activities. Even though these surveys are not precise, they do provide an indication about where industrial activities might be heading and can be useful if investors are aware of their limitations. Tracking these forward-looking indicators allows investors to judge if the demand and supply gap is expected to widen or narrow in the future. This can support investors' decision-making when investing in industrial properties or when negotiating new leases with prospective tenants.

A.3.6 Other Segments

While this text only covered the key real estate segments, other segments may be analyzed using similar approaches and the analytical processes described above. For instance, investors can determine the drivers of demand and supply, consider indicators that will affect revenues and costs, and explore the risks and returns of every segment as was exemplified earlier. The fundamental principles of real estate analysis do not differ greatly between segments even though each segment has its own nuances.

Other real estate segments not covered here include, but are not limited to:

1. Co-living and share houses
2. Hostels and dormitories
3. Retirement housing
4. Co-working spaces
5. Healthcare clinics, medical centers, and hospitals
6. Educational establishments
7. Industrial townships
8. Mixed developments where a development has multiple segments such as retail, office, hospitality, and residential sitting on a single site
9. Tightly regulated segments, such as agriculture, forestry, and mining

Interested readers may look for specialist reports and industry papers to get insights into these segments.

A.4 Real Estate Valuation

The previous discussion on the drivers of demand and supply for each real estate segment offers readers a glimpse into the indicators that affect revenues and costs. The knowledge of the cash flows at the property level will support the learning of the three main real estate valuation methods that will be described below: the income approach, the cost approach, and the sales-comparison approach.

A.4.1 Valuation

Real estate valuation is the process of determining the current worth of a real estate asset. Given that properties are non-fungible and infrequently traded, real estate valuation is a complex undertaking, part-science, part-art, that is usually performed by licensed appraisers.

The term value holds various meanings within the real estate sector. As a result, a property's value can be determined in a multitude of ways, depending on the needs of all parties involved in a transaction. For instance, the property valuation required by a lender may be different than the one required by a tax assessor. The three main measures of real estate value are:

1. **Market value:** The value that a typical investor is willing to pay and a typical seller is willing to accept for a property. This measure fluctuates greatly since it is heavily influenced by the sale of comparable properties during a given time period. The market value is central to real estate transactions, as it is the price that a buyer and seller must agree upon before signing a Purchase and Sale Agreement. Lenders also find market value to be an extremely important measure, as it provides an estimate of what can be reasonably expected for the sale of the property in the event of a default and foreclosure. Note that market value and valuation are frequently confused but are two distinct concepts and values. An investor should be careful never to mistake a property's valuation for its market value.

2. **Investment value:** The worth of a property to an investor. Investment value may be above or below the market value depending on an investor's motivations and how well the property fits into their portfolio, risk tolerance, and tax circumstances, among many other factors. For example, a strategic investor could be willing to pay a little higher than market value if the acquisition allowed him to amalgamate an adjacent property into a larger plot for redevelopment at a much higher profit.

3. **Value in use:** The value of a property when used for a specific purpose. For example, the ground floor shop space could be used as a restaurant, as a hair salon, or as an office. The value in use of this shop can vary widely, depending on its tenant and the activities.

In addition to the above, the same property would have a different insurance value, forced-sale value, depreciation value, inheritance value, taxable value, accounting value, and so on. Given these various definitions of value, investors should ensure that all parties in a transaction are aligned with the same definition to avoid potentially costly misunderstandings.

A.4.2 Highest and Best Use

The most profitable use of a property is known as its highest and best use. Properties should always be valued at their highest and best use, regardless of their current use. To determine a property's highest and best use, an appraiser must compare multiple use cases for a given property to discover which one will yield the highest return to an investor. For instance, an appraiser may assess a vacant site based on three potential use cases: apartment, office, and retail property. The appraiser would calculate the expected value after construction for each property type. The cost of construction would be subtracted from each expected value to calculate the implied land value. The use case with the highest derived land value would be deemed the highest and best use for the land.

A.4.3 Valuation Method 1: The Income Approach

The income approach is the most popular method of real estate valuation. This method equates the value of a real estate asset to the present value of the sum of its expected future net operating income (NOI). Appraisers may derive the property value either by discounting the future cash flow stream or by directly capitalizing the NOI.

A.4.3.1 Net Operating Income (NOI)

The term net operating income (NOI) is used extensively in real estate investments. Its main application is in the analysis of properties that already generate income (i.e., completed properties that are tenanted). Understanding what constitutes the NOI is essential to the subsequent step of estimating the property value by discounting future cash flows or by direct capitalization.

The NOI may be quickly calculated by taking the total annual revenue of a property minus the annual operating expenses of the property.

The total revenue of a property includes rent, car park charges, advertising income, such as billboards and multi-media displays, management fees charged to tenants, and so on. The total operating expenses relate to costs which are required to keep the property running (i.e., utilities, waste management and cleaning, security, maintenance, insurance, property tax, municipal charges, agents' fees, administration, etc.). Capital expenses related to the property, such as spending a million dollars upgrading the lobby of an office building, will impact the cash flow, but not the NOI.

NOI = Total annual revenue − Total operating expenses

Thus, the NOI measures a property's profitability before accounting for non-operating expenses. In a way, the NOI is similar to the more familiar accounting item called EBITDA (earnings before interest, tax, depreciation, and amortization).

This is the most common way to calculate the annual NOI. However, in the United States, landlords calculate NOI with an additional step. First, the potential gross income (PGI) is estimated based on the assumption that the property is fully leased with tenants paying rents at the market rate. Then vacancy and collection loss are subtracted to derive the effective gross income (EGI). Finally, the NOI is found by subtracting the operating expenses from the EGI. The additional information for the vacancy and estimated collection losses is useful for some investors.

A.4.3.2 Discounted Cash Flow (DCF)

For investors, a property's value is equal to the sum of its expected cash flows. This sum is equal to the income generated by the property during its useful life. All investors want to purchase a property at a value below the sum of its expected future cash flows, so as to make a profit from the investment.

Given that real estate investments require large capital sums to be invested upfront while the profits and returns are paid out progressively over the future months and years, the analysis of a property's returns has to take into account the fact that inflation will diminish the value of future cash flow returns. The effect of inflation means that a dollar of profits in 10 years' time has less purchasing power than a dollar of profits today.

However, investors **do not** merely want to invest for a return that matches inflation. That would imply that the investor has only managed to achieve break even across the entire investment period. Most investors would target to make an additional margin above the expected inflation rate. This additional margin should be sufficient to cover the potential risks that the investor would be exposed to during the investment period, as well as pay the investor a reasonable profit upon divestment of the property. Examples of the potential risks considered by investors are interest rate risks, policy risks, market risks, and in some cases foreign exchange risks.

The combination of inflation plus margin provides investors with a "hurdle" rate, alternatively seen as the opportunity cost of capital. This hurdle rate is applied as the "discount" in the Discounted Cash Flow (DCF) model. This discount factor is applied to each of the future year's cash flow in order to transform them to present-day value. Summing up all the present values of cash flows from the future years will allow an investor to determine if a property will generate sufficient profits to make the investment worth considering.

Using this measurement to ascertain the present worth of a project is helpful when evaluating several projects with different cash flow patterns. Taking two similar-sized office buildings in the same city, Building A might generate low cash flow in the initial years which could increase significantly in later years. The cash flow of Building B might be the reverse. Assuming the same discount rate applied to both office buildings, Building B should be preferred over Building A.

Setting an appropriate discount factor is crucial to performing the DCF analysis. The appropriate discount factor is generally viewed as the opportunity cost of capital, or the minimum rate of return required by the investor. Fixing a discount that is too high, either because of the inflation outlook or asking for a high profit margin, will result in a deflated sum of future cash flows, causing investors to incorrectly conclude that a property will generate returns below its market value. Underestimating the discount factor, however, can also be dangerous. A low discount value will yield a larger sum of cash flows in present value terms, leading investors to believe, unrealistically, that the property can generate large profits, and thus overvaluing the property.

One final note on the DCF formula. This formula requires investors to estimate the terminal value or divestment value of the property. This value is determined by considering the long-term outlook of the property market and making an educated estimate about its value when the property is sold to the next owner at the end of the investment period. The estimated value may be supported by extrapolating trends of the recent past property cycles and by taking the final year's expected cash flow and dividing it by the target capitalization rate for divestment.

A.4.3.3 Direct Capitalization

The direct capitalization formula is given as:

$$\text{Capitalization rate} = \text{NOI} / \text{Property Value}$$

where the capitalization rate (or cap rate) is expressed as the annual percentage returns of a property derived by dividing the NOI by the value of the property. While the formula looks simple, there are many factors encapsulated in the variables which require deeper consideration. The cap rate is influenced by a wide variety of factors that impact either the NOI, such as vacancies, rents, and operating costs, or the property value (e.g., new land policies, new amenities around the property, etc.).

Investors using the direct capitalization method should expect to calculate both entry and terminal cap rates. The entry cap rate, which is measured at the time of investment, is calculated based on the existing NOI and purchase price. Unlike the entry cap rate which is derived from actual figures, the terminal cap rate is an estimated figure, or a target that is set to be achieved. It is calculated based on assumptions of the future NOI and the target divestment price.

A cap rate may also be used as a hurdle rate or as an expectation of annual returns when we apply the DCF method. In this sense, the cap rate can be thought of similarly as the discount rate.

The relationship between the three variables in the direct capitalization equation can be visualized using the pyramid in Figure A.11. A key takeaway from this pyramid is that cap rates and property values are inversely related, meaning that if the NOI were held constant, a high cap rate will yield a low property value and a low cap rate implies a high property value.

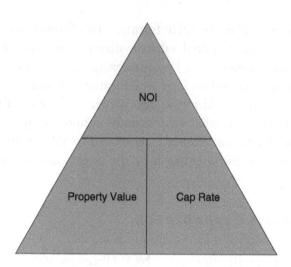

FIGURE A.11. Pyramid relationship of net operating income, cap rate and property value.

A note of caution. Knowing that a property has a high cap rate does not necessarily mean that investors should rush to acquire it for the attractively high income. We need to delve deeper.

A high cap rate can be the result of a low property value or a high NOI. Poor tenant quality, deteriorating equipment, and poor amenities can cause a property's value to drop, while high rental rates and low vacancies can increase the NOI. In a similar way, a low cap rate does not necessarily mean that an investor should immediately shun the investment. The cap rate could be low, and go even lower, because the property's value has been increasing perhaps due to improved public infrastructure or new development plans in the vicinity that brought a surge in investment demand. Cap rates could also be low due to a drop in the NOI after an anchor tenant has departed, leaving a large vacant space which took many months to fill.

While factors such as prime locations and comprehensive neighboring amenities would cause property values to increase (i.e., they are positive for investors), factors such as increased vacancies and declining rents would cause the NOI to drop and are negative for investors. These opposing factors, however, are linked with *decreased* cap rates. So, knowing that the cap rate is increasing or decreasing alone does not provide enough information about the attractiveness of an investment opportunity. Instead, investors should investigate the reasons for the change, based on the specific context of the property and its environment, to determine the investment merits.

A.4.3.4 Stabilized NOI

Investors must be careful when using the direct capitalization method to ensure that the NOI is truly representative of the property being analyzed. For instance, they should consider if the NOI is comparable to other similar properties in the vicinity or impacted by short-term and once-off factors, such as renovations. To work around the temporary impact on cash flow, an appraiser will use a stabilized NOI, which is based on the income-generating potential of the property accounting for vacancy loss.

For example, an appraiser may be valuing a 10-story office building where two stories are under renovation. It would not be fair to use the current NOI when performing direct capitalization calculations as the NOI would underestimate the office building's value once the renovations are completed and new tenants have moved in. In this case, the appraiser should use a stabilized NOI, based on the expected income after renovations are completed, to provide a more reliable estimate.

A.4.3.5 Drawbacks of the Income Approach

This valuation approach is the most widely used and it is applicable to a large majority of properties that are completed and generating cash flow. However, it is not the preferred approach when investors consider properties which are under construction or under extensive renovation, or properties which have large seasonal variations in income and expenses (e.g., ski resorts, convention centers). Within a residential enclave which is mainly filled with owner-occupied homes, it is also challenging to apply the income approach to appraise the value of the apartments and houses, as scarce data are available on the cash flow from renting those homes.

A.4.4 The Cost Approach

Performed by estimating the cost of rebuilding an existing real estate asset from scratch, the cost approach is typically used when locating comparable properties is difficult, for example, a single retail mall in the middle of an industrial park. The logic applied here is that an investor should not pay more for a property than the cost of acquiring a vacant site and developing a comparable property themselves. In reality, however, investors may be willing to pay a small premium for an existing property to avoid the time-consuming and resource-demanding nature of construction.

The following are the steps involved when using the cost approach to appraise the value of an existing property:

1. The cost of the land is estimated.

2. The replacement cost of the entire building is estimated, taking into account the current standards of the building specifications and the current market prices of construction.

3. The replacement cost of the building is then adjusted to account for depreciation of the existing building.

For the final step, there are four types of depreciation that investors should take into consideration. These are physical deterioration, functional obsolescence, locational obsolescence, and economic obsolescence (Figure A.12).

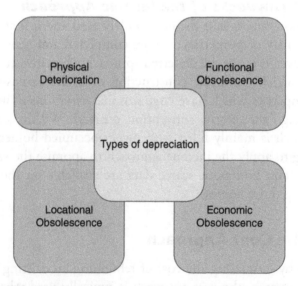

FIGURE A.12. Types of depreciation to consider in real estate.

A.4.4.1 Physical Deterioration

Physical deterioration is caused by aging and natural wear and tear of properties over time. It can be further classified into two types: curable and incurable.

Curable physical deterioration refers to issues where the value of fixing exceeds the cost of fixing. In other words, it is the effects of aging or natural wear and tear that are worth spending money to fix through improvements, renovations, or remodeling. For example, the value added to an apartment building after replacing its façade may exceed the cost of replacement, which means that the weather-worn façade is considered a curable physical deterioration.

Incurable physical deterioration is the exact opposite. The effects of aging and wear and tear on a building are severe enough that the financial returns will not be sufficient to warrant spending money to fix the damage. Incurable physical deterioration also needs to be accounted for by an appraiser. Their role will be to calculate the loss in value caused by the deterioration. This step is necessary because an astute investor would not pay the same price for a building affected by incurable physical deterioration as they would for an unaffected property.

A.4.4.2 Functional Obsolescence

Functional obsolescence occurs in buildings that do not meet current regulatory or operational requirements due to outdated or inefficient designs. These buildings become less desirable than their newer and more efficient counterparts and, thus, generate a lower NOI due to lower rents and possibly higher maintenance costs.

An outdated security system serves as an example of functional obsolescence for buildings marketed toward top-ranked IT companies, since many of these companies require buildings to meet their security standards before they would consider leasing them. If an older building is not able to meet these companies' standards, then the landlords will lose the IT companies to better quality buildings in the vicinity. Energy inefficiency is another example of functional obsolescence, as many companies are now more cognizant of their environmental footprint and may require their office landlords to meet the latest energy-efficiency standards.

Once functional obsolescence is identified, the value of its impact can be calculated as the estimated NOI impact divided by a cap rate deemed appropriate by the appraiser. This amount should then also be subtracted from the replacement cost of the building.

A.4.4.3 Location Obsolescence

Location obsolescence occurs when a property's location becomes less desirable due to a variety of factors, such as a precinct's aging demographics, leading to lower consumption power or a change in zoning law, resulting in the property generating a lower NOI.

Many mining towns became irrelevant once the minerals and commodities being mined were depleted. In other cases, small towns serving the needs of long-distance commuters along transport routes ceased being relevant after new national highways and high-speed railways were constructed, bypassing these towns. Many of the town's residents would lose their jobs and relocate to other cities which offer better economic prospects. The retail, office, and residential buildings will decline in occupancy and generate lower NOIs.

Once determined by an appraiser, the value of location obsolescence should be subtracted from the replacement cost.

A.4.4.4 Economic Obsolescence

Economic obsolescence is the result of economic conditions that make it impractical to construct a new building. This is typically caused by market conditions that lead the cost of construction to exceed the value generated by the building. An example of economic obsolescence can be seen from examples of cities that could not recover from high unemployment rates and high crime rates, leading to poor maintenance and general degradation of properties in those cities.

A.4.4.5 Drawbacks of the Cost Approach

Given the potential for error when estimating the magnitude of physical deterioration, functional obsolescence, location obsolescence, and economic obsolescence, the biggest shortcoming of the cost approach is the subjectivity of these estimates. The degree of error is more pronounced for older properties or properties with a large degree of obsolescence. These cases require a highly skilled and experienced appraiser to provide the best estimates. The cost approach is better suited for determining the value of newer properties with modern designs in a market with a reasonable number of land transactions, as well as availability of construction cost data.

Additionally, a key assumption of the cost approach is that an investor would never pay more for an existing building than the cost to acquire the land and construct a comparable property, but this assumption is not always accurate. Quite often investors actually do pay a premium for an existing property rather than build a new one, for example:

1. Constructing a new property would be take too much time and management resources.

2. A long gestation period is expected, e.g., for planning, design, and approvals.

3. Other valuation methods derive a higher property value than the cost approach.

A.4.5 The Sales Comparison Approach

The sales comparison approach determines the value of a property based on the transaction data of similar, and comparable, properties in the current market. The intuition behind this approach is that an investor will not acquire a property if he or she could purchase similar properties for less.

Properly identifying comparable properties is essential to using this approach, but it is difficult as no two properties are identical. To improve on what is considered "similar," investors should take these attributes into account: location of property, age, land size, built-up area, land tenure, type of use, and the physical condition of the property. Once similar properties have been identified, adjustments must be made to account for any differences. Examples of adjustments include:

1. **Age:** A property's value tends to decline with its age, so an older property will typically yield a lower price per square foot than a newer property. Even with regular maintenance and renovations, constant wear and tear will cause parts of the building and equipment to suffer incurable deterioration.

2. **Location:** A property in a sought-after location is expected to be more valuable than a property elsewhere. Hence, a well-located property will likely be valued higher, on a dollar per square foot basis, than a property in a less desirable street block or precinct.

3. **Condition:** A property judged to be in good condition is typically more valuable than a property that has visible signs of deterioration. An old building could be renovated and repainted so that the visible flaws are covered up but an inspection of the mechanical and electrical (M&E) installations, such as plumbing, cables, and other equipment, could reveal a lot more about the condition of the building.

Finally, the dates of transaction of the selected, comparable properties need to be considered. Recency is prioritized as the more recent transactions would hold better relevance due to ever-changing market conditions, including interest rates, government policies, population, and so on. The data from sales of comparable properties could include transactions from the recent months or as far back as five years. Adjustments have to be made to account for movements in the market since the dates of sale.

A.4.5.1 Drawbacks of the Sales Comparison Approach

The sales comparison approach's largest shortcoming is its heavy reliance on the transaction data of comparable properties. In certain markets where transactions are infrequent and the property assets vary in shape and size, little transaction data are available. And even where available, they may not be comparable. For example, within a single industrial park, the sizes of factories and the sizes of the land plots they are built on could vary from 10,000 square feet to 1,000,000 square feet. Out of the dozens of factories in that industrial park, there could be one transaction every one to two years, and they are of different sizes and built to different specifications. In this scenario, appraisers will not use the sales comparison approach to provide valuation reports to their clients.

The sales comparison approach works best in active and liquid markets that produce large volumes of transaction data. Even under these conditions, however, sufficient data may not be available for specific property types, such as retirement facilities and mixed development buildings.

Another drawback of this approach is its assumption that all investors value properties equally. In reality, the motivations and circumstances of investors vary, leading each investor to value the same property higher or lower depending on their investment intent and management capabilities.

A.4.6 Reconciliation Between Different Valuation Approaches

Applying the income, cost, and sales comparison approaches to a property will usually result in three different values. This divergence is the result of the three approaches relying on different datasets, and imperfect data and assumptions. Market inefficiencies also contribute to this variation. An appraiser must reconcile these differences and, as best as possible, draw on previous experience to objectively qualify the opinions to arrive at a final property value.

Often, appraisers utilize two or all three approaches before concluding on the final property value. Where a valuation approach may not be meaningful due to insufficient conditions being met, an appraiser must determine the most accurate valuation approach and explain why that approach provides a better representation of the property's value. In a case where the cost approach is chosen, all the adjustments arising from deterioration have to be qualified, explained, and justified so that interested parties reading the valuation report (e.g., investors, financiers, tax officials, etc.) may understand the appraiser's rationale in deriving the property value.

A.4.7 International Valuation

It is becoming increasingly common for firms to invest internationally in this globally connected economy in search of diversification and higher returns. Investors need to familiarize themselves with the different practices and property laws applied to property valuation across countries. It is important to note that despite cross-border differences, such as currencies, laws, and building standards, the underlying principles and characteristics of international real estate and the valuation approaches are still applicable.

For instance, appraisers in Germany and Japan will value a property by summing the value of the building and the value of the land it sits on, possibly using the income approach for the building and sales comparison approach for the land. In Singapore and Australia, properties are commonly valued as a single asset without differentiating the value of the land component.

Many real estate and finance terminologies differ between countries. Investors need to familiarize themselves with the proper terms in which they are investing to avoid potentially costly miscommunication. For instance, units of measure vary by country. Real estate professionals in Japan, Korea, and Taiwan measure floor area in tsubo, pyeong, and ping, respectively. A tsubo in Japan (which is equal to a pyeong in Korea and a ping in Taiwan) is approximately 3.3 square meters or 35.5 square feet.

Conversion of units of measures may complicate communications too. A Canadian investment analyst comparing two investment opportunities, say, an office building in Sydney, Australia, versus an office building in Tokyo, Japan, would need to carefully convert the rents in Sydney, quoted in Australian dollars per square foot per year, and the rents in Tokyo, quoted in Japanese yen per tsubo per month, to Canadian dollars. Getting definitions correct is the foundation of good investment analysis.

International investors must also understand legislative differences. These could be the local tax laws, safety and engineering standards, or land tenure and land ownership restrictions. For example, industrial properties in Singapore can have land tenures ranging from 30-years leasehold, 60-years leasehold, 99-years leasehold to freehold.

A.5 Due Diligence

Due diligence is typically performed by multiple parties in a transaction, but primarily by investors, appraisers, and lenders for the purpose of an acquisition. Given the time and the efforts required from various parties, due diligence is only performed once a transaction is likely to be consummated. Typically, when an investor decides to invest in a property, they will provide a letter of intent to the seller to confirm the interest. The letter of intent will include a statement that the offer is subject to a round of due diligence checks. If any substantial issues are revealed during this process, the investor may renegotiate the price or withdraw from the transaction.

Due diligence performed on the property involves checking on:

1. **the physical property:** for example, inventory list, visible signs of deterioration, procuring the services of a qualified engineer to provide an engineering audit report, etc.;

2. **the legal contracts tied to the property:** such as tenancy agreements, suppliers' service contracts, property and land titles, etc.;

3. **the financials of the property:** such as terms of the loans, revenues and expenses, taxes, bank account balances, late collections, controls and governance, etc.;

4. **the management of the property:** for example, checks on credit quality, track record, and reputation could be done on the quality of the asset manager, the property manager, and other service providers.

The scope of work in due diligence is very wide. Astute investors need to be thorough and attentive in checking on the investment property before proceeding to complete the acquisition. In other cases where the property investment is indirect, through a fund manager, additional due diligence would have to be performed on the quality and experience of the fund management company and the team in charge of this investment opportunity. Readers may refer to Chapter 1, Section 1.2.5 for further discussion on this topic.

A.6 The Four Quadrants of Real Estate Investment

The first half of this chapter has provided an overview of the range of real estate segments and the drivers that contribute revenue, costs, demand, and supply to each segment. That was followed by a brief outline of several real estate valuation approaches and the process of due diligence prior to investing capital in real estate assets. Having established the foundations, the next step in the investment process is for the investor to consider where to allocate capital.

A.6.1 Categorizing Real Estate into Four Quadrants

In a 2003 article entitled "Why Real Estate? An Expanding Role for Institutional Investors," in the *Journal of Portfolio Management*, Susan Hudson-Wilson, Frank J. Fabozzi, and Jacques N. Gordon[3] stated that the primary reasons for investors to include any new categories of assets in an investment portfolio are: (1) to reduce the overall portfolio risk by including assets that respond differently to market fluctuations; (2) to earn returns well above the risk-free rate; and (3) to hedge against unexpected inflation or deflation.

In several research publications, Hudson-Wilson advocated that institutional fund managers should include real estate as a part of their investment portfolios because real estate as an asset class reduces an investment portfolio's risks and enhances the cash returns of the portfolio, outperforming stocks and bonds. The traditional investors narrowly defined real estate investments as private real estate equity (i.e., direct ownership of properties) and private real estate debt (i.e., loans or mortgages provided against properties). Given the expanded availability of securitized real estate assets, Hudson-Wilson suggested a broadened definition of real estate to include public real estate equities (i.e., shares of Real Estate Investment Trusts or Real Estate Operating Companies that are listed on stock exchanges) and public real estate debt (i.e., debt or bonds backed by properties or by real estate companies, sometimes structured as commercial mortgage-backed securities, and tradable on public markets).

Categorizing real estate investments based on their public and private trading characteristics as well as by the bundle of rights to real estate, either through debt or through equity, provides investors with the four quadrants approach of allocating capital to real estate.

The framework for the four quadrants of real estate investment is illustrated in Figure A.13 by Timbercreek Asset Management, a multibillion-dollar real estate fund manager. The four quadrants approach considers institutional investors allocating capital to real estate from a large multi-asset investment portfolio. The funds set aside for real estate investments could be divided among several or all four quadrants.

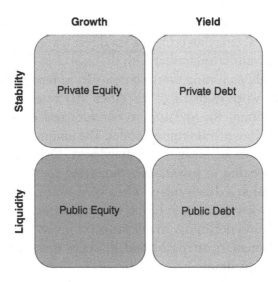

FIGURE A.13. The four quadrants of real estate investment.

Source: Timbercreek Asset Management, https://www.investmentexecutive.com/in-depth_/partner-reports/4-quadrant-approach-to-real-estate-investing/, accessed July 26, 2022.

This framework may also be seen from the standpoint of a fundraiser. The four quadrants offer a framework for thinking about project financing for fundraisers such as real estate developers and fund managers. For instance, a listed real estate developer looking to buy a significant property might think about funding the purchase using a combination of public equity (by issuing more shares), private equity (through a joint venture with a real estate fund), public debt (by issuing public bonds), and private debt (via a loan from a bank).

This section's primary focus is from the perspective of an investor deploying capital, not from the point of view of a fundraiser.

A.6.2 Investing in the Real Estate Quadrants

Each of the four quadrants is not as accessible as the others, and due to the difference in risk-return characteristics, attracts different investors. The size of initial investments in certain quadrants, such as private equity, can be large and prohibitive. Additionally, the risks and investment duration of each quadrant may be appealing for some investors but may not work for others.

Less-experienced real estate investors may lean toward private equity deals. Real estate investments via direct ownership of properties are, for most investors unfamiliar with the asset class, the most intuitive option. After all, collecting monthly rents from tenants is what many people picture when thinking of real estate investment.

It is important for investors to consider real estate investments beyond the obvious private equity model. The uniqueness of each quadrant brings its own advantages and drawbacks. Depending on market conditions, investing in private debt financing for an office building could be viewed as a disadvantage when economic conditions are hot, or it could be viewed as a safe haven investment when market conditions are weak and declining. Many property investors take advantage of the complementary strengths and diversify their real estate assets across multiple quadrants.

One more point to highlight before we move on to discuss the pros and cons of each quadrant. The quadrants represent four methods of investment in real estate assets. Each quadrant has its own characteristics which bring about its unique risks, returns, and investment time periods. The risks and returns of real estate assets also vary according to the segments that are chosen.

For example, let us consider a US$20 million private equity investment for a warehouse, situated in an industrial park, which is under construction with an investment period of two years (i.e., it will be divested after the construction is complete and tenants installed). On the other hand, we have a US$20 million private equity investment in a Grade A office building in the CBD with a holding period of five years. Both are similar-sized private equity investments but the risks are vastly different. First, the industrial property segment is generally considered more volatile than the office property segment. Second, the warehouse is located in an industrial park where the land value and the liquidity of land transactions are likely to be inferior to those of the offices in the CBD. In the case of an economic downturn, it would be challenging to divest the warehouse, especially since it is still under construction. The office building in the CBD will be less challenging for the investor to divest.

The example above illustrates another dimension of investment selection: the physical attributes of the property. The warehouse is still under construction and therefore the intrinsic value of the investment is the value of the land. The office building has tenants and a steady cash flow from monthly rents being paid to the investor and therefore, on a comparative basis, the risks are much lower than that of the warehouse development project. Real estate investors classify properties as core, core plus, value-add, and opportunistic to reflect the different risks-returns profiles based on the physical states of the property (Figure A.14).

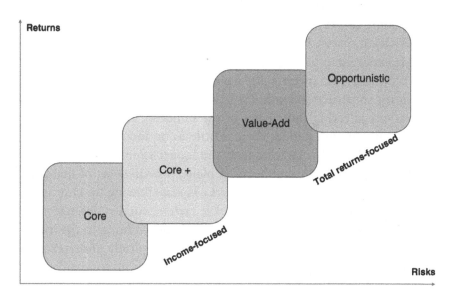

FIGURE A.14. Expected risks-returns characteristics of real estate in various physical states of development.

In the above example, the office building is a core asset, which is described as a conservative investment that has low risks because the property is in a good quality location, has creditworthy tenants, and is in a well-built condition, such that no significant upgrading or renovation expenses are expected in the next 5–10 years. Operational risks and market risks will still be present. Otherwise, the risks of losses are relatively low and therefore the expected returns are low as well.

Core plus properties have most of the characteristics of core properties except that their risks are higher due to one or a few factors such as a need for façade enhancements, or improving the quality of management to uplift rents to market levels, or to rebrand the building to improve the tenant mix, and so on. A core plus asset owner is usually able to generate a higher NOI through active management of the asset.

Value-add properties have higher risks than core plus and require additional capital investments to upgrade the asset. In this context, upgrading means extensive renovations to the building, such as changing the electricals and wiring to reduce energy usage and upgrading the communications infrastructure, enhancing accessibility for tenants and visitors who are physically challenged, upgrading sanitation facilities, and so on. During the renovation period, the asset owner may have to forego some rental income as new tenants may not be willing to take up the vacant spaces. However, post-renovations, new and renewal tenants are expected to pay significantly higher rents of, say, 30% or more.

Opportunistic investments have the highest risks as they involve significant construction works for new property development or major renovations affecting most parts of the building. During the renovation or construction period, there is little to no income and cash flow is negative. Risks also increase with the longer time period from land purchase, approvals for architectural plans, procurement of materials, and construction works until revenues can start flowing in. During the construction period, a range of market factors, such as interest rates, inflation, and government policies could change, adding to the investment risks. Opportunistic investment risks are typically undertaken by experienced professionals and property development companies that are well backed by capital.

In summary, investors in real estate need to consider three dimensions for their capital allocation strategy:

1. **The real estate segments to focus on, e.g., residential, office, retail, hospitality, industrial, etc.**
2. **The physical attributes and risks-returns profile of the assets: core, core plus, value-add, and opportunistic.**
3. **The method of investment: the four quadrants of private equity, private debt, public equity, and public debt.**

Due to the specialist knowledge required in managing real estate portfolios, investors may allocate their capital to a mix of the four quadrants but sharply focus on specific segments and physical attributes. For example, a private equity fund manager may be focused on opportunistic investments in the hospitality segment, which means the fund manager invests in land to build hotels, resorts, and serviced apartments. A public listed property developer could choose to focus on opportunistic investments by building offices. As with any investment, the best returns will go to investors willing to assume the highest risks. Investors who prefer safer assets will be compensated with lower returns.

Putting all the information above together, if we combined the four quadrants and the four risks-returns characteristics, the following matrix will result (Figure A.15).

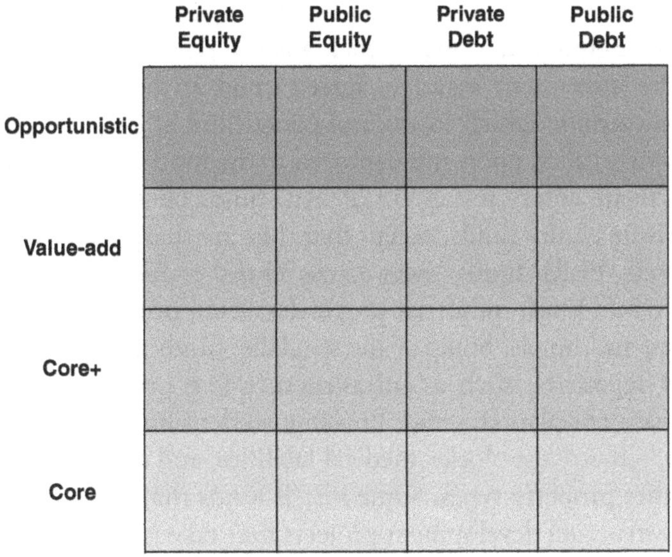

FIGURE A.15. 4x4 matrix of real estate portfolio allocation.

These classifications will allow real estate portfolio managers to frame their thinking about how their funds could be allocated and invested. Filling out the cells with the percentage of funds invested in that cell may highlight the concentration risks in a particular area, or reveal the gaps which could be tapped to improve portfolio returns or reduce portfolio risks.

Applying dates and timelines to this matrix may also guide a portfolio manager on how the invested funds may shift in allocation over the next few years. This is because property investments that will be maturing and then divested will see their capital and profits (or losses) returned. Frequently the bulk of these funds are reinvested in other debt, buildings, and projects in the same cell. However, sensing new opportunities or concentration risks, the fund manager could shift the funds to another cell.

A.6.3 Private Equity

Private equity investments involve large capital investments in the direct ownership of real estate. Given that they are not publicly traded, these investments are illiquid but offer the potential of stability and capital gains in addition to regular cash flow yield.

Private equity fund managers manage a pool of resources according to the investment mandate agreed upon at the fund's inception. Investors commit capital to the real estate fund at its outset, which is subsequently called upon and deployed in the fund's first years of operations. Private equity real estate (PERE) funds operate similarly to all other private equity funds, except that they are sharply focused on real estate assets. PERE funds invest across all real estate segments, including office buildings, industrial properties, retail properties, apartment buildings, and hotels. Some of the specialist funds also invest in niche property segments, such as infrastructure (e.g., toll roads, airports, water treatment plants), senior housing, student hostels, workers' dormitories, self-storage blocks, medical facilities, and data centers among many other property types. Some PERE funds that invest in property and infrastructure development projects may take two to three years to draw on the capital committed by investors.

Real estate investors may skip PERE funds and acquire real estate directly. Funds held by insurance companies, especially premiums paid for life insurance, are mainly invested in long-term, stable assets. Pension funds have the same needs. Managers of insurance and pension funds invest the bulk of their funds in real estate-related assets for 10 years or 30 years and longer. Real estate is one class of assets that allows the insurance and pension fund managers to match the long tenure of their funds with the steady long-term returns provided by real estate assets. It is common to see insurance and pension funds investing in office, retail, and residential buildings and holding them for decades.

A.6.3.1 Investing via Private Equity

To begin the investment process, investors should define their investment objectives clearly. The objectives, such as the period of investment, minimum returns hurdle, cash flow, and so on, will delineate the types of real estate segments and opportunities to select. The objectives will also determine if the investors might buy assets directly or invest through PERE funds which have similar investment objectives.

Investing directly in a physical asset is relatively straightforward. For investors choosing to invest via a PERE fund, there are a few more steps to complete. First, the investor should review the fund mandate. This spells out the controls and limits of what the fund may invest in and what the fund managers are authorized to do. Some examples of these controls and limits are concentration limits on a particular segment, loan-to-value limits, extent of discretion for the manager to spend on renovations and building upgrades, regularity of dividend payments, and so on. Since each fund has its own set of investment mandate, and its own controls and limits, PERE funds vary greatly in style and approach.

Second, investors need to consider the track record and quality of the management team. This step is crucial, as the success of a fund is dependent on its managers' ability to manage the property investments, maximize revenue opportunities, and ensure that the objectives of the fund are met. The manager also needs to be knowledgeable about the relative risk-reward dynamics and market trends which could affect the performance of the assets. For instance, the retail segment was once booming, but the growth of e-commerce and the Covid-19 pandemic have greatly harmed the segment. A good manager would not only be tracking the trend closely but would take action to reconfigure the tenant mix or divest the property before revenues decline further.

Most importantly, investors need to conduct thorough due diligence on the fund management firm and its track record. This review should cover the fund's property selection process, the property acquisition process, the asset management process, the valuation policy, the risk management, legal and compliance procedures, financial controls, and reporting. This list is far from exhaustive, and investors should do as much research on a fund, and its fund manager, as possible before investing.

A.6.3.2 The Benefits of Private Equity

The key benefit of private equity real estate investments is that property valuation does not change by the day and its returns are not highly correlated with public market returns. This makes PERE investments an excellent tool for injecting stability when diversifying a standard investment portfolio of stocks and bonds.

PERE investments tend to yield higher returns than other asset classes especially if we include opportunistic and value-add investments, such as the development of land or the major upgrading of a building. Development of a building from the ground up usually results in an asset with a value much higher than the costs of land plus construction. An opportunistic investor creates new value on a land site just as an entrepreneur creates new value by growing a new business.

The private equity route also offers an increased amount of control to investors. An investor who is the direct owner or the lead investor of the property can decide how the operations and management of the building are to be run and can respond to changing economic conditions.

A.6.3.3 The Disadvantages of Private Equity

Despite its many benefits, private equity has its disadvantages. One of the biggest deterrents is the illiquidity of physical real estate. The time taken to acquire a building, from studying the opportunity to making an offer, through to due diligence and finally the contractual completion, takes at least three months. Even when economic conditions are rosy, a building changes owners only once every 5–10 years. When economic conditions are bleak, there are fewer buyers and financiers in the market. So investors who need to divest buildings during a slow economy may take several months to find interested buyers and then another three months to complete the transaction. This means that during recessionary periods, PERE investors who are hard-pressed for cash are unable to liquidate their real estate assets in a short time.

Another disadvantage of private equity is that it requires more active management and oversight than investing in debt and mortgage products, or in publicly listed instruments. This is especially true for investors who have direct ownership of buildings. The investment managers must be capable of selecting profitable investments, investing in the buildings, and then getting their asset management colleagues to manage the assets. A good quality asset management team will enhance the value of the properties over a few years, increasing rental returns, improving operational efficiency, and keeping a lid on costs. Finally, after five or more years of holding the assets, the investment manager will divest the assets at or above the targeted returns.

An additional disadvantage of investing in private equity in the area of property development is that it requires investors to accept negative cash flows in the early stages. The initial payment for land acquisition is significant. Subsequently expenses are racked up for architecture design, and planning approvals, construction of the foundation, the building structure and then the interiors, the façade, landscaping, and general facilities. When the construction is within about six to nine months to completion, the pre-leasing activities can begin and prospective tenants who sign up will pay a deposit to secure the space that they wish to occupy. So, only after three years of negative cash flows will investors begin to receive some cash inflow, and the deposit money is not even recognizable as income. Investors would have to wait until the building is certified for occupiers to move in, then rents can be collected from tenants who have signed up. Positive cash flow may only be seen after the building is sufficiently occupied, which could be a year after the construction is completed. The lack of positive cash flows in the early years increases uncertainty, and some investors are deterred from invest- ing in development properties. For other investors, the uplift in the asset valuation (i.e., the increase in the value of the building after it is fully tenanted minus the total cost of land and construction) could represent a paper profit of more than 50% during the three to four years of the property development period. Investors could then hold the completed building for many more years to enjoy the positive cash flow from rental collection. Alternatively, investors could divest the building within two years of completion as the expected future increase in property value will be modest once the property is fully tenanted.

To some investors, the disadvantages described are seen as a strength of PERE investments. The added benefits of diversification of risks, higher potential returns, and management control make PERE investments lucrative for investors who have sufficient risk appetite and resources.

A.6.4 Public Equity

In the public markets, real estate investing takes the form of acquiring the common shares of Real Estate Operating Companies (REOCs) and Real Estate Investment Trusts (REITs). Exchange-traded funds (ETFs) that are focused on REOCs and REITs offer another route for investors who want exposure to real estate through public equity. Real estate ETFs may also allocate a small fraction of their funds to companies that provide real estate services. The public equity quadrant is considered to be the most liquid form of real estate investment.

In many public markets around the world, REOCs are known as property developers. For a property developer, listing the company's shares on the stock market is one major source of funding to expand on development activities such as land acquisition and construction or acquiring a rundown neighborhood for gentrification and upgrading. Examples of large property developers are Berkeley Group, listed on the London Stock Exchange, Daiwa House Industry Co, Ltd, listed on the Tokyo Stock Exchange, and New World Development Company Limited, listed on the Hong Kong Stock Exchange.

A REIT is a legal entity, structured in the form of a trust, which invests and holds property assets on behalf of investors. It is similar to a closed-end fund with income-producing real estate as its main investment focus. Most of the REITs are listed on stock exchanges and are accessible to all the retail investors and institutional investors. Hence, REITs are generally considered public equity instruments. In jurisdictions where REITs are given significant tax advantages, wealthy investors and PERE funds could create REITs to hold their property assets so as to benefit from the tax advantages. These REITs may remain private REITs (i.e., not be listed on stock exchanges) until the owners decide to list them on the market or divest the assets held by the REITs. Examples of listed REITs include Avalon Bay Communities Inc., listed on the New York Stock Exchange; CICC GLP Warehouse Logistics, listed on the Shanghai Stock Exchange; and Goodman Group, listed on the Australia Stock Exchange.

The advent of blockchain technology has brought a new trend to the real estate investment world. Property ownership may now be structured and securitized inexpensively on a blockchain platform. The securities, also known as tokens, are backed by real estate. The tokens may be traded on the blockchain platform which acts as a public exchange in which a large number of investors can participate. This process is also known as the fractionalization of real estate, breaking down what used to be lumpy expensive properties into smaller bite-sized assets so that more investors can invest in real estate. The trend of real estate tokenization was discussed in Chapter 4, Section 4.5.

A.6.4.1 Understanding Listed REOCs and REITs

To understand the public equity quadrant of real estate investing, investors should be familiar with the characteristics of companies listed on the stock exchanges. A listed company issues shares to investors through a stock exchange. These shares can be traded on the exchange on any business day and the share prices could be different at the end of every business day. A company may be listed only if it complies with securities regulations and the rules of the exchange. It could also be delisted if it fails to meet exchange requirements. Depending on the jurisdictions under which the exchanges operate, listed companies need to provide quarterly or semi-annual financial reports to their investors and the exchanges.

Investors in the stock markets generally look out for a common set of financial indicators (e.g., Earnings Per Share (EPS), Debt Equity Ratio (D/E Ratio), Profit Margin Ratio, Price Earnings Ratio (PER), Growth Earnings Multiple, Return on Assets (ROA), Return on Equity (ROE), etc.).

However, given the characteristics of real estate (illiquid, large chunky investments, long gestation periods with negative cash flow in the initial years, variances in valuation, etc.), there are several important financial indicators that investors need to pay attention to when reviewing the financial reports of REOCs and REITs.

Merely analyzing changes in a publicly traded real estate company's revenue, however, is not enough. Investors must also consider the factors influencing revenue across the various business activities over the past few years. This step is especially important for REOCs, which often undertake a range of real estate activities, such as property development, asset management, etc.

Investors should also research a company's strategic plan before investing, again paying attention to changes over time. For instance, if a publicly traded real estate company is decreasing its investment in the hotel segment, then an investor might question why. Typically, a company's strategic plan changes in response to industry changes. So, perhaps the hotel segment's profitability has declined in recent years, prompting the firm to invest elsewhere. In fact, simply noticing a trend is not enough; investors must also be knowledgeable of the drivers behind a trend to make a proper investment decision.

A.6.4.2 *Valuing Publicly Traded Real Estate Assets*

Just as there are various valuation methods for individual properties, several methods are used for valuing listed real estate companies. As real estate assets are illiquid, we need to pay attention to the companies' cash flow and how they use debt. In addition, we will discuss two indicators commonly used to measure the health of listed REOCs and REITs: the Net Asset Value Per Share (NAVPS) and the Funds From Operations (FFO).

A.6.4.3 *Debt Used by REOCs and REITs*

Debt is an important factor for investors to consider before investing in a listed real estate company. To assess the attractiveness of REOCs and REITs, investors look at the amount of debt versus the amount of equity that a company deploys to finance its investments and operations. Key questions around debt include: how much has the company's debt grown or shrunk over the past few years? How much of this year's financial growth is funded by the company's operating cash flows and how much is funded by borrowings?

Additionally, investors should be careful investing in a company that has massively increased its borrowings over a short period of time. Sudden increases in borrowing are typically negative and analysts should research and question the reason for borrowing before making their investment recommendations.

If the ratio of debt versus equity is 1-to-1, we would consider the REOC or REIT as a low risk and safe company. In simple terms, a debt-to-equity (D/E) ratio of 1-to-1 means that the asset value is comprised of one part debt and one part equity, or a gearing of 100%. In simple, practical terms, this is equivalent to a REOC or REIT that is worth US$1 billion but has a total debt of US$500 million. If we applied this metric to a single building, such as an office tower that is financed by one part debt and one part equity, we would say that the building has a loan-to-value (LTV) ratio of 50%.

A D/E ratio of 2-to-1 implies a gearing level of 200% or an LTV of 66.7%, while a D/E ratio of 3-to-1 implies a 300% gearing and an LTV of 75%. It is generally considered risky to go beyond a gearing of 300%. However, during the past two decades of low interest rates, businesses and investors tended to take on higher levels of debt because cheap debt could enhance the ROE significantly.

There is no standard benchmark for what is considered "safe," but let us consider this example. If a company owned just a single building worth US$100 million and the building is financed by a loan of US$75 million and shareholders' capital of US$25 million, the building has an LTV of 75%, and if the company has no other assets or loans, the company has a gearing of 300%. When the market condition weakens and the value of the building drops to US$90 million, the bank loan of US$75 million is still backed by an asset that is worth US$90 million but the gearing has increased to 500%. However, if the value of the building drops to, say, US$80 million, even though there is still US$5 million of equity in the building, the lender may start to get nervous and negotiate with the company to repay or reduce the loan. If the value of the building dropped to US$75 million, the lender would probably have to take legal action to seize the asset, sell it, and recover the loan. The lender might recover less than the US$75 million it provided to the company while the shareholders would be left with negative equity in the company (i.e., essentially a bankrupt company).

In this example, the company and the building having 75% debt versus 25% equity are considered safe from the viewpoint that property values have to decline by 25% or more before risking a default on the loan. However, where market conditions may be more volatile, lenders may feel that a 25% margin is still too risky and therefore only lend to borrowers who require 70% or lower LTV.

Maturation of debt is another factor for investors to consider. Investors should consider the debt repayment profile of the REOCs and REITs to understand whether there could be cash flow bottlenecks in future. Most financing terms require a large repayment of principal at the end of the loan period, and the company's income streams may not be sufficient to repay its obligations. In such cases, refinancing of the debt would be required at the end of the loan period, failing which, the company may be pressed to divest an asset to meet its obligations.

Given the heavy capital investments required to invest in property assets, debt plays an important role in REOCs, REITs, and direct single building investments.

A.6.4.4 NAVPS

The net asset value per share approach (NAVPS) is useful for investors entering the public equity quadrant. The approach entails subtracting a company's total liabilities from its tangible assets to derive the net asset value, or NAV, and then dividing the NAV by the number of shares issued:

NAVPS = Net Asset Value / Number of Shares Issued

Another simplistic way of looking at this indicator is that an investor who owns one share of the company will receive the equivalent of the NAVPS amount of assets should the company go into liquidation. For this indicator, non-tangible assets, such as goodwill and deferred tax liability, are not included in the NAVPS calculation, since these would be difficult or impossible to sell upon liquidation.

This method is related to the concept of the "book value" which is reported by listed companies. In the case of real estate companies, the book values may include goodwill and other intangible assets, such as IT services and high-tech equipment for data centers, and therefore it is better to estimate the NAV of the company instead of accepting the book value as reported.

The inputs into the NAV calculation consider current market values rather than book values as the book values could be based on historical values, at time of acquisition or at cost, which may not reflect the current values of the properties. For public REOCs and REITs, the appraisals of the asset values will be included in the quarterly or half-annual financial reports made publicly available by the company. If the appraised value of an asset seems outdated or appears inaccurate, perhaps due to a recent extensive renovation exercise, investors can use one of the three valuation methods explained in Section A.4 "Real Estate Valuation" to make adjustments to the reported value.

Hence, NAVPS calculations involve more than simply relying on the listed company's reported numbers. In the case of REOCs that have assets in various stages of development, from land sites, to semi-constructed projects, to completed buildings that have tenants paying rents, the companies are constantly increasing in value as the construction works progress. As such, most investment analysts studying the valuation of REOCs will estimate their NAVs using a DCF approach.

Applying the DCF approach to estimate the asset values of REITs and REOCs provides analysts with a fundamental baseline value of these companies' physical assets. The assumptions about future market conditions and discount rates have to be applied consistently. Analysts may also take into consideration other factors affecting the companies and make adjustments to the asset values to derive estimates for what they think the companies are worth (i.e., the companies' market values). These factors may include the management team's expertise, changing trends of revenue streams from the properties, possible changes to construction timelines, ability to secure land sites, and so on.

If the share price of the REOC or the REIT on the stock exchange is higher than the NAVPS that is estimated by the investment analyst, the company is said to be trading at a premium. Conversely, when the NAVPS is greater than the share price on the stock exchange, the REIT or the REOC is said to be selling at a discount, which means that the stock could be attractive to investors since it signals that stock market players have undervalued the company. The stock prices trading at a premium or a discount to the NAVPS could also mean that investors have a different view about the near-term financial performance of the company. This disconnect between market valuation and asset valuation is the result of various factors affecting the outlook of the company.

While the NAVPS approach is used to value both REOCs and REITs, it should be noted that REIT portfolios are primarily made up of income-producing properties, which makes it easier to value each of the REIT's assets using the DCF approach. A substantial portion of REOCs' assets, on the other hand, could be bare land or buildings under construction, where cash flows could be lumpier. Applying the DCF approach would involve many more assumptions in terms of the timing of expenses and revenue.

Given that accounting definitions and standards can vary drastically by country, an analyst using the NAVPS approach must begin by understanding the accounting practices of the region in which they are investing. For instance, the International Financial Reporting Standards (IFRS) records asset values based on the fair value of the investment property. Under the US Generally Accepted Accounting Principles (US GAAP), however, investments are recorded based on their historical value. NAVPS is most useful when accounting is based on fair value rather than historical value. Analysts need to be cognizant about the accounting methods applied to the asset values so they can be confident about the value of an REOC or REIT.

A.6.4.5 FFO and AFFO

Many businesses fail due to cash flow issues, and in real estate, the lumpy nature of land and building acquisition and property development requires careful cash flow planning. An REOC could be profitable, but if the timing of cash flow is not properly managed, it could still seize up. Cash outflow from land purchase, construction, interest payments, and other operating expenses needs to be timed properly to align with cash inflows from bank loans, sales of properties, and rents. Delays to construction work, weak income from sales and rents, and an inability to secure financing or refinancing would see an REOC at risk of being in default of payments. To a lesser extent, REITs are also exposed to cash flow challenges. REITs are committed to pay out more than 90% of their profits as dividends, and they have relatively low levels of retained profits to buffer against unexpected expenses.

Therefore, analysts rely on another investment metric called funds from operations (FFO) to analyze the health of REOCs and REITs. The FFO is an indicator reported by REITs and REOCs, particularly in the real estate industry in the United States. It is calculated using the profits, or net income of the company, adding back the losses from property divestments and the expenses from depreciation and amortization, and subsequently less the gains from property divestments and the income from bank interest.

Building on this, analysts also use the adjusted funds from operations (AFFO) to fine-tune the FFO formula to account for a variety of factors, such as provisions for routine maintenance capital expenditures, and leasing commissions. No fixed AFFO formula exists, as the needs of different investors and the structures of different companies mean that each investment requires its own unique set of adjustments. When making adjustments, analysts have to be cognizant of changes to, for example, tax laws and depreciation items. Forecasting and making provisions for the needed capital expenditures for the next few years are extremely difficult. As a result, two skilled and experienced analysts using the AFFO method may derive widely different price estimates when examining the same REIT.

The FFO and the AFFO valuation methods aid analysts:

1. Examining the cash flows gives a more accurate picture of a REIT's or REOC's performance since standard accounting measures under IFRS and US GAAP treat depreciation as an expense. Furthermore, property assets in different countries would have different tax and depreciation treatments, so looking at the cash flow is a better way to assess the health of property companies.

2. The FFO and the AFFO are widely accepted as relative value indicators within the real estate industry. Thus, they serve as common valuation metrics for analysts and investors.

3. These multiples may be used in tandem with other valuation metrics, like NAV, to give a broader valuation of a REIT or REOC.

4. The FFO and the AFFO provide investors with a quick method of comparing REITs and REOCs at different valuation levels as well as to industry-average price multiples, allowing investors to quickly identify undervalued or overvalued securities.

However, there are downsides of evaluating REOCs and REITs using the FFO and the AFFO:

1. Investors should not use these metrics as the sole valuation criteria on which to base their investment decision. In isolation, the FFO and the AFFO valuations can paint a skewed picture of a REIT's and a REOC's financial health. These data points must be considered in the context of the underlying property assets of a company to get a more complete picture of its performance.

2. FFOs and AFFOs account for the cash expenses and cash inflows but they do not account for the value of real estate assets owned by the REIT or the REOC. If a property is under development or renovation, its valuation will increase after the construction works are completed. The increased revenues will be captured in the FFO or AFFO calculations but the additional value of the asset will have to be reflected in other financial indicators.

3. While the formula for the FFO is relatively straightforward and the numbers are easily obtained from financial reports, the AFFO requires adjustments made by analysts whose opinions and assumptions could vary widely.

A.6.4.6 Real Estate Investment Trusts (REITs)

REITs offer investors an opportunity to invest in professionally managed real estate portfolios consisting mainly of properties with stabilized rental income. REITs are attractive to investors because of the requirement that REITs pay at least 90% of their taxable income as dividends to their shareholders.

A REIT is structured as a trust vehicle, and a share of a REIT is called a unit. The shareholders of a REIT are known as the unit holders (Figure A.16).

Depending on the jurisdictions where the properties are located and where the REIT is listed, for tax efficiency, REITs acquire properties through special purpose vehicles (SPVs). For each property that the REIT acquires, the REIT sets up an SPV and uses the SPV to acquire the title of the property. The SPV could be an onshore corporate entity or it could be a company registered in an offshore, tax-efficient jurisdiction. The advantages of taking this extra step are multi-fold. When the REIT manager divests the property in the future, they can do so in an efficient and straightforward manner by selling the shares of the SPV to the buyer rather than transferring the property title. In addition, the SPVs accounts and financial statements relating to the property are neat and not co-mingled with other funds, making it easier for the buyer to perform their due diligence prior to investing.

Some REITs are created and majority-owned by large conglomerates or REOCs. These "sponsor" companies are able to develop new

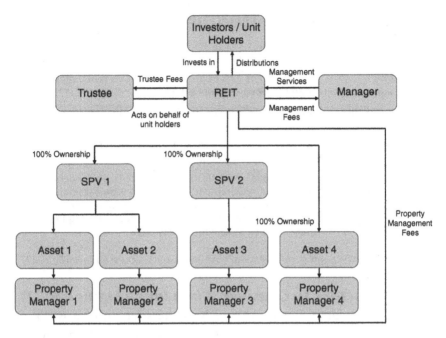

FIGURE A.16. An example of a REIT structure.

buildings, fill them with tenants, stabilize the cash flows, and then sell the buildings to the REITs that they own. This is especially useful for new REITs, as having strong sponsors boosts investor confidence in the stability of the REIT as well as its access to a pipeline of properties for future acquisition. The key characteristics of US REITS are listed in Table A.2.

The REIT manager plays an outsized role in the success of a REIT. A capable and diligent REIT manager will not only ensure that the portfolio of properties is profitable, they will also add value to the assets by improving rental returns and minimizing costs. In order to maximize the assets' returns, REIT managers appoint active property managers and leasing and marketing managers to ensure the efficiency of the daily operations and attract good quality tenants.

Given that a well-managed asset with reputable tenants has good capital gains potential, a REIT manager will always strive to add value through active management. For example, for a retail REIT, regularly hosting consumer events in a mall will attract more shoppers, which will, in turn, attract better tenants and increase revenue. A higher NOI could result from increased revenue, thereby increasing the value of the property and the REIT.

TABLE A.2. Key characteristics of US REITs

Investment type	Invest at least 75% of their total assets in real estate, cash, or US Treasury securities
Main income	A minimum of 75% of gross income from rents, mortgage interests, or sale of real estate
Dividends payable	Pay at least 90% of taxable income as dividends to unit holders
Volatility of income	Low. REITs own properties that have long-term tenants that provide relatively stable revenue streams
Frequency of equity offerings	More frequent than REOCs. Due to the large dividend distribution requirement, REITs retain little earnings to finance new acquisitions. Many of their significant acquisitions have to be financed through offering new shares as well as taking on new debt.

Source: https://www.reit.com/investing/how-invest-reits, accessed July 15, 2022.

A.6.4.7 Factors to Consider When Investing in a REIT

The earlier paragraphs have covered how the strength of a REIT or an REOC may be measured by their debt levels, the NAVPS, and the FFO. In addition, due to the unique characteristic of REITs, investors look closely at their ability to pay dividends regularly.

The main investment objective for most REIT investors is receiving a steady dividend stream derived from the rentals of the property portfolio. A secondary objective could be to derive capital gains from the price of the REIT units that are traded on the stock exchange. Some investors go a step further and look at the potential of whether dividends may continue to grow year after year.

In addition to looking at the absolute amounts paid out in dividends, investors look at the dividend yield. This is derived from the dividend per unit (DPU) paid out per annum divided by the current price of the units. So, for a REIT that is expected to pay 5 cents of dividend in the next 12 months and investors could buy a unit of the REIT for a dollar today, the forward dividend yield is 5% per annum. The inverse of this is the price-to-dividend ratio which could be viewed as an investment of a dollar today will take 20 years to be paid back in dividends.

Investors prefer the DPU to increase at a steady or sustainable rate over time. So, when a REIT acquires an additional building for its portfolio, the REIT manager should ensure that the acquisition is yield-accretive for the investors. That is, the profits contributed by the newly added building should result in a DPU higher than before the acquisition. Given that most REITs finance new acquisitions by issuing new units, the result is that the total dividends will be distributed across more units, diluting the DPU. This is a balance that the REIT manager needs to strike, such that the overall result of the acquisition is a net increase in the DPU and dividend yield.

While investors tend to favor increasing dividend yields, it is important to understand the reasons behind any increase. A rise in dividend yield can be caused by an increase in the DPU, which is a positive outcome if the rental returns have improved or if the expenses have gone down. Conversely, an increase in yields could be a negative signal because it could be the result of a decrease in the unit price caused by investors selling down the units as they expect a weaker outlook for the REIT caused by high interest rates or loss of tenants.

REIT investors who intend to hold REITs over the long term, say for five years and more, may also rely on the dividend discount model (DDM) to value the REITs. This assumes that the value of a REIT unit is worth the present value of the total future dividend stream, discounted for the rate of return that the investors expect. Investors could assume that the dividend stream will be constant (i.e., zero growth) or they could assume a constant growth to the future dividends. The constant growth DDM is also known as the Gordon Growth DDM, and an assumption is made that the REIT will pay dividends that grow at a constant rate into perpetuity. This method of valuing the price of a REIT is similar to the DCF method, and for both these methods, there are several similar weaknesses, such as assumptions made about terminal values and discount rates and not being able to account for share buybacks.

As with investing in any company, investors should thoroughly research a REIT before investing. Analysis should include the REIT's history, management, portfolios, and financials, among other things. Additionally, a REIT's portfolio could span across real estate segments and geographies, so investors need to be cognizant about the country- and sector-dependent context of their investment. Geopolitical trends could also affect the REIT's performance.

A.6.4.8 Variations of REITs

REITs come in different forms. In Australia, REITs were listed on the Australian stock exchange as early as the 1970s, and they were called listed property trusts (LPT). The most common structure of the LPT is a "stapled security" where the listed entity is a combination of two or more legal entities, usually a REIT and an REOC, that are bound together contractually. Each of the legal entities brings their strengths to the listed company: the REIT with its tax advantages and steady cash flow and the REOC with potential for large capital gains derived from property development.

In this structure, the different parts of the stapled security are bound to their respective legislation. Thus, only the portion of an investment portfolio that adopts the REIT model will be subject to REIT regulations and tax incentives. Stapled securities are therefore only obliged to pay unit holders the 90% minimum of rental income as a dividend for properties structured under the REIT entity.

In Singapore, hospitality REITs are listed as stapled securities, which are combinations of a REIT that owns hotels or serviced apartments and a business trust which may be used to smooth out the rents and cash flows from the seasonal variations of the tourism market. The business trust may serve several purposes: to provide rental support to the hotels held by the REIT during the low seasons, to manage hotel operations during interim periods between the out-going and incoming hotel operators, or undertake construction of a new hotel asset, and so on.

Property trusts are similar to REITs as they are considered collective property investment vehicles, having portfolios of income-producing real estate and paying out regular dividends to unit holders. However, these listed property trusts do not qualify as REITs and do not enjoy the same tax privileges. Therefore, they are not bound to pay out 90% of their profits as dividends and they do not have the same restrictions on loans or property development activities. In a way, a property trust is similar to an REOC except that an REOC is a legal entity that is governed under the Companies Act, but a property trust comes under the Trustees Act, which is a regulatory framework that governs the operations of trusts and trustees.

Additionally, REITs in the United States can be categorized into two main types: umbrella partnership REITs (UPREITs) and Down-REITs. An UPREIT is the most common form of REITs in the United

States. The UPREIT structure allows property owners to exchange their assets for units in the UPREIT, and the property owners can defer capital gains taxes on their exchange of the properties for UPREIT units. DownREITs evolved from UPREITs. DownREITs also allow property owners to defer capital gains taxes when contributing the properties to the REIT. However, DownREITs are less popular because they involve a more complicated partnership arrangement between real estate owners and the REIT.

China is a recent entrant to the REITs world, having floated nine REITs on the Shanghai and Shenzhen stock exchanges in June 2021. The REITs are backed by infrastructure projects and industrial parks but they are structured a little differently to the REIT structures that investors are familiar with. They are a unique financial structure that pools investors' money in a closed-end fund, and the fund then invests in asset-backed securities which represent ownership of the underlying assets. In other words, a China REIT does not own the assets directly, but via the ownership of shares of a project company that owns the infrastructure assets.

A.6.4.9 Advantages and Disadvantages of Investing in Public Real Estate Equities

The biggest advantage of investing in listed real estate companies is that they offer greater liquidity than direct investments in properties. Additionally, listed stocks offer more flexibility in timing the realization of cash values and gains or losses than private equity investments.

Another key advantage to publicly traded real estate companies is the smaller amount of capital necessary for investment. Purchasing a share of a real estate portfolio requires far less money than purchasing one building. Thus, more investors are able to enter the real estate investment market through public equity.

Additionally, given their limited liability status, investors in REITs and REOCs bear no liability for the debt and obligations of these companies beyond that of their capital investment. Direct ownership of real estate, on the other hand, leaves owners fully liable for expenses and debt.

Publicly traded real estate investments also offer investors exposure to a wider range and quality of properties. Some iconic and institutional-grade properties cannot be easily acquired, as they are expensive and seldom change ownership. The public equity route allows investors to gain exposure to such properties in their portfolios.

Another advantage of these publicly traded real estate investments is diversification. These companies own a portfolio of properties, and especially for REOCs, from income-producing properties to projects that are in various stages of construction. Many of these companies also spread their risks by diversifying across geographies and real estate segments. Investors can add international properties to their portfolios without having to navigate the legal and tax complications of cross-border investments.

As with all publicly traded instruments, listed real estate companies share the same macro-economic risks, such as market risks, liquidity risks, among others. Even though REITs and REOCs have hard physical assets on their balance sheets, their shares are publicly traded on stock exchanges and are subject to the supply and demand of equities investors in the public markets. Hence, investing in REITs and REOCs may be unprofitable for investors as stock prices may fall even if the underlying properties are performing well.

Owning real estate via REITs and REOCs means that investors have assigned the control, management, and operations of the properties to the companies' management teams and employees. These managers are overseen and guided by the board of directors to ensure that they perform in the best interests of the shareholders and other stakeholders. However, investors do need to review the track record of the management team and see how well they have managed costs. Has management taken on more risks through aggressive land bidding? Have they purchased assets above market prices in the past? Have they taken on very high levels of debt to fund the expansion of the real estate portfolio? Investors need to consider if management decisions have consistently demonstrated that they acted in the shareholders' best interests. A competent management that has a strong sense of responsibility to shareholders and stakeholders (e.g., suppliers, staff, policy-makers, etc.) will bring long-term success and profitability for a REIT or an REOC.

A.6.4.10 Comparing Private and Public Equity

Despite their similarities, private and public equity do vary. For instance, a primary difference between the two funds is their control over decision-making. As publicly listed companies, public equity funds must often call for a vote for important decisions, which can be a costly and time-consuming process. Private equity funds, on the other hand, have greater control over decision-making since they have a smaller number of shareholders. Another difference is that it tends to be easier for publicly listed firms to borrow from lenders, since regular public disclosures improve transparency about the financial strengths of the listed entity. Since it is more difficult for lenders to value PERE firms, PERE firms may find it more challenging to secure long-term loans at low interest rates that are as attractive as what the public companies can obtain.

To further accentuate these differences, Table A.3 compares the main characteristics of private and public equity.

TABLE A.3. Comparison of characteristics of private and public equity

Criterion	Private equity	Public equity
Organization	Small to medium-sized companies with a few to a hundred employees. Special purpose vehicles (SPVs) for tax benefits. Company ownership is private.	Medium to large companies with a few tens to tens of thousands of employees. Company shares are listed and traded on stock exchanges.
Control	Committee of Investors Contractual obligations to investors	Board of Directors Exchange regulated
Information disclosure	Severe informational asymmetry	Quarterly or half-annual disclosure as required by stock exchanges
Investment process	Intensive due diligence	Security analysis
Management of risk	Diversify across projects, stages, real estate segments and countries	Diversify across real estate segments and countries
Liquidity	Highly illiquid	Liquid/marketable
Returns and dispersion	Highly varied returns across years	Relatively stable long-run returns

A.6.5 Private Real Estate Debt

Private debt is debt undertaken by individuals or private companies through a variety of forms, such as bank mortgages, student loans, mezzanine loans, subordinated loans, promissory notes, and debentures. The term private means that this debt is not publicly traded, usually directly between a borrower and a lender. However, it is possible for private debt to become public debt by pooling together multiple loans and securitizing them, which will be discussed in Section A.6.6.

Several years of excessive borrowings and weak oversight in the home loans market created a US housing bubble in the mid-2000s. The fallout resulted in the collapse of renowned financial institutions, such as Bear Sterns and Lehman Brothers, and culminated in the 2008 Global Financial Crisis (GFC) with financial institutions and real estate businesses around the world bleeding severely. The recovery from the economic downturn required the US interest rates to remain low as money printing machines went into overdrive. According to data from the Federal Reserve, also known as the central bank of the United States, commercial and multifamily mortgage debt totaled US$3.4 trillion in 2008, more than double the US$1.6 trillion in year 2000. The total debt declined to US$3.1 trillion in 2012 but on the back of near-zero interest rates climbed to US$5.0 trillion in 2021. In the United States, banks are the largest holders of real estate debt, accounting for half of all the loans. Other categories of real estate debt holders are insurance companies, securitized debt listed and traded on exchanges, and government-sponsored entities (Freddie Mac and Fannie Mae).

Private real estate debt refers to loans secured against real estate, (i.e., loans which are backed by real estate as collateral). The majority of these loans are underwritten by banks, for example, commercial loans secured against a building or a plot of land, or home loans secured against residential properties. Private debt may also be provided by non-bank lenders that are financial services companies and investment funds, such as housing societies, credit unions, and cooperatives. In some countries, property agencies may provide bridging loans to home buyers who are in the middle of purchasing a new home while selling the current home.

To invest in the private debt quadrant, one must understand the needs of the borrower and the lender. Before taking on debt, the borrower must weigh up the cost of debt relative to the cost of equity to ensure that a loan makes financial sense and enhances the investment returns. The borrower needs to be confident that the building or the development project will generate enough income, either through recurring cash flows from rents or from an eventual sale, to be able to fulfill the repayment terms of the loan.

On the other hand, the lender aims to minimize risk by ensuring that the collateral for the loan provides sufficient security in case the borrower defaults on the covenants of the loan contract. The lender undertakes due diligence on the borrower and the asset to verify that the borrower is creditworthy and has no credit issues or previous history of loan defaults and that the asset provided as collateral has a value in excess of the loan amount. Before the borrower can draw down on the loan, the lender and the borrower will enter into a loan contract which spells out the covenants that the borrower needs to abide by. Some examples of loan covenants include the borrower having to maintain an interest coverage ratio where the NOI is at least 1.5 times the annual interest expenses, a loan to value ratio of less than 70%, a bank account maintaining a minimum sum of cash deposits from which interests are paid out, sufficient insurance cover taken out for risks of fire and accidents, and so on.

A.6.5.1 Loan to Value Ratio (LTV) and Interest Coverage Ratio (ICR)

Investors need to understand the key characteristics of real estate debt. The loan to value (LTV) ratio and interest coverage ratio (ICR) are two primary parameters describing the debt taken out on a property. Lenders typically set limits on the loan size using the LTV ratio and the ICR so as to minimize their risks.

The LTV ratio is expressed as the principal amount of the loan divided by the appraised value of the property. Banks lending as senior lenders tend to prefer LTVs of below 75%. This means that if the economy is weak and the borrower goes into liquidation, the bank can seize the property and sell it at 75% of its previously appraised value and still be able to recoup the loan in its entirety. Investors in real estate debt who look at this from the lender's angle may interpret the 75% LTV ratio as a 25% "margin of safety" where asset prices have to drop by 25% before their investments will be in the red. The LTV ratio may be applied to properties in various stages of readiness, from land sites to buildings under construction or buildings under renovation and to completed buildings.

The use of ICR is somewhat more limited as it applies to completed buildings which are investment properties with tenants. The ICR is derived using the annual NOI of a property divided by the expected interest payment for the year. In the case of a building that is occupied by the owner, the ICR may be estimated based on the cash flow and the EBIT (earnings before interest and tax) of the owner's business operations. A variation of the ICR is the debt service coverage ratio (DSCR). In the DSCR, the total debt service includes both the principal and interest payments. Most lenders require borrowers to demonstrate an ICR of above 1.5. An ICR of below 1.0 would mean that the NOI of the property is unable to pay the interest expenses of the loan.

A.6.5.2 Leverage Illustrated

Home loans, commonly referred to as mortgages, make up a large portion of the real estate private debt quadrant. Home loans are taken out by homeowners who purchase the residential properties for their own enjoyment, and they are also taken by investors who have purchased residential properties for investment.

The following is an example that illustrates the power of using debt to enhance the returns on an investor's capital.

Investor A purchases an apartment for $1 million. The apartment generates an annual NOI of $40,000 and attracts an income tax expense of, for illustration purposes, $4,000 per annum. To finance the purchase, the investor uses $300,000 of their own capital and borrows $700,000 from a lender (i.e., the LTV ratio of the loan is 70%). The loan comes with an interest rate of 2.5% per annum. Using this information, we can compare the effects of leverage (Tables A.4 and A.5).

We see that the NOI yield of the apartment, or the cap rate, is 4.0%. This also represents the ungeared, pre-tax returns that the investor would have gotten if they had paid for the $1 million apartment fully and not taken any loans. The returns on the $1 million of capital is reduced to $36,000 (or 3.6%) after accounting for the $4,000 income tax.

With a loan of 70% LTV ratio (i.e., a gearing of 2.3 times) the after-tax returns on the $300,000 capital invested increased to 6.3%

TABLE A.4. Ungeared purchase example

Ungeared purchase		Formula	Comments
Capital invested ($)	1,000,000		The price of the house and related acquisition costs.
Net operating income (NOI) ($)	40,000	Annual rent income – operating expenses	
NOI yield (also seen as cap rate) (%)	4.0	NOI/Capital Invested = $40,000/$1,000,000 = 4.0%	
Tax expense ($)	4,000		This is an arbitrary number assigned for illustrative purposes only.
Net profit ($)	36,000	NOI – Tax expenses = $40,000 – $4,000 = $36,000	
Gearing used (i.e., loan-to-value [LTV] ratio)	None		
Return on capital invested (%)	3.6	Net profit/Capital Invested = $36,000/$1,000,000 = 3.6%	

(Table A.5). Note that with the interest expense, the profit before tax is reduced and therefore the tax is also lower.

Next, assume that Investor A added on a junior loan, or a mezzanine loan, of $200,000 and thereby reduced the amount of capital they invested from $300,000 to $100,000. The gearing on this investment has increased significantly, to 9.0 times. The interest expenses increased, once we add on the interest rate of 5.0% per annum on the $200,000 mezzanine loan. With a lower profit before tax, the income tax dropped to, for example, $3,000. In this scenario, the returns on the invested capital increased to 9.5% per annum (Table A.6).

This simplified example illustrates how gearing increases an investor's return on capital. Without any debt, Investor A would make about 3.6% on their capital of $1 million. Their return on capital increased to 6.3% after taking out a mortgage with a 70% LTV ratio. When Investor A increased the borrowing to 90% LTV ratio, the return on the $100,000 capital that was invested jumped to 9.5%. Having access to debt at a relatively low cost helped Investor A increase their rate of return while reducing the amount of capital they had to inject.

TABLE A.5. Geared purchase using senior loan only example

Geared purchase (using senior loan only)		Formula	Comments
Gearing used, i.e., LTV ratio (%)	70	70% × $1,000,000 = $700,000	
Capital invested ($)	300,000	Capital invested = Total house price − loan taken = $1,000,000 − $700,000	
Net operating income (NOI) ($)	40,000		
NOI yield (also seen as cap rate)(%)	4.0	$40,000/$1,000,000 = 4.0%	
Tax expense ($)	3,500		This is an arbitrary lower number assigned for illustrative purposes only.
Interest expense for the first year	17,500	Interest rate × loan taken = 2.5% × $700,000 = $17,500	Interest rate of 2.5% per annum
Net profit ($)	19,000	NOI − tax expense − interest expense = $40,000 − $3,500 − $17,500 = $19,000	
Return on capital invested (%)	6.3	$19,000/$300,000 = 6.3%	

If Investor A had $1 million of capital to invest, they could conceivably purchase 10 apartments by investing $100,000 and borrowing $900,000 for each apartment. They will receive a total profit of $95,000 a year for the $1 million of capital invested. This return is 2.6 times more than the $36,000 of profits made without leverage.

Furthermore, if the property market trended up by 5% after a year, each apartment will be worth $1.05 million and Investor A would be sitting on a very large capital gain of $500,000 for the 10 apartments. The capital gain amounts to 50% of the $1 million capital that was invested to acquire the apartments.

However, Investor A should be aware that gearing magnifies gains, and similarly magnifies losses. Excessive gearing results in high interest expenses and leaves the investor vulnerable to cash flow negative situations if the following events occur:

TABLE A.6. Geared purchase using senior and mezzanine loan example

Geared purchase (using senior and mezzanine loan)		Formula	Comments
Gearing used, i.e., LTV ratio (%)	90		Total of $900,000 in loans, consisting of $700,000 in senior loans and $200,000 in mezzanine loans
Capital invested ($)	100,000	$1,000,000 − $900,000	
Net operating income (NOI) ($)	40,000		
NOI yield (also seen as cap rate) (%)	4.0	$40,000 / $1,000,000 = 4.0%	
Tax expense ($)	3,000		Do note that this lower value is arbitrarily assigned to reflect lower tax paid on lowered profits for illustrative purpose
Interest expense for the first year	27,500	Total interest expense = senior loan interest + mezzanine loan interest = 2.5% × $700,000 + 5.0% × $200,000 = $27,500	Interest rate of 2.5% per annum
Net profit ($)	9,500	$40,000 − $3,000 − $27,500 = $9,500	
Return on capital invested (%)	9.5	$9,500 / $100,000 = 9.5%	

1. Rentals fall short when a tenant moves out before another tenant is found.
2. Rents decline.
3. Tenants default on payments.
4. Interest rates increase.
5. Property expenses increase.

If the investor could not meet the loan covenants, the lenders could move to foreclose on the property.

In addition, other than interest payments, valuation declines will affect the borrower too. In this example, Investor A purchased the

$1 million apartment by borrowing a total of $900,000 debt. If the apartment's market value dropped to $900,000, Investor A would lose the capital invested in the apartment if the lenders forced a sale of the property at market value to recoup the principal they had provided. Industry norms dictate that senior debt must always be paid before junior debt and therefore Investor A must repay the mortgage lender and the remaining sum paid to the lender of the mezzanine loan. Investor A's capital is completely wiped out by a 10% value decline in the property market.

We then consider the more realistic situation where the property could not be forced-sold at market value. Under a foreclosure and urgent sales scenario, the highest offer from any interested buyer could be, for example, $800,000. Investor A has to allocate the first $700,000 of the sale proceeds to repay the mortgage lender. The remaining $100,000 will go to the mezzanine lender. Not only will Investor A's capital be wiped out, the mezzanine lender would have lost half of the principal. This is the reason why junior lenders demand higher interest charges to cover for the higher risks they face as compared with senior lenders.

Investors of real estate debt placing funds with junior lenders and senior lenders need to understand the risks of the loan portfolios they are investing in, how lenders create the loan portfolios, and how the lenders manage the borrowers' risks.

NOTE: In good times or bad, the revenue generated by real estate is never certain, but the requirement for timely repayment of debt is always certain. Thus, with real estate being a lumpy and capital-intensive asset class, the mismatch of expenses versus cash inflows is a risk that investors need always to bear in mind. What led to the crippling of global financial institutions during the GFC were loans written up by aggressive lenders who provided borrowers with high LTV ratio (say, 90–110%) on top of very generous valuations (V in LTV) for their properties. These highly leveraged properties provided lenders and debt investors with little to fall back on when they seized properties from borrowers who had defaulted on payments and property values fell.

A.6.5.3 The Cash Flow Waterfall and Capital Stack
Understanding the order in which a property's income is paid out is crucial to investing in real estate. As mentioned above, senior lenders are always repaid before junior lenders, both of whom are entitled to repayment before the borrower (i.e., the property investor and the

shareholders). The order in which cash flows are distributed is illustrated as a "waterfall chart" in Figure A.17. Operations and maintenance are entitled to the first cut of a building's revenue because these expenses need to be paid in order that the building is able to operate smoothly and generate income. These payments will include utilities, the salaries of maintenance workers, security operations, waste management, parts for the repair of fixtures, and so on. Property and municipal taxes fall under this expense category.

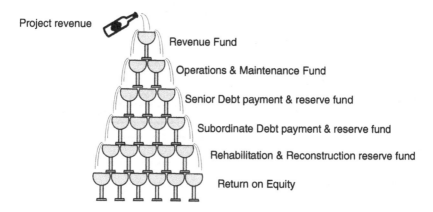

FIGURE A.17.　The cash flow waterfall.

After ensuring that the operations of the building are taken care of, senior debt lenders are next in line to receive payments for interest charges and principal repayments, if any. Subsequently, the junior lenders are paid their interest charges and principal and then the rehabilitation, reconstruction, and capex provisions fund is topped up. Finally, income taxes are paid on the profits of the building, and if there is any money left in the pot, the shareholders receive dividends which represent the return on their invested equity. Each tier must be paid in full before the next tier below can receive their share of the money.

Another method of illustrating how various stakeholders of a real estate asset are arranged is via its capital structure. Also known as a real estate capital stack, it represents how an asset is paid for via a mix of equity and debt. The various tranches of liabilities and shareholders' equity are stacked up in order of highest risks for equity investors at the bottom of the stack, to the lowest risks for debt investors at the top of the stack.

Figure A.18 shows the key characteristics of each tier of the capital stack. The risks and the expected returns run in a continuum from the lowest at the top to the highest at the bottom. In the middle of the stack are quasi-equity and quasi-debt, instruments for financing that have blended risks and blended returns as they are structured with characteristics of both debt and equity, for example convertible loans.

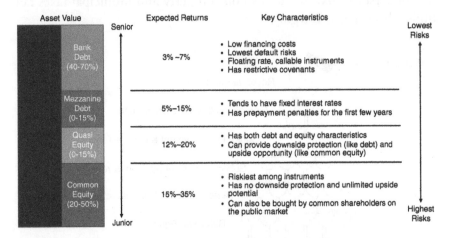

FIGURE A.18. Example of a capital stack financing a property or a real estate project.

The cash flow waterfall and how different tranches of equity and debt are stacked up form the foundation for the risks and rewards of real estate investments.

A.6.5.4 The Risks of Private Debt

For a loan that is secured against an asset, such as a building or a land site, the borrower risks losing these assets if the borrower defaults on the loan covenants, such as being late on payments, not maintaining a minimum LTV level, and so on. In cases of default, the lenders have a claim on the properties that were pledged, and they can sell the properties to recover the principal and any outstanding interests.

An investor in real estate debt is buying debt that has been originated by a lender. The investor shares most or all of the risks with the lender. In exchange, the investor earns the bulk of the interest and fees paid by the borrowers. Investors will better appreciate the characteristics of buying real estate debt if they know the risks faced by borrowers and lenders (Table A.7).

TABLE A.7. Risks of private debt for borrower and lender

Borrower	Lender
Interest rates rising quickly may impact cash flows	Late or missed payments
Penalties on late or missed payments	Needs to issue costly legal demands in case of default
Needs to provide property as a security to the lender and may need to provide additional security in the form of corporate guarantees or bank deposits	If the borrower goes into liquidation, the lender might not be able to recover the full principal of the loan when the asset is force-sold
Where the loan principal is not fully paid at the end of the term, refinancing the principal might be challenging	The borrower may not be able to repay the residual principal at the end of the term

A.6.5.5 How Lenders Reduce Risk

In addition to the loan contract, lenders may further reduce their risks through securitizing the debt and selling them to debt investors, or syndicating each loan with a few lenders and/or debt investors. Both methods allow lenders to share their risks, and their returns, with other debt investors.

Under the securitization method, a lender may pool together a large portfolio of real estate loans and create mortgage-backed securities (MBS), as shown in Figure A.19. Investors keen on getting exposure to real estate debt may buy into the MBS. The lender passes on the bulk of the interest payments from the borrowers to the MBS investors and takes a small cut of the interest. At the same time, the liabilities and risks of these loans are also transferred from the lender to the MBS investors.

A large portfolio of loans may be sub-divided into multiple tranches of the MBS based on their levels of risk. Senior secured tranches bear the least risk and thus have the lowest expected returns. These are followed by mezzanine secured tranches, which bear slightly more risk and offer slightly higher returns. The mezzanine tranche is followed by the unsecured tranche, which has the highest risk and offers the highest returns. Even within each tranche, there can be further sub-division

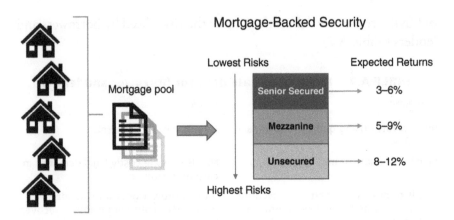

FIGURE A.19. Structuring the MBS.

based on the risk profile of the loans, such as the credit history of the borrowers, the monthly income and mortgage-servicing capability of the borrowers, and the loan-to-value ratios of the mortgages versus the value of the assets. These variations provide investors with a range of options to invest in MBSs that match their risk appetites.

Alternatively, some real estate debt investors may like exposure to the blended risks of the entire mortgage pool. In this case, the lender could stack the mortgage pool based on the risk levels described above but subsequently "slice" the tranches vertically to be sold to investors.

MBS were blamed as the primary cause of the 2008 Global Financial Crisis. The financial instrument itself should not be blamed. In truth, it was the corrupted process of securitization that tainted the reputation of MBS. High-risk lenders provided mortgages to home buyers with poor credit scores in the early to mid-2000s and then sold the risky mortgage portfolios to investment banks that repackaged them into MBSs to be sold to investors. Bad practices, such as low-quality loan origination and inadequate risk disclosures, misled investors into believing that these pools of mortgages and property collaterals were safe. In reality, the years leading up to the crisis were marked by a large number of defaults on poor-quality loans with high LTVs. As a result, many investors suffered financially during and after the economic turmoil.

In addition to MBSs, a lender may reduce risks by syndicating loans. For example, a borrower may seek $300 million of loan against a building that is worth $500 million. A lender could take the lead to underwrite the loan but partially sell down $250 million of the loan to a few more lenders. Having multiple lenders finance a single loan ensures that no sole lender bears the full risks of the loan and the asset that backs the loan. Each of the lenders participating in the syndicated loans may further sell down their risks to other debt investors.

The risks of private real estate debt may also be bundled up and sold to investors in the public debt markets via mortgage REITs and debt-focused Exchange Traded Funds.

A.6.6 Public Real Estate Debt

Public debt, as the name suggests, refers to debt instruments that are publicly traded. Public real estate debt refers to publicly listed entities that own large pools of loans and mortgages which are secured against real estate assets. These mortgage pools receive regular, monthly payments, consisting of interest and repayments of principal, from borrowers. Profits are derived from the interest income, and investors of such publicly listed entities receive dividends that are distributed. Therefore, such investments offer relatively stable returns to investors and are considered less volatile than publicly listed equity investments. Additionally, when demand from investors increases and interest rates move down, investors could enjoy capital gains on the price of the listed entities.

In the quadrant of public real estate debt, the main investments instruments are MBS traded as mortgage REITs, debt-focused Exchange Traded Funds, corporate bonds, and medium-term notes issued by real estate developers or real estate funds securitized against their assets.

A.6.6.1 Mortgage-Backed Security (MBS)

MBSs are securitized pools of mortgages backed by properties. Securitizing a financial asset, in this case, a pool of real estate mortgages, turns the asset into fungible shares that are smaller in value per share and more easily tradable. Securitization allows the mortgage lenders to reduce their risks, by shifting default and prepayment liabilities onto the investors who purchased the securities.

MBSs may be classified according to their risk levels, from least to most risky, which are the senior tranche, the mezzanine tranche, and the unsecured tranche. In addition to selecting MBSs based on risk, investors may also select MBS investments based on their property-collateral types. Two main types of properties back-up MBSs: Commercial MBSs (CMBSs) and Residential MBSs (RMBSs). CMBSs are securitized against mortgages on income-producing properties, whereas RMBSs are securitized against mortgages on owner-occupied properties. Other types of MBSs exist, collateralized against other financial assets, such as credit-card loans, car loans, student loans, and so on.

MBSs may also be defined based on their payment structure with the two primary models being pass-throughs and collateralized mortgage obligations (CMO).

Pass-through MBSs are the predominant kind of MBSs traded on the secondary market. They are a security that is created when mortgage lenders, such as banks, pool their loans into an entity and sell shares or participation certificates in the entity to debt investors. The cash flows from the mortgage pool are then "passed through" to the investors monthly, both interest and principal. In exchange for these cash flows, however, investors bear risks that would typically fall on the lender, such as prepayment and default risks. Early prepayment of the principal is considered a risk to investors because the interest income will be reduced when borrowers pay down their loans ahead of schedule. This often occurs during periods of reducing interest rates when borrowers could refinance their mortgages for lower interest with other lenders.

CMOs, on the other hand, are repackaged pass-through MBS whose cash flows are distributed based on priority, as outlined in the structure of the bond. These MBSs are organized according to maturity dates and risk levels. Thus, the key difference between pass-through and CMO investments is the process in which investors are paid. Under the pass-through structure, investors receive a monthly pro-rata distribution of any principal and interest. The CMO structure, however, substitutes a principal pay-down priority schedule among tranches for the pro-rata process. Thus, investors in the senior tranche will be paid first and the balance will be trickled down to the junior tranche investors, as illustrated earlier by the payment waterfall and the capital stack diagrams.

Note: MBSs may be issued as private debt or they may be tradable as public debt in secondary market through brokers. Investors who like fixed income instruments may also access MBSs in the public markets through Exchange Traded Funds that focus on MBSs.

A.6.6.2 Exchange Traded Fund (ETF)

ETFs are bundles of marketable securities that track the performance of various indices through diversified portfolios of financial assets. Investors gain access to a diversified portfolio in a single investment of any ETF. There are ETFs for a wide range of underlying securities, including ETFs for airlines, banks, technology stocks, and of course for REITs and REOCs too.

Public real estate debt investors may consider ETFs that are focused on MBSs and Mortgage REITs (mREITs) as a way to diversify their debt investments across multiple types of property loans. As ETFs are traded on exchanges, they experience price fluctuations throughout the day, providing better liquidity and lower investment fees for investors who like diversification and flexibility.

ETFs are passive investment funds that track indices. They do not manage properties or real estate debt and therefore their expense-to-asset ratios are low, allowing them to charge lower fees. Despite the diversification, ETFs have their inherent risks. Investors should note that it is often difficult to track market indices closely because it is not possible to purchase each security in the same proportion as a basket of stocks tracked by the indices.

As with all investment instruments, due diligence is key and investors should scrutinize the funds and the fund managers carefully. For example, an ETF of MBSs is a derivative of a derivative, that is, an ETF of MBSs is a collection of MBSs which are themselves pools of mortgages backed by real estate. The credit quality of the MBSs within an ETF could vary widely, making some of these high-yielding investments relatively risky even for fund managers with well-established track records.

A.6.6.3 Mortgage REITs (mREITs)

If a REIT entity is mainly invested in MBSs, they are also known as mortgage REITs (mREITs). Generally, mREITs focus on either CMBSs or RMBSs and are most popular in the United States and Australia. mREITs offer investors a portfolio of mortgages with different yields and different maturities. Additionally, mREITs collect monthly mortgage payments from the borrowers in the CMBS and RMBS pools, and pay to their investors a steady income in the form of quarterly dividend payments.

While investors in mREITs are not exposed to the full liabilities of property ownership, they do still bear a substantial amount of risk. As previously mentioned, MBSs are subject to prepayment risk, in which a mortgage's yield is not fully realized if repaid before the maturity date, and default risk, in which investors are unable to collect in the event of a default since they are not owners of the debt itself. There is also a reinvestment risk, which refers to the possibility that the mREITs managers are unable to reinvest some of the principal repayments or, in the case of a declining interest rates environment, may be forced to reinvest the funds at lower-than-current yields. If the mREITs' management took on long-term loan instruments, investors will also be exposed to interest rate volatility risks.

Being a REIT, mREITs are similar to equity REITs in that they are required to pay at least 90% of their profits as dividends to unit holders instead of retaining more for reinvestment. Otherwise, mREITs and equity REITs differ in that mREITs own real estate debt while equity REITs own physical real estate. With real estate, equity REITs can enjoy price growth from higher rents which translate to increased dividends and increased property valuations. As investors are willing to pay a higher price for the growth potential, equity REITs usually pay a lower dividend yield than mREITs.

A.6.6.4 Corporate Bonds and Medium-Term Notes (MTNs)

Bonds are a form of debt issued by corporations and governments, and they can be publicly traded or private. Investors of a corporate bond are essentially lending money to the corporation, and the bond comes with a promise of regular, usually six-monthly, interest payments and principal repayment at the end of the bond term. This is a major source of capital for many businesses as corporate bonds are preferred over share issuance and bondholders do not share in the profits of the companies.

Notes, such as bank notes and promissory notes, are legal papers that represent a borrower's obligations to repay a lender the amount of money borrowed. A medium-term note (MTN) is a form of a fixed income security, similar to a bond, that has a maturity period of 5–10 years.

As popular forms of public debt, corporate bonds and MTNs have many similarities. For instance, both investments are non-callable, have fixed interest rates or coupons, and have investment ratings. Such debt instruments are attractive to investors because in the event of bankruptcy, debt holders are paid before shareholders, which reduces the risks of total loss.

Just like cash and stocks, bonds and notes are considered mainstream debt instruments and are therefore not covered as alternative investments. Readers should be cognizant that bonds and notes issued by real estate entities carry different risks compared to those that are issued by businesses from other industries and non-business entities, including governments and not-for-profit organizations.

REOCs and REITs issue corporate bonds and MTNs, and they do so for a wide range of purposes: land acquisition, property development, purchase of buildings, or for general working capital. For example, bonds and MTNs of three- to five-year terms are particularly suitable for financing the construction and development of land sites after which the newly completed building could be financed based on its new valuation. The borrowing period could be timed to coincide with the construction schedules, and any delays to the projects may pose risks to the bond holders.

Investors need to pay attention to the yields and credit ratings (if the debt issued is rated). Higher yields might indicate that the company, or the tranche of debt issued, is riskier than their peers in the industry.

While public debt instruments may come with better and more regular financial disclosures as compared to private debt, the large size of the loan pool and the aggregated data of borrowers' profiles and securitized assets mean that it is difficult to assess the risks with confidence. Investors need to stay vigilant and conduct regular reviews of the profile of the borrowers and the quality of the assets backing these loan portfolios as these evolve with time due to old loans being retired while new loans are taken into the loan pool.

Notes

1. https://www.businesstimes.com.sg/companies-markets/manulife-us-reit-manager-eyes-hotelisation-of-office-assets-amid-dour-outlook.
2. https://www.businessinsider.com/retail-lose-track-time-shopping-malls-gruen-effect-transfer-ikea-department-stores-2016-12.
3. Susan Hudson-Wilson, Frank J. Fabozzi, and Jacques N. Gordon, "Why Real Estate?: An Expanding Role for Institutional Investors," *Journal of Portfolio Management*, 29(5) (2003): 12–25. https://jpm.pm-research.com/content/29/5; https://jpm.pm-research.com/content/28/1/20.

About the Website

Thank you for purchasing this book.

You may access the following additional complementary bonus resources provided for your use by visiting:

www.wiley.com\go\dearth\gsialternativeinvestments

Password: Dearth123

At this link, you will find the following bonus materials for the book:

- an appendix on ESG and Sustainable Investing;
- a collection of additional materials organized according to the structure of the book;
- due diligence checklist for real estate investments.

We do hope that you enjoy both the book and the bonus content!

Index